CORPORATE FINANCE HANDBOOK

**The Confederation
of British Industry**

CORPORATE
FINANCE
HANDBOOK

CONSULTANT EDITORS:
CHRISTOPHER GASSON & ADAM JOLLY

**KOGAN
PAGE**

Publisher's note
Every possible effort has been made to ensure that the information contained in this handbook is accurate at the time of going to press, and the publishers cannot accept responsibility for any errors or omissions, however caused. All liability for loss, disappointment, negligence or other damage caused by the reliance on the information contained in this handbook, or in the event of bankruptcy or liquidation or cessation of trade of any company, individual or firm mentioned, is hereby excluded.

Published in 1999

Kogan Page Ltd
120 Pentonville Road
London N1 9JN
kpinfo@kogan-page.co.uk

© Kogan Page and contributors 1999

British Library Cataloguing in Publication Data
A CIP record for this book is available from the British Library
ISBN 0 7494 2746 9

Typeset by Saxon Graphics Ltd, Derby
Printed and bound in Great Britain by Bell and Bain Limited

Contents

Foreword

Corporate finance is probably the single most important determinant of the success or failure of a business, yet very few executives actually understand how it works. Most executives do not come from a financial background, and many of those who have trained as accountants do not have a great deal of experience of finance itself beyond their everyday dealings with their bank.

Instead, most executives have to learn about corporate finance the hard way: an acquisition, a financial crisis, or a development opportunity precipitate a flurry of approaches and presentations to City institutions. Several disappointments later, the way ahead is discovered, but the learning process is almost always traumatic.

This book aims to give executives a glimpse of what is involved in corporate finance, so they can find their way around the brick walls which confront anyone trying to raise money.

All too often the lack of understanding of the rules of finance has undermined the relationship between industry and the City. The truth is that the two are mutually dependent: the City needs opportunities to invest in growing businesses as much as growing businesses need investment.

The largest and most established enterprises have, in general, got this relationship right. It is the small and medium-sized businesses, particularly those that are getting involved in activities which can no longer be financed by their high street bank, that this book is aimed at. Additionally there are also a number of managers within large established corporations who are suddenly finding themselves involved in corporate finance as their parent companies reorganise, throwing up buy-out opportunities.

For many people, corporate finance involves a new range of professional advisers, often speaking an unfamiliar language. It is not surprising that many executives find themselves bluffing their way through it and hoping that their professional advisers are going to make the right decisions for them.

The CBI Corporate Finance Handbook is an outsider's guide to the subject. It explains the issues comprehensively and accessibly for anyone approaching them for the first time. It covers not only issues of structuring and raising finance (sections 1–4), but also the areas of executive management most closely associated with corporate finance, namely mergers and acquisitions and turnarounds.

Each chapter is written by an expert on the subject, concisely and without jargon. There are some areas of overlap, but only where it is beneficial to approach the issue from more than one point of view. The final section contains a directory of professional advisers, including an indication of the size of deal that they have been involved in. This is because the size of a new client in comparison to a professional firm's existing clients is probably the best indicator of the level of attention a new client can expect.

About the Contributors

Arthur Andersen – Financial Restructuring Division

Financial Restructuring is one of the teams within the London Investment Banking group. It is a small team of seven highly experienced practitioners offering:

- strategic and commercial analysis of businesses
- assessment of underlying value
- critical appraisal of business plans and assessment of viability
- financial appraisal
- management of the financial restructuring process
- exit management.

The team will typically be seeking to act for the management or equity stakeholders of underperforming corporates.

The team also provides Arthur Andersen's input to *The Thames Fund* ("TTF"). TTF is a debt fund jointly owned by Arthur Andersen and HSBC Investment Bank plc. It invests in companies experiencing financial problems where traditional sources of funding are no longer available.

By combining its financial resources with the turnaround and financial restructuring skills of its shareholders, TTF can support recoveries in underperforming companies. TTF is a high risk fund that will consider:

- Replacement of existing debt
- Partial replacement of debt
- Short term liquidity funding
- Provision of new debt.

The Partners responsible for Financial Restructuring are David Duggins and David Lovett. Directors responsible are Joanne Holland

and Adrian Wolstenholme. Assistant Directors are Laura Barlow, Russell Pope and Chris Steed.

Contact details: Arthur Andersen, 1 Surrey Street, London, WC2R 2PS. Tel: 0171 438 2491

Robin F Baum Consultants

Robin Baum is a consultant specialising in assisting businesses through a period of problems or expansion. A commercial lawyer by training, but with extensive experience as a merchant banker with Grindlays Group, N M Rothschild & Sons and English Trust PLC, he has operated as an independent consultant since 1991.

Bertoli Mitchell

Established in 1994, Bertoli Mitchell is an M&A boutique specialising in the publishing sector. For further information, please contact Christopher Gasson. Telephone 0171 394 0424, e-mail: cg@bertolimitchell.co.uk.

Biddle

Biddle is a 34 partner City law firm with specialist expertise across a range of practice areas, including corporate, tax, employment, pensions and property. The corporate department has an active and growing client base of public and private companies, generally in the £1m to £100m range. The department's 1:1 partner to solicitor ratio is intentionally high and reflects clients' appreciation of the firm's partner-led approach. Particular areas of expertise are mergers and acquisitions, corporate finance and private equity. Recent publicly-announced transactions include the sale of Routledge Publishing to Taylor & Francis plc, the acquisition of the Ross Breeders poultry business from Hillsdown, the sale of Flying Colours Leisure Group to Thomas Cook, the flotation of City North Group plc and the MBO of the Perfect Pizza chain.

For further information, please contact Roger Fink (0171 667 0081) or Martin Lane (0171 667 0118).

Business Dynamics

Business Dynamics acts as hands-on business advisers to companies, business schools, banks and business links. It was founded by Brian

Warnes, who had previously set up and run a small-ticket, fast-acting development capital fund for the Midland Bank. As a result of this experience, the effect of an equity injection in helping a company's bankers be more supportive became self-evident. Seeing the need for an educational exercise for the management teams concerned, coupled with upgraded and reworked management information, he founded Business Dynamics in July 1987.

Deloitte & Touche Corporate Finance

Deloitte & Touche Corporate Finance provides a full range of advisory services and support for transactions including: mergers and acquisitions; disposals; management buy-outs/buy-ins; capital raising; sponsorship and new issues; valuations; due diligence; bid defence; public to private partnerships; and capital consulting.

Its clients include listed and unlisted public companies, individual shareholders, venture capitalists, management teams and government bodies in the UK and overseas. Independent advice, specialist skills, quality of service and innovative solutions to business problems are hallmarks of its work.

Thirty partners and over 200 staff dedicated to corporate finance work serve its clients from across the UK. They have backgrounds and relevant experience in accounting, taxation, merchant banking, venture capital, management consultancy and industry.

Forward Trust

Forward Trust Limited is one of the UK's leading providers of asset-based services and finance, employing some 1,200 people. From vehicle fleet management to complex asset financing for major projects, Forward Trust has the experience and expertise to provide solutions for commercial organisations.

A wholly owned subsidiary of Midland Bank, itself a member of the HSBC Group – one of the world's largest banking and financial services organisations – Forward Trust has assets in excess of £5bn.

Forward Trust operates brands within three strategic market sectors: rail, cars and commercial vehicles; and their respective related services. Forward Trust has a strong commitment to providing added value services. The need to differentiate and generate a competitive edge through the quality of customer service is a key priority.

Greig Middleton

Greig Middleton's Corporate Finance team specialises in advising smaller and medium-sized quoted companies with growth aspirations. It is Stockbroker to over 60 mainly fully listed companies and Financial Adviser to a considerable number of these. The Corporate Finance team is particularly experienced in advising and preparing companies for flotation and other services include secondary equity issues, acquisitions, mergers, disposals, public takeovers and defences, reorganisations and restructurings. The team's success in the smaller and medium-sized companies market is attributed to its members achieving a clear understanding of clients' needs in order to work closely with them in seeking to achieve their goals.

Greig Middleton is a member firm of the London Stock Exchange and is regulated by the Securities and Futures Authority. Greig Middleton is a recognised sponsor for the London Stock Exchange's Official List and is a listed Nominated Adviser for AIM.

KPMG

KPMG offers growing businesses a total business advisory service that is designed to help owner managers maximise the potential of their business by advising and providing solutions on a wide range of issues that impact on competitiveness.

KPMG's teams are organised to give the very best commercial and professional advice based on two clear principles: the provision of teams dedicated to the sector and its delivery through locally based advisers who are supported by KPMG's national and international network.

Lloyds Development Capital

Lloyds Development Capital is the Venture Capital arm of Lloyds TSB Group plc. LDC invests between £0.5m and £10m in unquoted companies with a turnover typically in excess of £5m.

It makes investments in a full range of equity products including ordinary shares, preference shares, convertible preference shares and loan stock. It invests money from the bank's balance sheet, so it does not suffer the same pressure as some other venture capital funds to seek a rapid return of its money.

LDC has invested in over 200 businesses in its 16-year history across a wide variety of industry sectors, of which IT forms a large proportion of its portfolio. It invested £46 million in 20 deals in 1997 across the UK.

LDC is now ranked fourth amongst UK venture capital companies, by number of deals in the £1m – £50m market segment (source Corp Fin UK+ January 1998).

NMB-Heller Limited

NMB-Heller is a unique provider of structured finance for businesses. The company's products include: Invoice Finance, to which can be added Credit Control, Credit Protection, Stock Finance, Trade Finance, Term Loans and Treasury Management. Used alone or in combination, these are designed to offer flexible working capital solutions for changing circumstances such as periods of rapid growth; a planned acquisition; possible refinancing; or MBO/MBIs. In conjunction with its associates, working capital finance can be made available through-out Europe.

NMB-Heller Ltd is a wholly owned subsidiary of NMB-Heller Holding, a company jointly owned by ING Group and Heller Financial Inc., a wholly-owned subsidiary of the Fuji Bank.

NatWest Equity Partners

NatWest Equity Partners is a leading European provider of private equity. It has been investing in unquoted companies for almost 30 years and specialises in structuring and leading buy-out transactions and acquisitions with management.

It has six offices in the UK, in Bristol, London, Leeds, Birmingham, Manchester and Glasgow, as well as teams on the ground in Madrid, Düsseldorf, Milan and Paris, and a Scandinavian team based in London. With around 60 investment professionals, it is well placed to transact national and cross-border deals.

NatWest Equity Partners has around £2 billion under management, £1 billion of which is for future investment.

Pannell Kerr Forster

Pannell Kerr Forster is the eighth largest accountancy practice in the UK, with a network of 26 offices throughout the country. Its primary target market is small and medium-sized developing businesses, ranging from privately owned to fully listed companies. Using dedicated personnel with experience gained from outside as well as within the profession, it provides a comprehensive range of corporate finance services including fund raising, flotations, management buy-ins/buy-outs, acquisitions and disposals, due diligence and valuations. Pannell Kerr Forster is authorised by the Institute of Chartered Accountants in England and Wales to carry on investment business. For further information contact, in the first instance, Nick Whitaker on 0171 831 7393.

PricewaterhouseCoopers Global HR Solutions

PricewaterhouseCoopers is the world's largest professional services organisation, employing more than 135,000 staff globally. In the UK, it has over 700 consultants in its global human resource solutions service, focused on helping clients to create value with their people. Its specialists include lawyers, taxation experts, pay and reward specialists, human resource consultants and actuaries.

Combining practical HR experience with a detailed knowledge of the regulatory requirements, it helps organisations make their people a source of competitive advantage.

It also gives UK and global advice on: strategic HR consulting services, including organisational effectiveness and people performance; management assessment, development and training; human resources information technology; pensions, including valuations, investment strategy and administration; PAYE and social security planning; cash and share-based incentives, including tax favoured schemes; employee benefit design and communication; employment law, including immigration and nationality law; expatriate advisory services, including tax planning and compliance; and personal financial planning for senior executives.

About the Editor

Christopher Gasson is a corporate financier and financial journalist. After reading Politics and Economics at Oxford, he joined the *Local Government Chronicle* as City correspondent, primarily focusing on the fund management sector. From there he moved to *The Bookseller*, where he was financial news editor. After a spell as managing director of an Internet information business, he joined Bertoli Mitchell as an associate. He is the author of the leading textbook on valuing media companies, *Media Equities: Evaluation and Trading.*

Section One
An Introduction to Corporate Finance

KPMG ADVISES MORE OWNER MANAGED BUSINESSES IN THE UK THAN ANY OTHER FIRM

OMB

So, if you want your business to grow, call
Peter Mamelok on 0171 311 1000, Jack McLaren on 0141 226 5511,
Ken Smith on 0121 232 3000 or Mark Munton on 0113 231 3000

means business

1
An Introduction to Corporate Finance

John Eggleston,
KPMG

Structure

Corporate finance involves advising a company or its shareholders on the issues around the finance structure. The principal objective of most corporate finance transactions is to help create or maximise value through the establishment of the most appropriate finance structure. As a consequence, its focus is most often on raising money, buying or selling companies and share structure.

The financing structure can make or break the business. An appropriate one means that the business is driving the structure. The consequence of having an inappropriate structure is likely to be cash flow difficulties and results in underperforming against expectations. Management time is diverted to solving the problem and to meeting repayment schedules and, in extreme circumstances, this can lead to insolvency. The issue needs frequent monitoring. What was an appropriate funding structure two years ago might no longer be right for the current needs of a business.

Structure is covered in detail in Chapter Two.

Values

In order to help companies arrive at the right finance structure, corporate financiers have to understand the vision and objectives of the business they are advising; for example, whether it wants to grow steadily or whether it has to grow quickly to take advantage of a particular situation. They have to work in accordance with the ethos of the company. Most often this is concentrated on increasing share value, but for some companies it might mean protecting ethical principles or its role in the local community. They also need to appreciate what the worth of the company is based on and this valuation is a key to finding the right finance. This is composed of an increasingly complex mix that includes: product or service, brand value and quality of the management team.

Valuation techniques are covered in more detail in Chapter 18.

Change

When the corporate financier is involved, the catalyst is always change and most often concerns a change in ownership for the owner managed business. However, whether it's a large or a small company, the approach is invariably the same and is founded on examining why the money is required and assessing what is the most appropriate form of finance.

Corporate financiers' advice has to be timely and to be able to provide this they need to understand the impact of change. The financial market thrives on change and political, social, economic and technological change are all factors which impact on the availability of finance and the conditions on which it is given. 'Global contagion' describes the effects of globalisation, which increasingly influence the UK market place. Currently the behaviour of the American President, the chaos in Russia and the crisis in Japan are all influencers. Loss of confidence is one of the results of this particular combination of situations and at the time of writing it is very difficult, for example, to get a major line of debt from a single source. It is evident that effects of globalisation are difficult to predict, but it does seem to mean that different industries are affected in different ways. This makes it even more important for the corporate financier to have in-depth knowledge of industry sectors and of certain individual marketplaces. Informed decisions are best made with local, national, international and sector specific advice.

Balance

The principle that guides the activity of the corporate financier is one which seeks to create a financial structure that enables a company to achieve its objectives in the most cost-effective way. Essentially there are two forms of finance: debt and equity, with a whole range of financial tools to bridge the gap between the two. The purpose of this book is to provide a comprehensive guide to these techniques.

Debt is a relatively low risk, low return form of finance and requires security, servicing and repayment. Equity is the permanent investment capital of the business. It is a high risk, high return form of finance and represents an investment for the lender. In its purest form there is no fixed rate of return and no guarantee of return, but it gives the lender a stake in the company. Owner managers should remember that the least expensive form of equity is to be found by ploughing back profits into a company. (The benefits of this are examined in more detail in Chapter 6.)

In the search for the best structure, the corporate financier needs to find the balance between debt and equity. Too much debt and the lender begins to own you; too much equity and the business may not be maximising its ability to use debt. This assessment of debt, of under-gearing and over-gearing, is one of the guides that analysts use in judging how well a company is managed – and the better managed a company, the more likely it is to get the funding it seeks. (Debt is covered in section two of this book.)

This balance, or the situation that is best, is different for every company, depending on its short and longer-term objectives. Traditionally, private businesses have been content with steady growth. They have wanted independence and have tended to rely more on debt finance. However, there is an enlarging band of entrepreneurs who want fast growth, and they need high-risk money to achieve their ambitions. Their challenge is to find the equity. (The issues involved in raising equity are covered in sections three and four.)

Applications

Corporate finance is not an end in itself, although sometimes those who direct their entire corporate strategy toward a flotation on the Stock Exchange might mistake it for one. It is a tool of corporate strategy, which facilitates the development of shareholder value. As such it is involved at each major event in the life of a corporation: its birth, its coming of age and its marriages.

Mergers and acquisitions are perhaps some of the most important applications of corporate finance. Not only that, but mergers and acquisitions are the most critical events in the life of most businesses. Get them wrong and everything else can often be put at risk.

Mergers and acquisitions are covered in section five. Turning around failing businesses is the subject of section six.

John Eggleston is Head of KPMG's Owner Managed Business Practice.

2
Raising Finance – Making the Right Choice

Stephen Bayfield
Pannell Kerr Forster

Introduction

The directors of a company seeking to raise finance have an over-whelming choice. There are numerous types and sources of finance available in the market place. However this does not mean that raising finance is easy. This article explores how to go about raising finance and how to identify the most appropriate source or sources that fulfil the requirements of both the company and its shareholders. It is aimed at those businesses which are not of a sufficient size to operate a sophisticated in-house treasury department and accordingly does not cover the specialist financial products only generally available to large multinational companies.

The business plan

The first step in the fundraising process is the preparation of a suitable business plan. The purpose of this is twofold. It should provide potential investors with sufficient information to enable them to make an initial assessment of whether or not to consider providing finance. It should also identify how much finance is required and how and when it is to be utilised.

It is beyond the scope of this article to go into detail on the contents of a business plan. The key points to get across include the following:

- the amount of finance required and why;
- a description of the business, its history and its products;
- the marketplace and the company's position within it;
- the organisation's structure and people;
- the strategy; and
- the financial projections.

It is of particular importance that the directors manage to get across their understanding of the marketplace in which they operate and the opportunities and risks that are present within it. The strategy must be deliverable and convincing. It should be borne in mind that, in many cases, experts acting for the financier will review the plan.

Care should be taken over the circulation of the business plan, as it constitutes an investment advertisement under the provisions of the Financial Services Act. Distribution to established finance providers such as banks, leasing companies and venture capitalists is exempted, but if the plan is circulated to non-specialists or individuals (however sophisticated an investor they may be) the document must, at the very least, be verified or approved by an authorised person. Failure to comply is a criminal offence.

Choosing the most appropriate sources of finance

Having established how much funding is required, it is then necessary to determine the nature of that funding. Selecting the right type of finance involves consideration of the following:

- what is realistically available and achievable;
- the likely terms;
- what is suitable for the business;
- whether the type of finance is flexible enough to cope with the future requirements of the business;
- whether the type of finance is compatible with the personal aspirations of the shareholders and the directors; and
- the costs associated with raising the finance.

Seeking finance of a type that is not suitable can involve considerable time and energy and, inevitably, disillusionment with the whole process. Selecting a type that is not compatible or flexible enough to cope with future plans can be disastrous for the development of the business and shareholders' aims. Notwithstanding this, many businesses raise finance that achieves the immediate aims but does not address future needs – in other words, it provides a quick fix.

An important matter to bear in mind is that investors require the ability to recover their investment, together with a return commensurate with their risk, at or before a given time or in certain circumstances. If the investment is in the form of debt, it is important that the cash flows of the business are robust enough to cope with the repayment profile or the alternative sources of finance are available. If the investment is in that form of equity then, with the exception of those companies whose shares can be freely traded on a stock market or equivalent, the investor is likely to require comfort on the proposed exit strategy and the likely timescale for achieving it.

Selecting the appropriate funding structure

The funding structure of the vast majority of businesses comprises working capital, term debt and equity. Working capital and debt require the granting of appropriate security and servicing and repayment out of the cash flow generated by the business, whereas equity is the permanent capital of the business. The security available and the cash flow profile of the business will determine the balance between equity and debt, after making due allowance for the anticipated growth of the business.

The structure of the funding and, in particular, the repayment profile should also take into account the seasonality of the business and its impact on operating cash flows.

Types of debt finance

Debt finance is typically required to provide working capital for the business and to assist in the funding of fixed assets and acquisitions.

Working capital

Working capital is normally provided by way of a bank overdraft or a factoring or invoice discounting facility. The bank overdraft remains the most common and simple source of working capital and has the distinct advantage of being available from the provider of the company's clearing facilities.

Factoring and invoice discounting are becoming increasingly used (see Chapter 3). The one time image of this type of finance as being the last resort before insolvency is gradually disappearing. Factoring can be particularly attractive to smaller businesses as it not only provides working capital but also effectively outsources debt collection and administration to the factor. Divisions of most banks and a number of specialist organisations provide factoring and invoice discounting facilities.

Term debt

Term debt is used to provide funding to acquire fixed assets or other businesses. It is repayable over an agreed period of time and is normally secured on the assets of the business. There are various forms of finance available ranging from mortgage, asset finance through to securitisation and acquisition finance.

A mortgage is the traditional method of financing property and remains widely used.

For most businesses acquiring equipment the main decision is whether to purchase or lease the assets concerned (see Chapter 4). Deciding what is the more appropriate in any given situation will depend on a number of factors, including cash flow, the company's tax position and the nature of the asset concerned.

Acquisitive companies and many MBO/MBIs will be funded by loans which, whilst secured on the assets of the business, will be greater than the value of those assets. These lenders, typically specialist divisions of banks, will place far greater emphasis on the cash flow of the business than on asset values. Larger MBO/MBIs may also incorporate an element of mezzanine finance. Such finance ranks behind senior debt in terms of security, in return for which the funder earns a higher return through a higher rate of interest and equity participation.

Many specialist forms of finance are available for larger businesses seeking funding in tens or hundreds of millions of pounds. These are usually packaged in the form of bonds, typical of which is securitisation whereby companies with predictable cash flows, e.g. leasing and property investment companies, parcel their receivables from a block of assets in a debt instrument which is then sold to institutional investors.

Revolving credit facilities

In an ever-increasing competitive environment to lend to good quality businesses, many banks and other lenders are increasingly seeking to distinguish their packages from the rest of the field. One such product is the revolving credit facility. This typically will provide funding based on an agreed percentage of a company's debtors, stock and fixed assets. The percentage will vary according to the type of asset and the proportion relating to fixed assets is repayable over an agreed period. The working capital element of the facility is not repayable over an agreed period, but is designed to vary with the levels of stock and debtors at any given time. This type of finance can be very attractive to the growing business.

Other considerations

Selecting the most appropriate types and sources of debt finance is not simply a question of finding the lowest interest rate. All loans are made subject to terms and conditions, and the provisions relating to default can be crucial. Particular attention should be given to the covenants, usually expressed as ratios such as pre-tax profit/interest payable (interest cover), loan/net asset value (asset cover) and cash flow/debt service (cash flow cover), as breach of any of these could lead to a renegotiation or withdrawal of facilities. If these covenants are drawn too tightly, management time can easily be diverted from developing the business into crisis cash flow management. Covenants are usually based on financial projections made by management; over ambitious forecasts can thus lead directly to difficulty in compliance.

As better deals can usually be struck by shopping around, it is likely that covering debt finance needs from a variety of sources will be less expensive than a single source. However a balance should always be struck between flexibility and cost. Too many sources of debt finance can lead to a lack of co-ordination between lenders, particularly in difficult circumstances, causing severe problems for management. The author recalls one high profile situation in the early 1990s. A company, struggling in the recession and in the process of negotiating a refinancing package with its principal banks, was forced into receivership as a consequence of action taken by a small leasing company to impound one of its assets.

Equity finance

For most businesses looking to expand, the initial source of equity finance is the existing shareholders. However many businesses will reach a time when equity finance is required from third party sources, usually triggered by one or more of the following events:

- one or more shareholders are seeking an exit, but the sale of the whole company is not an option;
- the company requires finance to grow organically or by acquisition;
- the company is subject to an MBO/MBI;
- the company is a start-up or in an early stage of its development and needs access to capital; and
- the shareholders/directors are attracted by the status of being a quoted company or want to create a market in the shares.

There are a considerable number of providers of equity in the marketplace, but finding the right backer(s) can be a time consuming and frustrating process. The following are the principal sources of external equity finance:

- private individuals (or business angels). These are wealthy individuals who in many cases have sold their own business and are seeking to reinvest and possibly play a non-executive role in privately-owned companies. These individuals will often be seeking tax relief on their investment under the enterprise investment scheme (EIS);
- venture capital trusts set up to manage equity investments under the EIS;
- private equity or venture capital funds;
- trade investors; and
- financial institutions and the investing public at large through the stock markets.

Business angels

Business angels play a crucial role in the investment community. They are willing to take the time to consider investments in companies seeking comparatively small amounts of equity of £5,000 to £250,000. In addition many are prepared to consider investments in start-up or early stage companies. These are areas in which the corporate equity providers are reluctant to get involved, not least because it is uneconomic for them to invest small amounts.

Whilst there are probably in the region of 20,000 people who could be regarded as business angels, finding a suitable investor is not easy. Friends and business contacts of the directors should be considered first, particularly those who may have attributes that bode well for a long-term business relationship. Failing that, use should be made of one or more of the business angel introductory services that exist in order to make suitable contacts. The British Venture Capital Association will provide a list of such introduction agencies on request.

Venture capital trusts

These trusts exist to invest in suitable qualifying companies. Investments are typically in the range of £100,000 to £1 million in the form of ordinary shares and preference shares/subordinated loans. They provide a valuable source of equity finance to smaller growing companies. Directors of companies seeking finance from such trusts, or indeed from business angels requiring EIS tax benefits, should be mindful that the rules of the scheme may restrict their business activities over the appropriate qualifying period. It is important that the directors are aware of what needs to done, or avoided, to maintain qualifying status if such funding is obtained.

After the shares have been held for the relevant five-year period, the investors will be seeking an exit. This is likely to come from a trade sale, a refinancing or flotation.

Private equity/venture capital funds

There are a large number of venture capital funds willing to provide funding for companies in amounts ranging from a few tens of thousands to hundreds of millions. These funds generally have investment preferences that may relate to the size of investment (whether minimum or maximum), the nature of the transaction being funded and the sector/location of the business. Accordingly it is important to target the right fund(s) for the business concerned. Private equity is covered in detail in section two.

Trade investors

Trade investors are an important source of finance for early stage companies or those still developing their business. Investments are usually made in hi-tec businesses or, for strategic reasons, in businesses developing or operating complementary or competitive products.

In considering a trade investor, it is necessary to take into account the possibility that future exit options may be affected. The investor is the logical purchaser of the business and his presence as a shareholder may serve to deter other purchasers.

A clearly drafted shareholders' agreement is a pre-requisite.

Flotation

Flotation on a stock market gives access to the widest range of equity finance providers. It has the additional advantage of providing a market for dealing in shares in the company.

Whilst flotation is not appropriate or possible for a large number of companies due to their size or trading record, the development of junior UK markets such as AIM has increased the level of access to funding from institutional and private investors.

A stock market listing is particularly suitable for growing or acquisitive companies who will be able to issue new marketable shares to fund their growth. It is also attractive to larger established companies with an extensive shareholder list, in order to create liquidity in the shares. However, it should be borne in mind that without realistic growth prospects the benefits of listing can quickly be lost for the shareholders of such companies.

Flotations are covered in more detail in Chapter 14.

Summary

The range of types and sources of finance available can be overwhelming. However, time taken to consider what the business needs both now and for its medium-term needs, encompassed in a business plan, will greatly assist in determining what is achievable. Effort can then be concentrated on targeting those providers of finance that are relevant to the requirements of the business and its owners.

An ambitious, growing company is unlikely to be able to arrange a financing package that will be relevant throughout its existence. The package should be able to serve the company's needs to the next critical stage of its growth, and then be flexible enough to enable the company to enable a satisfactory refinancing.

In selecting appropriate financiers, the most important considerations are:

- *Knowledge of the business* – ideally a funder should understand the various issues that may affect the business and the markets in which it operates. This will assist in achieving a funding package that is tailored to business needs and takes into account the cycles to which that business may be subject.
- *Flexibility* – the funder should be able to cope with the current and future requirements of the business. It is also important to ensure that the terms on which finance is provided do not prevent or restrict future fund raising options, which can occur where an existing investor has reached the limit at which he is able or prepared to invest.
- *Personal relationships* – A good working relationship with your financiers can be crucial. It can have significant advantages both during and after the initial fund raising process.

Stephen Bayfield joined Pannell Kerr Forster as a corporate finance partner in May 1997, following three years as a director of an acquisitive group.

Section Two

Debt

3
A Glossary of Debt

Christopher Gasson
Bertoli Mitchell

Asset Cover is the ratio of net assets to total debt – i.e. total assets minus current liabilities/debt. It is used by banks to judge the security of their lending. The level of asset cover that a bank will feel comfortable with will depend on the nature of the assets: cash might be counted at 100 per cent, property at 80 per cent, stock and debtors at 50 per cent.

Bills of Exchange are instruments used in trade finance, typically used to provide finance between the time goods are delivered and payment is made. They are in the form of a promise to pay a fixed amount on a specified date (typically 3 months after issue). Most importantly they are tradable, enabling the vendor to realise the debt in cash by selling it on (usually to an accepting house). The price agreed will be discounted to reflect the prevailing interest rate.

Bonds are interest bearing securities which can be traded in the money markets. They are usually the cheapest source of debt for large companies. They consist of a coupon and a principal. The coupon represents the annual interest rate payable on the principal. The principal represents the face value of the bond which can be redeemed at maturity. They trade in the financial markets at a price which reflects the prevailing interest rate and expectations of the future interest rate. This process is described under **yield**, below. They are usually unsecured, but the borrower is required to have a **credit rating**. BBB- or Baa3 are considered the lowest investment grade rating. Money can still be raised in the high yield bond (or junk bond) market on lower ratings, but a higher interest rate is required. There will usually be covenants to ensure that the company does not subsequently take out higher ranking loans. The minimum amount that a company can raise in a bond is probably £50m. This is because the market prefers liquid (ie large) bond issues.

The bond market is a public market – ownership of bonds has to be registered and they are taxed at source. This has led to the growth in the Eurobond market. Eurobonds are bonds issued outside the domestic jurisdiction of the residency of the issuer. They are payable free of withholding tax and they can be bought and sold anony-mously. These tax advantages have made them a very popular means of raising debt among large corporations.

There are a number of different types of bond and Eurobond:

- *Commercial Paper*: bonds with a maturity of under one year. They offer no coupon. Instead they are usually sold at a discount to the redemption value which corresponds to the prevailing interest rate. They are used primarily by the largest, most credit-worthy institutions.
- *Medium Term Notes*: bonds with a maturity of between one and five years.
- *Floating Rate Notes*: bonds that pay interest pegged at a certain number of basis points (hundredths of a percentage point) above LIBOR.
- *Paid in kind*: bonds that issue more bonds instead of paying cash interest.
- *With Warrants*: bonds that give the right to acquire ordinary shares in the issuer after a certain period.
- *Zero-coupon bonds*: bonds that pay no interest. They are issued at a discount to their face value relating to the expected interest rate to maturity.

Charges represent security that a bank has in making a loan. They can be fixed or floating. A fixed charge is one that refers to a specific asset, e.g. a building or plant. In the event of default the lender can take con-trol of the asset and sell it to cover the value of the loan. A floating charge refers to all the assets of a business over which there is no fixed charge. It therefore ranks below a fixed charge in a liquidation. (See **Ranking** below.)

Committed facilities are agreements between banks and borrowers to provide funds up to a specific amount, at a specific interest rate (usually a fixed amount above LIBOR) for a specific period of time. Term debt (see Chapter 1) is generally in the form of a committed facility. Unlike uncommitted facilities such as overdrafts, they cannot be removed on demand by the lender. They do however usually entail covenants which, if broken, can mean that the debt has to be repaid on demand.

Convertibles are debt instruments that can be converted into equity in certain circumstances. They include convertible bonds, which give the bearer the right to convert the bonds into shares at a pre-defined ratio after a specified date. Another example is convertible loan stock, which is often used by venture capitalists to dilute the management equity should they fail to perform (see ratchets, Chapter 11).

Covenants are conditions imposed on loans and bonds to protect lenders against default. They stipulate things such as:

- a minimum level of asset cover;
- a maximum level of gearing;
- a minimum level of interest cover;
- that no prior ranking debt is subsequently arranged;
- that specified assets cannot be sold without the consent of the lender;
- that the lender has the right to review the loan in the event of the business being taken over or control otherwise changing hands;
- that the lender has the right to call in the loan in the event of the borrower defaulting on other loans.

Whether or not a company accepts the covenants proposed to it by its bank will depend on the strength of its negotiating position. The very largest publicly quoted companies can usually avoid most covenants, but smaller unquoted companies may find themselves having to agree to very restrictive covenants simply because there is less competition for their business.

Credit Rating is the means by which the public debt markets assess the credit worthiness of an issuer of debt. There are two main rating agencies, Moody's and Standard & Poors. The rating systems they use are slightly different:

Investment Grade

Moody's	Standard & Poors	Interpretation
Aaa	AAA	Highest quality
Aa1, Aa2, Aa3	AA+, AA, AA-	High quality
A1, A2, A3	A+, A, A-	Strong payment capacity
Baa1, Baa2, Baa3	BBB+, BBB, BBB-	Adequate payment capacity

Speculative-Grade Ratings

Moody's	Standard & Poors	Interpretation
Ba1, Ba2, Ba3	BB+, BB, BB-	Likely to fulfil obligations, on-going uncertainty
B1, B2, B3	B+, B, B-	High-risk obligations
Caa	CCC+, CCC, CCC-	Current vulnerability to default, or in default
Ca, D	C, D	In bankruptcy or default, or other shortcoming.

The lower the credit rating the greater the **yield** required to entice investors to buy the bonds. Speculative grade-rated bonds are often referred to as high yield or junk bonds. Such issuers usually require **credit wrapping** to get their bonds away. The market's attitude to different credit ratings is dependent on the prevailing attitude to risk. A high yield bond might trade at 300 basis points above LIBOR in a stable market, but in a highly risk averse market this spread might increase to 800 basis points. Sometimes it becomes effectively impossible to raise finance at all in the bond market without a triple or double A credit rating. The process of achieving a rating takes at least three months.

Credit Wrapping is a technique by which a bond issued by a company with a poor credit rating can be shored up with the assistance of an institution with a strong credit rating. It involves the institution (usually a large insurer with a triple A credit rating) agreeing to underwrite a proportion of the amount payable in the event of default in exchange for a premium. In many cases it is the only way in which ‣poorly rated companies can issue bonds.

Debt to Equity Ratio is a measure of the gearing of a business. It is calculated as long-term debt (usually including preference shares) divided by the shareholder funds. It is an important indicator for banks: they are extremely reluctant to lend money to businesses that are highly geared (see Chapter 6 on internal equity).

Discounting is a means of raising money against the value of unpaid invoices. A discounter will purchase invoices (bills) at a discount to their face value, hoping to make a profit on redemption. **Factoring** is the more common form of invoice finance in use today.

Debentures are secured long term. The security usually comes in the form of a floating charge over the assets of the business. This gives the holder of the debenture the right to appoint an administrative receiver in the event of default, giving it enormous powers over the business (see Chapters 7 and 8). The advantage of debentures for borrowers is that they generally pay a lower rate of interest than an overdraft, and they are **committed facilities**.

Eurobonds: see **bonds**.

Factoring is a means of raising working capital against trade debtors (see Chapter 4). There are two sorts. *With service factoring* involves assuming the credit risk for collecting debts, but only advancing the money as it becomes payable. *With service plus finance factoring* involves paying a percentage of the value of the invoice as soon as the goods are delivered.

Forfaiting is a form of invoice **discounting** used by exporters.

Gearing: see **debt to equity ratio**.

Hire Purchase is a means of structuring the purchase of capital assets such that ownership of the asset only changes hands once a certain number of instalments towards the final consideration have been made. (See Chapter 5.)

Interest cover is one of the most important ratios a bank will look at in determining whether to advance a loan. It looks at the number of times a company would be able to pay interest out of its earnings before interest and tax. It indicates at a very basic level whether or not a business will be able to service its debts. For this reason, it is more important than analysing the value of the security (i.e. asset cover) in reaching decisions about loans. The level of earnings at which most banks will start to get uncomfortable will be between two and three times interest.

Leasing is a means of hiring fixed assets. It is covered in detail in Chapter 5.

Letter of credit is a means of trade finance involving an importer's bank (the issuing bank) writing to a bank in the exporter's country (the negotiating bank) authorising the payment of a specified sum to the exporter on presentation of the shipping documents.

Loan stock is a tradable debt instrument that can either be secured or unsecured. Secured loan stock is a **debenture**. Unsecured loan stock is very similar to **preference shares** but it ranks above preference shares on liquidation. Loan stock is used in structuring venture capital deals and in situations in which loans to large companies are syndicated among a number of banks.

Mezzanine finance is a generic term for financial instruments that have the characteristics of both debt and equity. It may be secured or unsecured, and it may or may not involve a degree of participation in the up-side of the sale of the business. It usually comes in the form of variations on **preference shares** or **loan stock.** It is usually provided by mezzanine finance specialists to back management buy-outs and buy-ins.

Mortgages are loans secured against fixed assets, usually property.

Off balance sheet finance is finance that can be raised without declaring it on the balance sheet. Typically it would involve moving an asset into a separate company which then raises money against it and returns the cash to the original owner of the asset. Until Financial Reporting Standard 5 was introduced, there was no reason why such transactions should be disclosed at all in the company accounts, and it was a very attractive means for quoted companies to raise money without alarming their shareholders. Since FRS 5, companies have been required to divulge related party transactions and it is no longer so attractive.

Overdrafts are uncommitted facilities that exist to meet seasonal working capital needs. Although interest rates are higher, they are cheaper than using a term loan for the same purpose because interest is calculated on the basis of the account at the end of each day rather than the maximum amount borrowed.

Preference shares are equity instruments that behave like debt instruments. They pay interest at a fixed rate rather than dividends. Like debt, they do not participate in any increase in the value of the business, but unlike debt they are unsecured, and therefore vulnerable should the value of the business decrease. On liquidation, preference shares are ranked below loan stock and debentures, but above ordinary shares. Often they can be converted into ordinary shares if interest payments are not met. They do not usually have voting powers. They can be structured in various different ways:

- *Convertible preference shares*: these can be exchanged for ordinary shares under certain conditions or after a certain date. Convertible preference shares are often used by venture capitalists to structure ratchets. They enable the investor to dilute the management's equity if certain targets are not achieved.

- *Cumulative preference shares*: where interest payments are rolled into the principal, to be paid off on redemption. They are used by venture capitalists to ensure that a business is not over burdened by interest payments while it is not generating excess cash. Usually the accumulated interest is paid on exit.
- *Redeemable preference shares*: which can be exchanged for their value in cash on or after a specified date or event.

Ranking refers to the order in which holders of a company's securities are paid out in the event of liquidation. The order is as follows:

- Preferred creditors (i.e. PAYE, NIC, VAT and wages and salaries up to a maximum of £800)
- Holders of fixed charges over the assets (i.e. mortgagees)
- Holders of floating charges over the assets (i.e. debenture holders)
- Senior creditors such as trade creditors and other unsecured debt
- Subordinated creditors such as holders of unsecured loan stock
- Holders of preference shares
- Ordinary shareholders.

A lender will always want to ensure that there are more claimants ranked beneath it than above it. The debt to equity ratio can be seen as a measure of where a lender will be in the queue: a low debt to equity ratio means that there are plenty of equity participants at the back of the queue to absorb any risks, and therefore gives banks comfort. A high debt to equity ratio means that the bank's loans will be more exposed in the event of liquidation.

Receivership refers to the appointment of a licensed insolvency practitioner to realise the value of the assets to repay the value of the outstanding debts after a company has defaulted.

Revolving Facilities are debt instruments that combine the flexibility of an overdraft with the commitment of term debt. They are negotiated for a specific credit limit for a specific period, during which time they can be drawn down or repaid. As **committed facilities** they usually involve **covenants**. Interest is payable on the whole facility whether or not it is drawn, although there will usually be one interest rate for the drawn part of the facility, and another, slightly lower, interest rate for the undrawn part of the facility.

Securitisation is traditionally defined as the replacement of bank borrowing by bond issues, but in recent years it has a more specific meaning. It is the issuance of bonds against the security of receivables. It involves transferring legal title to an income stream to a separate company, which then issues a bond back by that income stream. Should the income stream be more than enough to cover the interest payments on the bonds, then the excess is returned to the original company; should the income stream be insufficient, then the bond holders have the right to sell-on the income stream. Usually the bond holders will be protected against default by **credit wrapping**. Securitisation has been one of the growth areas of finance in the late 1990s. It is used by leasing companies and mortgage lenders as well as pop stars (securitising their royalties) and utilities.

Syndication is used where one bank is either reluctant or unable to provide the full amount to be borrowed itself. It is usually required only for the largest loans, unless there is undue risk involved.

Yield refers to the income (expressed in terms of per cent per annum) from a bond, taking into account both the interest receivable and the discount from the redemption value at which the bond is purchased. For example a ten-year 8 per cent bond due for redemption in five years' time may be trading at £90. The actual income expressed in percentage terms will be different from 8 per cent for two reasons. First, because the coupon pays interest as 8 per cent of £100 rather than 8 per cent of £90, and, second, because when the bond is eventually redeemed the holder of it will receive £100 rather than the £90 it costs on the current market. Taking both of these factors into account involves some quite complex mathematics because, strictly speaking, the value of the discount should not be amortised evenly across the remaining life of the bond. Bond analysts use 'yield curves' to calculate the yield to maturity. When the price of bonds falls, the yields rise and vice versa.

4

Structured Finance

John Bagley
NMB-Heller

Introduction

Traditionally, corporate finance was the domain of a company's bankers, who would lend money for growth by way of overdraft facilities and loans, on the strength of the balance sheet – historic information based on the company's net worth. Now, growing businesses can take advantage of 'structured business finance', which is based on the value of a company's assets and is a more flexible source of finance than bank loans and overdrafts. Structured business finance is based on the principles of invoice discounting, taking the idea one stage further by financing other assets.

Invoice discounting is a source of business finance which advances cash against the value of sales invoices and which allows the business to run its own sales ledger and payment collection. Invoice discounting itself developed from 'factoring', the form of invoice finance that involves handing sales ledger administration over to the finance provider – and paying an administration fee for this service.

Structured business finance follows the route taken by asset-based finance in the United States and tends, in the UK, to be offered by those finance providers not owned by the high street banks. The product is driven more by asset valuation than by balance sheet valuation and, as such, is highly attractive to ambitious, expanding businesses. In general, structured business finance is used by medium to large SMEs (up to around £60–70 million turnover), which require a more flexible funding package than can be provided by mainstream banks.

Strategic structured finance

Increasingly, we are now finding that structured business finance provides an ideal solution for management buy-outs and buy-ins (MBOs and MBIs) and other financial restructurings. The more traditional use of structured business finance has tended to be for businesses that are highly seasonal – such as those which depend on the Christmas trade. Generally it is true to say that structured business finance is far more flexible than the bank overdraft, and levels of finance available are usually higher. This is because there is no monetary limit set on borrowing levels, as they are linked to assets such as stock and sales which are constantly moving. The finance provided, therefore, is matched to the assets available, not to pre-set limits. When structured business finance is provided by a company independent of the high street banks, it will generally tend to replace traditional bank overdrafts and loans.

In its present form, structured business finance has been in existence for the past two or three years and is becoming extremely popular. Although figures are not yet kept separately for this form of asset-based finance, statistics from the Factors and Discounters Association show a healthy growth in overall business volumes within the asset-based finance industry – over the last ten years a seven-fold growth from £7 billion in 1987 to nearly £50 billion in 1997. The greatest area of growth, in our experience, is in arranging MBOs and MBIs. Here, the level of flexibility which structured business finance provides is highly attractive to the corporate finance team involved in arranging the overall deal. Structured business finance can provide a source of finance for the buy-in/buy-out which enables the new management to retain 100 per cent equity in the business (rather than hand over a proportion to a venture capitalist) – an option which comes very high on the list of priorities of the new owners. The key to structured finance is the funding of invoices followed by the funding of stock. An agreed percentage is made available against both of these assets, normally up to 85 per cent against invoices and 30–50 per cent against stock. Interest costs can be less than those charged by a bank for an equivalent facility; however, they will depend on the complexity of the deal and there are administration fees. It is unlikely that the managers will be asked to provide guarantees.

Case studies

A couple of examples of structured business finance facilities for an MBO and MBI recently arranged by NMB-Heller illustrate how structured business finance works in practice, and how it can provide solutions to meet needs speedily and effectively.

Frith's Flexible Packaging Limited

The first shows how this structured finance approach was used for an MBI in David Watson's purchase of packaging specialist, Frith's Flexible Packaging Limited. Here NMB-Heller teamed with its associate company, ING Lease, to provide sufficient cash for the buy-in. David Watson worked with a corporate finance consultant, first to identify the best business to acquire, and then to source funding. Because this acquisition was intended as the first of several, a major objective was to avoid the need to raise venture capital, holding it in reserve for larger future deals. To achieve this they needed to find an asset-rich business for sale, where 100 per cent asset-backed funding could be raised, and found Friths to be the ideal choice. When it came to sourcing the funding, ING Lease was prepared to go to 100 per cent funding of the plant and equipment on its appreciation of the strength of the business plan and the competence of the incoming MBI leader. NMB-Heller was selected to provide working capital by way of a term loan and invoice finance, because NMB and ING Lease could work together to produce a fast track service, providing a turnkey funding solution that avoided the need for the client to cede equity to a third party. There was an 'agreement in principle' within 48 hours and the whole deal was completed from start to finish within three months.

Eurotec Automotive

The second example shows how Eurotec Automotive, a whole-sale distributor of vehicle parts based in Wakefield, was acquired in a management buy-out jointly undertaken by the company's management team and its major customer from French parent, the CFAO Group. The business has an increasing turnover of £8 million, which has grown over recent years from £1 million under the leadership of managing director, Ron Branton. Integral to the deal was the asset-based working capital solution put in place by NMB-Heller which has supported the buy-out team and allowed it to retain complete equity control over the business. The management team can now call upon a flexible funding package that includes working capital advanced against debtors and stock, a working capital term loan and Trade Finance to facilitate the import of goods on Letters of Credit.

Crucial to the success of the deal was the ability to meet the tight timeframe set by the company's original owners for the completion of the deal. The NMB-Heller support package was implemented within a six-week period from start to finish, and enabled the management team to successfully complete the deal on time. A rival buyer from within the trade had intended to absorb the business into its own organisation, which would have resulted in redundancies for Eurotec employees. However, the NMB-Heller deal has now secured the long-term future of the business.

Summary

The ideal profile of a company that will benefit from structured business finance is one that is growing or undergoing a period of change, with experienced and forward-looking management, where the net worth of the company is relatively low compared with its turnover, but the company has good debtors and a fairly large element of finished stock on its balance sheet. Structured business finance is built upon the lender's knowledge of, and confidence in, a particular business. Timescales will, therefore, have to take into account the familiarisation process. Before any decision to invest in a company can be made, the lender needs to understand the business and the management plans and evaluate the size and strength of the assets – the invoices, stock and other assets to be funded. Normally, however, this process should not take more than three to four weeks.

5
Asset Finance

Forward Trust

How to pay for today's assets with tomorrow's money

Funding the cost of growth need not be a headache. A recent Bank of England report highlighted concerns that many British businesses still fund the fixed assets they need for growth from overdrafts or even cash flow. But short or medium-term borrowing to fund long-term investment can seriously affect businesses' corporate profitability. Equally, to use the company's own capital resources for such purchases can prove short sighted. Capital safely invested against a rainy day that produces a solid return is far more useful to the company than money spent on an asset that will depreciate. Spending these funds on an asset, even though it may be key to the company's future, reduces the company's working capital which could be better used in many ways – perhaps buying raw materials, improving wages or paying suppliers.

Using a bank loan or, even worse, an overdraft to fund asset purchases can be problematic. Interest rates can be unpredictable when what your business needs is stability in order to plan ahead to compete. Furthermore, does it make sense to have a loan secured on an asset that will depreciate as time goes by?

In spite of this, almost two thirds of the capital investment in plant, machinery, vehicles, ships and aircraft is funded either through cash flow, bank loans or the capital of the company.

But the balance is changing. Increasingly, businesses are looking towards asset finance houses to fund capital equipment. The asset finance idea is well over 60 years old and some finance houses have been providing both practical advice and capital for development for many years. Already some £21 billion of assets are financed this way and the trend, given the tax advantages and the release of capital built into the systems on offer, is increasing.

Basically, there are two ways to acquire assets this way: leasing and hire purchase. The difference is as simple as the names suggest. With leasing you have the use, but not the ownership of the asset, and with hire purchase, you have the use and the option of ownership at the end of the term.

The system that is most advantageous for your business will depend on a number of factors. Every business has its own special needs and problems, so it is wisest to spend some time discussing your own circumstances with an asset finance expert, in order to compare options. All surveys demonstrate that, since tax is tax and interest rates are interest rates, the key factor in the choice of finance house is almost always its ability to add value to the financial package, combined with financial stability.

Nowadays, leasing companies tend to be part of one of the major banking and financial services groups, and have consequently become enormously sophisticated, providing advice on a wide range of subjects, from the tax implications of your decision to the maintenance contracts you may need for your particular kind of asset. You also need to look for what added value they can bring, for example:

- Do they understand your market and the assets you require?
- Do they know how your business operates?
- Do they know what customers you have and what assets you own already?
- Is ownership necessary or will hiring fulfil your purpose?
- Will the asset be coming from Britain or abroad?
- Do you have to pay a deposit?

The questions may seem endless, but there is a practical purpose behind them. The finance company should be aiming to produce a tailored plan for your business that takes into account three key factors:

- What income will be generated by the asset?
- What is its anticipated working life?
- What will its value be at the end of the term?

Simply put, the plan they produce should always match the repayments you have to make to the income that the asset will provide for your business.

So the agreement you enter into, whether it is a lease or hire purchase, can be tailored to suit your business. Today, some top finance houses have built up a track record of specialised experience in particular industries, bringing a particular understanding of the problems and opportunities facing your industry. This means that they can frequently point you to the best supplier for the asset you need, help you to specify the equipment that will suit your business best and can actually suggest ways of working that may not have occurred to you. Some companies in your market may even be able to improve or develop new products or services for you. In addition, if you choose to lease, the financial muscle of these finance companies often means that they have considerable buying power, helping you to minimise costs.

Of course, because financial engineering is their core skill, you should also consider the ingenuity of the finance house. Competition is such that lessors must always seek to provide a financial package that makes the most of every opportunity to cover work in your favour. As well as making the most of your own position, they should also optimise the way you pay interest. For example, you may imagine that two per cent over bank rate is the same, whoever the supplier; but some companies calculate the interest you pay quarterly. So, even though you may have repaid quite a considerable sum by the end of the quarter, the interest you are paying is still being calculated on the amount owing at the start of the period. Ideally, of course, your interest should be calculated on a day-to-day basis.

The finance period is also important. An experienced finance house will understand your business and, recognising that some assets have a longer life-span than others, will advise you what the best timing should be; usually anything from three to seven years. They should also recognise that this period may well need to involve the time taken to set up the equipment – a printing press for example – before it can begin to produce an income. If this is the case, the company you choose should be prepared to look at low initial repayments, rising to the full scale when the machine is operating at peak efficiency. They should also understand the need for seasonal payment for assets such as coaches or food processing equipment for a particular crop, and cars, a subject that interests managers in most companies, are a matter of much consideration; how many miles, what type of miles, what kind of servicing? These are the kind of details that any business should consider before pursuing a relationship with a finance house. But all financing, whether hire purchase or a lease, will offer your company similar, broad benefits, as well as the particular advantages offered by individual companies.

First, it allows companies to plan ahead and provide considerable reassurance for the financial director.

Second, a choice of repayment methods, including fixed rates, means that you can budget more accurately because all your costs are pre-determined, not simply in terms of the repayments you make, but, with contract hire, in terms of the costs of running the asset itself. If, for example, you have a vehicle that the finance company has arranged to be kept in good order, you can be sure it will be properly maintained and that you will have the vital use of that asset for your business. The maintenance package may be arranged through the finance house or even through the manufacturer of the asset itself. Cars, for example, would be covered by the finance company, but heavy manufacturing machinery could well be the subject of an agreement made between the finance house and the manufacturer, to keep the asset in good running order for you. Once again, the finance house should tailor the most suitable package for your company.

Third, your financing costs can be fixed. At the start of the agreement, you agree with the finance house the period of the agreement, the repayments that are necessary, and the rates you will have to pay.

Fourth, and possibly most reassuringly, this route is increasingly proving to be the best way to use a company's resources. Because it frees up your cash flow as well as your capital, asset finance can actually help your company grow. It is becoming an important part of the overall strategic plan for a great many companies; and, as its effectiveness is proved, it is increasingly being built into a company's strategy, rather than simply being used on an *ad hoc* basis. It puts your own money to work, doing what it should do: supporting your business.

You can also benefit from considerable tax advantages when using both leasing and hire purchase. Before outlining the major benefits of these, it is sensible to consider the basic question: do you need to own the asset eventually or do you simply need to have the use of it for a certain period of time?

Though the finance house will usually help you decide the answer to this question and will provide useful pointers, it is worth outlining the advantages of the two main routes.

Hire purchase

Hire purchase is a system whereby you pay a specified amount of money over a pre-determined period. At the end of the agreement, you pay the option to purchase fee that can be arranged to suit your business' financial situation. If ownership is really important to your company, this is the way to go.

The particular tax advantages it offers are that, although the asset does not belong to you until the end of the term, you can claim a tax deduction on all the interest paid against your profit and loss account. The other advantage is that you can claim the capital allowance, so a percentage of the cost of the asset can be offset against the tax you have to pay.

In addition, if your business is VATable, you can claim all the VAT paid on the asset as if you had bought it outright. The only exception to this rule is in the case of cars, which are regarded by the Inland Revenue as a separate case.

In all these three cases, the tax rights of ownership belong to your company, although the asset is actually owned by the finance house. This is called 'deemed belonging'.

As you are treated as the owner as far as tax and accounting are concerned, you can also claim depreciation in your books. As far as the Inland Revenue is concerned, there is no difference between an asset that is yours under a hire purchase agreement and one that you own outright. It is dealt with in just the same way as any other fixed asset.

Leasing

There are two forms of leasing: Finance Leasing and Operating Leasing. The decision to go the leasing route is also a matter for discussion with the finance house and your business advisers. You might, for example, prefer to lease if you cannot claim your capital allowance due to lack of profits. If this is the case, you can benefit from the tax allowances that the finance house can claim, as they will pass them on to you in the form of lower repayments. Or perhaps the way that you look at a discounted cash flow in your business might make it more financially viable to lease; and, of course, it is possible for a lease to be off balance sheet. There are many reasons you might consider.

Finance leases

Finance leasing is on balance sheet, and operating leasing is off balance sheet, and there are strict rules governing which of the two you can have. A finance lease is simply described as one where all the risks and rewards are transferred to the lessee. If you have benefited from all the tax benefits during the contract and, when the asset is sold by the finance house at the end of the lease, you receive some of the sale proceeds, then you have effectively received the benefits of the asset. Under a finance lease, the sale of the asset is carried out by the lessee, operating as the agent of the finance company. The money from the sale goes to the finance house, but they return up to 95 per cent of it to the client. So the client never actually owns the asset, rather it is seen as being loaned to the client and so should be shown on your balance sheet.

The other benefits are that the rental interest can be variable. Again, this is part of the risk and reward factor. If the bank rate falls, you will benefit; if it rises, you will have to pay more. That is a risk calculation you alone can make.

With a finance leasing agreement you don't pay VAT on the capital cost. But VAT is charged on the rental and you can recover the VAT paid. The leasing rental is classified as a revenue expense.

At the moment, finance leasing volumes are falling off, as companies look to other, less complex forms of leasing and because recent legislation has removed some of the tax advantages they once enjoyed.

Operating leases

An operating lease, with or without maintenance, appears off your balance sheet because most of the rewards and all the risks lie with the finance house.

The way it works is simple. The finance house will discuss the asset you need in just the same detail as with any other contract. In this instance, they will be seeking to find the exact use that you will put the asset to so that they can calculate what its value will be at the end of the term. This is called the residual risk. The finance house is using its experience to determine the value of the asset when the contract is over. The reason is that the repayments you make will be based on the difference between the purchase price and the amount they believe that they can sell the asset for when you have finished with it.

Suppose that you are buying a vehicle – say an HGV and trailer. The finance house will want to know all about your business, the loads you carry, journey times and distances, the qualifications of those driving, where the vehicle will be stored and how it will be maintained. With this knowledge they will decide its value in seven years' time, the period you have decided that you want the use of the vehicle for. You will make regular payments on the pre-determined value of the asset for this period – not the whole life. As a result you will pay a lower rental. Another consideration will be the maintenance of the vehicle to ensure it is to the standard required to achieve its predicted value at the end of your agreement, although this will form part of your contractual negotiations, as maintenance is one of the added value services many finance houses offer as part of their packaging.

You will also benefit from the fact that the finance house, because it actually owns the asset and has taken the risk of forecasting its value, will be able to claim the capital allowance on it and so will be able to charge a lower rental than might otherwise be the case. For hauliers who are non-tax-payers, this reduction can be particularly useful. Your company can also charge the cost of the rental against its corporation tax and, of course, your financial director will be delighted that the payments will remain predictable and that there is no question of any risk in estimating the re-sale value at the end of the term.

The only variation to these general rules applies to cars. Because they are regarded by the Treasury as part perk and part company necessity, they are assessed differently. As a result, you cannot deduct the rental costs against your corporation tax unless the car itself cost less than £12,000. In the case of cars, it is always sensible to discuss the exact use of your fleet with an experienced finance house as they can advise on the most tax efficient route, the timing involved and the maintenance package that will suit you best. Contract hire is also one of the best ways to remove a lot of the problems of maintaining your car fleet from the shoulders of your fleet manager.

The popularity of this method of asset financing is growing rapidly, partly because of its simplicity and the increasing trend to out-sourcing, and partly because the alternative route of finance leasing has become less attractive as the tax benefits have been reduced by successive governments.

In fact, so popular has contract hire become that some of the largest deals in the past few years have been on this basis. Planes and boats and trains, the big ticket assets, are very frequently financed in this way and clients have seen enormous benefits.

Case study

ScotRail

In a recent transaction with ScotRail, the client was able to afford to lease 40 trains when they had only expected to be able to lease 38. This was due partly to the construction of the financing and partly to the sheer financial muscle of Forward Trust Rail being a member of HSBC.

'Our buying power and strength in the marketplace enabled us to use the economies of scale in our negotiations with the rolling stock manufacturers,' said Peter Aldridge of Forward Trust Rail.

This particular transaction began with detailed discussions between Forward Trust Rail and ScotRail itself. If a financier is to provide the best results for the client, a detailed picture of every part of the customer's objectives needs to be established. Only when this is complete can a realistic proposal be made. The timing, specification and structure of the bid between Forward Trust and ScotRail were all ironed out prior to discussions with potential manufacturers. ScotRail specifically requested that the financiers give their best price in the tender response rather than getting involved in long, drawn-out haggling at a later date.

Time was of the essence throughout the transaction and was exacerbated by the fact that, as a result of a franchise commitment, ScotRail needed to have the rolling stock in service by March 2000. At the appointment of Forward Trust Rail, the two parties set about creating a detailed specification for the trains which was given to three manufacturers for tender.

'We had negotiated some 95 per cent of the contents of the lease with ScotRail before we even spoke to the manufacturer,' said Peter. At the same time, Forward Trust Rail negotiated both a spares and maintenance agreement with the manufacturers. Two of the 50 engineers who work for Forward Trust Rail were employed at this stage, as their expertise was vital. Forward Trust aims to work in partnership with its customers, providing a portfolio of services and knowledge in addition to finance.

The lease agreement does not require ScotRail to make payments while the trains are being built. However, Forward Trust Rail has already started paying the manufacturers in stages, with the largest payments made on delivery of the rolling stock. To protect and support the interests of both parties during the building process, four engineers from Forward Trust are working with ScotRail.

The finance house should always aim to make the purchase and use of the assets required to run your business as simple and as painless as possible. To do this:

- They need to have access to considerable financial strength because you want to be sure that they will continue to back you throughout the whole term of the contact.
- They should be independent. By not being tied to any one manufacturer, they will be able to shop around on your behalf and make the best buys for you.
- They should be able to offer you the benefits of buying in bulk that will serve to lower your costs.
- They should have the depth of expertise to be able to offer you more than just money.
- They should understand your business and the market you operate in. This will allow them not only to tell you where the best place to buy tyres can be found, but to advise you on market trends that might affect the way you run your own business.

As in so many financial markets today, it is the added value that counts; the service that goes with the cash should be the most important factor in your decision about which finance house to choose and which system will suit you best.

All reasonable care has been taken in the preparation of this article, but it is intended only to be a general guide. You should check the position of your own company, with regard to financing assets in this way, with a professional financial adviser; the treatment of leases, for example, can vary depending on an individual auditor's interpretation. You should also make certain that there have not been any fundamental changes in accounting, taxation or legal requirements.

Looking for
a new perspective
on fixed asset finance?

Forward Trust is one of the most experienced and respected asset finance companies. Totally in tune with today's economic climate and the business environment, we work closely with large and small companies to tailor asset finance to suit their present and future needs.

Six separate divisions staffed by skilled specialists give us a highly focused perspective on the specialised asset requirements of British industry.

If you'd like to discuss your asset acquisition plans with one of our experts, call 0800 614304.

Forward Trust Limited P.O. Box 5693, 54 Hagley Road Birmingham B16 8PL

6

Internal Equity

Brian Warnes MA FCA FRSA
Business Dynamics Ltd

Introduction

Venture capital or other forms of outside equity investment are often seen as being the key ingredient to successful growing companies. The truth is, however, that most of Britain's fastest growing companies have financed their growth from internal resources. A survey carried out by 3i of companies with sales of between £500,000 and £100m showing turnover growth of 25 per cent per annum over a two-year period, revealed that most are owner managed, with only seven per cent of the equity in these companies in the hands of outside investors. Only three per cent of the shares in these 'superleague' growing companies are owned by venture capitalists. Besides overdrafts and other forms of short-term loans, the most significant form of finance for all these companies was generated internally: 80 per cent of respondents used retained profits to finance their growth, 22 per cent used long-term loans. Retained profits are the most favoured means of financing growth for a number of different reasons:

- *Expense*: retained profits are self evidently the cheapest form of finance. No interest is charged on retained profits, and no shares need change hands. There are no professional fees to be paid.
- *Dilution of ownership*: owner managers are often very reluctant to sacrifice control of a business.

- *Time*: it can take several months to attract a suitable equity partner.
- *Success rate*: equity funds tend to be choosy, typically backing as few as one or two per cent of the propositions submitted to them.
- *Exit strategies*: private equity investors require an exit, typically within three to five years. This means trade sale or flotation is on the agenda as soon as such an investment is made.

On the positive side, there are all the benefits of having an experienced equity partner on board to steer the company successfully through all the problems (and dangers) of growth and change. Furthermore, companies which need finance for major acquisitions or to grow rapidly in areas which are particularly working capital intensive may have no option but to turn to private equity.

However, for companies which are looking to build to a perhaps substantial size over a 10 to 15 year period, whilst remaining within the control and ownership of the original shareholders and management team, retained profit will always be the preferred form of finance.

The multiplier effect

Retained profit is not just a significant form of finance in itself, it strengthens the balance sheet of a company so that bankers can be more supportive.

It is widely known that banks assess the credit worthiness of a business on the basis of the security and interest cover available. But there is another factor that goes into deciding whether or not to make a loan or extend overdraft facilities. It is the 'one-to-one' gearing rule, which says that a bank should not have more in a company than the owners themselves. This means that a bank may be reluctant to lend more to a company than the sum of the share capital plus retained profits. If share capital is to remain unchanged, the only way a company can increase the amount a bank will be prepared to lend is through increasing retained profit.

One-to-one gearing in principle means that a bank will only provide half the funding needs of a growing company, and then only if the other half is already present as shareholder funds. For companies that do not wish to issue additional equity, the inescapable conclusion is that for every £1 of extra funding need, the company must make and retain 50p of additional profit.

Once this is appreciated, the importance of retaining profit, rather than distributing it, becomes apparent.

The challenge

Many owner-managed businesses consider a five per cent return on sales after tax to be good. At the same time their working capital requirement might be in the order of 20 per cent to 30 per cent of turnover. Capital expenditure comes on top of that. The result is that the ability to fund growth, calculated as twice retained profits, falls well short of the funding requirement. The result is over-trading: companies running out of funding as their businesses grow, and blaming their banks for not being supportive enough.

Fortunately there is much that can be done to resolve the dilemma provided every member of the management team can come intuitively to understand the true nature of the problem and modify the operation of their company well in advance accordingly.

For example, slightly modify the approach to generate say 60p retained profit and a bank will be happy to lend another 60p, whether it is needed or not (it may lend even more because they will see that gearing is reducing as borrowing needs rise). The company then has £1.20 of extra funding to meet a need of only £1. There is 20p of free funding to put the business ahead of the struggle to meet its working capital requirement. It can be invested to boost longer-term profitability such as research and development and capital projects, creating a virtuous circle.

Slightly fall down on the approach, and generate say only 40p, and the bank will lend another 40p at the very most (it may not even lend that much as it will see that gearing is increasing as borrowing needs rise). Some, sensing a situation in which gearing is increasing, will become nervous and may well stop well short of 1:1 matching. Assuming the company is adequately funded at the outset (which may not be the case), it is only safe if it does not grow. The faster it tries to grow, the sooner collapse will be inevitable. Possibly as many as 90–95 per cent of company failures or companies who fail to grow as they should because of funding problems do so for this reason.

Holding on to profit

Virtually any company can be made self-sufficient in funding as it grows. The first step is to ensure that retained profit is not needlessly dissipated.

Company directors are tempted to talk down the bottom line:

- Many private companies are susceptible to the argument that the greater the profit, the greater the tax bill, and therefore find ways of understating or reducing profits wherever possible.
- Smaller owner-managed businesses are often attracted to the idea of reducing taxable profits by making large contributions to a self-administered pension fund which then lends the money back to the company.
- Profits are often considered to be some sort of surplus whose main purpose is to provide for dividends and bonus payments.

The pressures are legion, particularly on the corporation tax aspect, even though successive governments, recognising the importance of retained profits in helping overcome the perceived 'equity gap' in the economy, have reduced tax rates on retained profits to non-penal levels.

The tax arguments for not retaining profits may make sense for companies that do not have significant funding requirements, but they are counterproductive for companies that do. £1 less profit may save 21p to 31p in corporation tax, but at the cost of reducing the funding available for growth by £2.

Retaining profit is essential in situations where:

- the present equity base is inadequate to support current funding needs;
- the company is experiencing rapid growth.

Once the equity base catches up and growth slows, progressively more profit can be distributed.

Conclusion

As long as the management team understands the urgency of maximising retained profits, then there is no reason why any business cannot, with matching bank help, be made fully self-sufficient in funding as it grows, however fast it wants to grow.

It requires very close planning and monitoring of cash flows, particularly on the working capital side (ie stocks, debtors and creditors), and a good understanding of the relationship between growth and profitability within the business. In exchange it offers a powerful, benign answer to funding problems of growing businesses.

But there is only the thinnest dividing line between growth which funds itself, and growth which does not, and therefore threatens the whole future of the business. Internal equity is therefore not just about providing the comfort of full control to owner managers who might otherwise have to seek external equity investors, it is also about the necessity of survival and success.

Case study

In the mid-1990s, a company making £370,000 pre-tax profit on a turnover of £7.1m with a positive equity base of nearly £300,000 decided on a strategy of growth. Overheads were increased, margins reduced. Turnover 'improved' to £9.7m. A pretax loss of £640,000 emerged, wiping out the company's equity base and with it its borrowing capacity. At the same time its turnover-related funding need also increased.

The following year turnover increased to nearly £14m. By hardening margins and cutting costs, profits were at least restored to breakeven. But the turnover-related funding need had by now nearly doubled against the still heavily negative equity base. The company survived only through a substantial injection of funds by the owners, who borrowed heavily against their homes to do so. Had the company collapsed, their homes and livelihoods would have disappeared with it.

Fortunately, in both years, despite loss of bank confidence, high turnover at least enabled factoring and invoice discounting to hold the balance. Even so, the first factor pulled out after the loss-making trends became apparent and a second had, with considerable difficulty, to be found. Bank support fell away completely. Margin improvements and cost cutting continued, with the twin aims of:

- Deliberately reducing turnover, which fell to £11.6m, through a still tougher margin policy, coupled with much tougher control of stocks and debtors, both combining to reduce the turnover-related funding need.
- Increasing retained profits. Profits improved to over £300,000 pre-tax, £200,000 post-tax. The consequent equity-base strengthening, although still negative, substantially restored the confidence of the bank, the twin aspects of the balance between funding need and funding availability moving towards each other favourably.

The trend continued in the current year, with further reductions in turnover and improvements in profitability taking place. Margins have had to be eased to cope with weakening markets, reducing the rate at which retained profits are being built up, but weakening turnover is at least further easing the situation in terms of lower funding need.

Brian Warnes has spent 30 years in the venture/development capital industry. Having previously set up and run a development capital fund for the Midland Bank, Midland Bank Venture Capital Limited, he founded Business Dynamics in 1987. Further information is available from "The Genghis Khan Guide to Business," published by Osmosis Publications (0181 855 5497) or from Business Dynamics direct on 0181 852 6560.

7
Banks and Distress

Robin Baum
Robin F Baum Consultants

Understanding banks

The most common complaint of entrepreneurs in a cash flow crisis is that their banks do not understand them. Very few of them consider that if they had made more effort to understand their banks, perhaps they would not have found themselves in such difficulties in the first place.

Banks are lenders to entrepreneurial businesses, but they are not entrepreneurial themselves. Banks finance the working capital a business needs to bridge the period of time between producing the goods and being paid for them. They are large organisations whose profits are more dependent on financial control than creativity. There are a number of specific points about the culture of banks of which all entrepreneurs should be aware.

The manual is supreme: Each bank has a central credit risk department that is responsible for producing a manual and policing its implementation. This lays down the criteria and ratios that are relevant to investment in each industry sector. It usually incorporates a computer credit scoring programme, which will determine credit limits and flag up a potential problem the moment a business gets into difficulty. Managers who deviate from the manual are putting their careers on the line: if things go wrong, they are finished.

Managers are not rewarded for taking risks: Bank managers have their time and targets directed towards generating new accounts and new business. It is very rarely cost effective for them to get involved in rescuing a failing business, they are not incentivised to do so, and as individuals they are not attracted by taking unnecessary risks.

Jobs are on the line: Banks are always seeking to reduce their costs to improve profitability. Their main cost is people. Over the past five years the banking sector has seen massive cut-backs in staff numbers. It is difficult to understate the impact of staff redundancy programmes on the attitudes of bank managers. There may be political pressure to support struggling businesses, but the threat of retrenchment has ensured that no manager is prepared to stick his neck out too far.

Banks do not provide risk capital: In 90 per cent of cases, when a business gets into difficulties it needs more risk capital. Banks do not provide risk capital. They provide finance secured against assets. Because they do not take the same risks as equity providers, the margins are lower. A bank will aim to make a two to three per cent margin over the base rate, while an equity provider is generally looking at an internal rate of return on its investment of between 20 and 30 per cent per annum.

Banks and security

When things start to go wrong, banks have a comfort zone, which is the value of the security they have taken in exchange for the loan. As long as the value of the asset taken as security exceeds the value of the loan by a reasonable margin, then the bank will not take a loss.

In many cases the security will come in the form of a debenture or fixed and floating charge over the assets of the business. This gives them a lot more control than most of their customers realise. Specifically, it gives them the right to appoint a receiver to dispose of the assets at a moment's notice. That threat alone puts them in a very much stronger position than the shareholders of a company, who stand to lose all their investment should a receiver be appointed. It also puts them in a stronger position than the trade creditors.

In calculating the value of the floating charge, a bank will typically take 70 per cent of the value of fixed assets such as property, 50 per cent of the value of the stock and 50 per cent of the value of the debtors. This gives an indication of the amount it is likely to realise on the appointment of a receiver.

When things go wrong

A problem is typically brought to the attention of the bank when an interest or principal payment is missed, during an annual review of an account, or when an overdraft limit is broken. The bank manager may also investigate after receiving messages from the credit risk department suggesting that certain business sectors are experiencing difficulties and should be looked at more closely.

When a problem is brought to light, the bank manager will first and foremost look at the security cover and the income cover for his loan interest. Then he will consider the plan for the business over the next 12 months including budgets and forecasts and cashflow projections ("the Business Plan").

The Business Plan must give the bank the confidence to continue its support and, to this end, include a staged reduction of gearing from reducing costs or disposal of assets as well as looking at the possible introduction of new equity capital. The presentation of this plan to the bank often becomes the key to getting its continuing support (see Chapters 7 and 8). The information is fed into the bank's computer, which advises on appropriate credit limits.

If further investigation is required, the bank will commission an accountant's report into the feasibility of the Business Plan and the past management of the business, and an independent valuation of the security. The cost of carrying out these checks is borne by the business rather than the bank. The bank will then decide whether or not to push the receivership button.

The equity solution

Nearly all businesses that get into difficulty have lost their capital base and are illiquid. They almost always need more equity and cash. The problem is that it is quite difficult to get new investors into a business that is in trouble quickly enough.

It could come from existing shareholders, either by them putting in cash or collateral (such as their houses) which can be used to raise an additional or increased loan.

It is usually very difficult to get new shareholders in at this stage. The venture capital market is increasingly dominated by low risk, big ticket management buy-outs. Struggling businesses are not attractive propositions: the risks are too high and the size of the deals generally too small. The venture capitalists that get involved in distress situations (known as 'vulture capitalists') tend to focus on larger deals, and tend to require substantial, and usually unacceptable, dilution of the existing shareholders.

Elsewhere in Europe, banks operate rescue funds which provide equity in these circumstances, but such funds have yet to take off in the UK. Banks are very well placed to take equity or options to increase the rewards of successfully supporting a struggling company, but they choose not to. The reason usually given is that there would be a conflict of interest.

The crunch

The lack of equity funding available for struggling businesses usually concentrates the friction between the bank and the proprietor of the business. By this stage there has usually been a complete breakdown of trust between the two parties and face-to-face encounters turn into slanging matches.

Things are exacerbated by the fact that the banks do not seem to appreciate the personal pressures they put on people. Proprietors have often given personal guarantees and have taken out additional mortgages on their houses. Banks will often ask for these as a sign of extra commitment when things first start to go wrong. Typically, proprietors of businesses in this situation are people who have been living to a pretty high standard and everything is falling around their ears.

While receivership often entails a massive loss of status and welfare for the proprietor, it is often the quickest and cheapest option for the bank.

Avoiding the crunch

Liquidity only becomes a crisis if problems are not identified early and appropriate action taken. Banks will need to be informed, but first one should prepare the Business Plan projecting the way forward for presentation to the bank. While banks frequently complain that they have not been warned of problems early enough, it is not uncommon for them to withdraw their support simply because the Plan has not been presented clearly, confidently and credibly.

Although it is possible to develop a turnaround strategy that will win the support of the bank on one's own, it is usually better to bring in an experienced outside adviser known to the bank. Such an outsider is better placed to see where the business has gone wrong, and will add credibility when presenting the Business Plan to the bank.

The problem is that most proprietors or chief executives believe that they are the only ones who know how to run their business and are very reluctant to involve outsiders until the last minute. Furthermore, there is concern about keeping the costs down.

I am often asked what key items I look for when I consider taking on a business. My answer is the product and the management; the product must have a unique selling point and the management must be experienced and totally convinced of the product and its ability to succeed. These are the basics on which one can build a successful turnaround strategy.

Case study

Andre Deutsch

Andre Deutsch was founded in 1950 by the publisher of that name. In 1984 he sold a controlling interest, a substantial part of the cost being lent to the purchaser by a clearing bank secured by a fixed and floating charge over the assets of the business including two central London office buildings occupied by the company and the personal guarantee of the new proprietor.

In the late summer of 1991, the bank had a revaluation of their security carried out which showed that their loan of £2.6m was uncovered and they commissioned an Accountants report on the business. Current exceptionally high interest rates had helped to plunge Deutsch into substantial trading losses. Should the bank have chosen to appoint a receiver at that point, they would have received no more than a few pence in the pound for their debts.

At this time Robin Baum was introduced to the proprietor of Deutsch and asked to assist in preparing a recovery strategy that would be acceptable to the bank. This strategy was devised and Robin Baum joined the Board of Deutsch and was retained to oversee the implementation of the recovery strategy.

Over the next 18 months the debt was reduced by £1m from cost reductions and disposals of assets, including one of the freehold buildings.

By this time Deutsch had returned to a trading profit after meeting the bank interest charges but the balance of the debt could only be cleared in the near future from a disposal of the business or major injection of new share capital.

Robin Baum set about trying to identify an investor and identified VCI plc, which was seeking to acquire a well-known quality publishing house. A sale was agreed which not only paid off the bank debt but also provided an attractive package for the proprietor, including a long-term service agreement.

Robin Baum is a Company Doctor who specialises in helping Corporate Borrowers through trading difficulties by giving hands on assistance; often his appointment follows a recommendation from their bankers. He has covered a wide field of industries including Publishing, Media, Medical education, Computer Software and high technology.

8

Legal Issues for Failing Companies

Jonathan Reardon
Biddle

Insolvency and the law

When is a company insolvent?

A company is insolvent if:

- it is unable to pay its debts when they fall due (cash flow basis).
- the value of its assets is less than its liabilities (balance sheet basis).

What are the responsibilities of directors when a company becomes insolvent?

Once a company becomes insolvent, a director's primary duties are to the creditors rather than the shareholders. Directors have a duty to minimise the potential loss to creditors.

What are the penalties for directors of companies who continue to trade whilst insolvent?

Directors of limited liability companies may be personally liable to contribute to the company's assets and may be guilty of the following statutory offences if trade continues after there is no reasonable prospect of avoiding insolvency:

- wrongful trading;
- fraudulent trading;
- preferences (in favour of particular creditors);
- transactions at an undervalue;
- misfeasance.

Directors may also be liable for disqualification for committing wrongful trading. Further, in liquidations, the conduct of the directors will be reviewed by the Official Receiver.

Directors may be liable on personal guarantees given in connection with bank loans, leases, HP/lease agreements.

What are the classic mistakes that people make?

- Not seeking professional advice early enough.
- Not being alert to potential problems (e.g. loss of market share, increased bad debts, extended credit to customers, rising work-in-progress, increased overdraft, reduced cash balances, lack of management information).
- Insufficient internal management (e.g. no regular auditing of accounts, annual projections and cash flow forecasts, no current business plans).

Checklist to keep directors out of jail

- Take advice from a licensed insolvency practitioner or a solicitor. They will often prepare a viability report at the request of the company or the bank.
- Communicate with your bankers, suppliers and advisers. (Banks will often be reluctant to put companies into an insolvency procedure and would rather use a constructive approach to maximise their return.)
- Minute all board meetings recording discussion of the problems and the action taken.

Options for failing companies

There are five categories of insolvency procedure for UK companies:

- Company voluntary arrangement (CVA)
- Administrative receivership
- Administration

- Compulsory liquidation
- Creditors' voluntary liquidation (CVL)

The first three can be used for business rescue, whereas liquidation is a terminal process. Two procedures, which are often used with solvent companies, are not scheduled in this list. Members' voluntary liquidation (MVL) only applies to solvent companies and is instituted by the shareholders. It is used to wind up companies that have outlived their usefulness. Schemes of Arrangements often follow on from a liquidation or administration. They are a compromise or arrangement between a company and its creditors or its members, which has been sanctioned by the court.

1. Company voluntary arrangement (CVA)

A CVA involves a plan of reorganisation sanctioned by the court which may include delayed or reduced payments of debt, capital restructuring or an orderly disposal of assets. It is proposed to creditors and shareholders at a creditors' meeting. The scheme is under the control of an insolvency practitioner acting as a supervisor. As obtaining the consent of all creditors is difficult, CVAs are relatively rare.

2. Administrative receivership

Administrative receivers are normally appointed by a bank which has a charge over the whole (or substantially the whole) of the company's assets. There is no court involvement.

   The administrative receiver may continue to trade and sell the business as a going concern, often back to existing managers by way of an MBO. His aim is to secure repayment to the bank that appointed him, rather than the general body of creditors.

3. Administration

Administration gives a company 'breathing space' to formulate a rescue plan or maximise asset realisations. An administration order is an order of the court appointing an insolvency practitioner as an 'administrator' to manage the affairs of an insolvent company. It can only be made for one or more of the purposes specified in the Insolvency Act 1986:

- survival of the business (or part of it);
- better realisation than from a winding-up;
- approval of a CVA or arrangement with creditors which the court is satisfied has a realistic prospect of success.

It creates a moratorium restraining creditors from exercising their rights against the company. Any secured creditor with the power to appoint an administrative receiver has the power to veto. Administration is a useful alternative to administrative receiverships where there is no such chargeholder.

4. Compulsory liquidation (or compulsory winding-up)

This is ordered by the court, usually on the petition of a creditor, the company or a shareholder. Initially, the Official Receiver (a civil servant and an officer of the court) is appointed. If the assets are likely to cover the administrative costs, he will call a creditors' meeting to appoint an insolvency practitioner as liquidator. The liquidator will realise the assets of the company for the benefit of all creditors.

5. Creditors' voluntary liquidation (CVL)

This is commenced by a resolution of the shareholders. However, it is under the effective control of the creditors, who can appoint a liquidator of their choice. This is the most common way for directors and shareholders to take action and thus minimise the risk of personal liability.

Jonathan Reardon is a partner in Biddle's Corporate Department with wide experience of corporate recovery and restructurings.

Section Three
Private Equity

The UK Mid MBO/MBI Market

The British Venture Capital Association (BVCA) definition of mid-sized MBO/MBIs is an investment of between £2m-£10m equity in any one transaction. In 1997, £525 million was invested in 116 UK midsized MBO/MBI transactions, representing 26% of the total amount invested in the UK in all MBO/MBIs, accounting for one third of all MBO/MBI transactions.

Murray Johnstone's target market is the UK mid-sized MBO/MBI market in the UK. We have one of the largest private equity networks in the UK with five offices - in Birmingham, London, Glasgow, Manchester and Sheffield. We are in an excellent position not only to source deals through our offices but also to provide finance on-the-spot to companies in the regions. We are conscious that if you are running a business in Yorkshire, you don't want to go to London to find the finance; with the excellent intermediary services now available in the major cities in the UK today, this is no longer necessary.

We started our private equity department in our Head Office in Glasgow in 1981 and since 1989 have opened the additional offices listed above. We have 15 investment executives with a range of investment experience and a portfolio management team of seven spread throughout our offices. Since 1981, we have made over 520 investments throughout the UK.

We manage some £370 million of private equity in a variety of funds - Limited Partnerships, Venture Capital Trusts (we are now the UK VCT market leader), investment trusts and the segregated private equity portfolios of UK pension funds. This range of funds is rare in the UK and gives us the ability to provide equity finance from £500,000 to £20 million, normally up to a total transaction size of £50 million. We like to invest in a range of industrial sectors, although we avoid high-technology and property deals, sectors in which we have no expertise.

To give you an idea for the kind of companies we back and the role we can play, here is an example.

We were introduced to Greater Manchester Buses North in the summer of 1993. At the time, the company was facing significant pressure with the bus deregulation in 1986 causing increased competition. However the sector was developing rapidly and we could see considerable potential provided the company could reduce its cost base. The employee and the management team were strong - they knew what they had to do and with the support of the unions and the workforce, we knew we could assist with a business plan which would turn the company round. After fierce competition from British Bus plc, the MBO team secured the business with our backing for around £27 million. The implementation of the agreed strategy showed immediate benefits, with the company, which had been breaking even, returning a profit of £2.3 million in its first year of trading. Investment in new vehicles gave customers an improved quality of product and service. In April 1996, the company proved an excellent acquisition target for First Bus plc which was keen to consolidate its position in the sector and bought the business for £68 million.

In the last five years we have made over 170 investments all over the UK. These have been in a range of industrial sectors at various stages of development requiring varying amounts of equity finance. To name a few; Dobbies Garden Centres (garden centre operators), Duport Harper (foundries), Ineos Group (speciality chemicals manufacturer), New World Domestic Appliances (gas cooker manufacturer), Moves (commercial and domestic removals and courier services), Aberdeen Football Club, London Pride (tourist sightseeing bus operator), Integrated Dental Holdings (dental practices and laboratories), John Kennedy (Civil Engineering specialist in laying, relining and refurbishing of water, gas, sewer pipelines), Card Warehouse (regional card retailer), Walmsley (regional furniture retailer), Ferranti Technologies (engineering), Pilkington's Tiles (ceramic tile manufacturer), Rank Amusements (amusement centre operator) and Scotia Haven Food Group (importer/packer of food products for home baking).

We have a rigorous approach to making investments. Every week we meet via a telephone conference call to review all our investment proposals to ensure that we are conversant with the deals under investigation and, most important, to allow us to exchange ideas and experience. Our due diligence process is extremely rigorous - all investment proposals are examined and completed by two executives, one of whom is a Director of Murray Johnstone Private Equity (MJPEL). Recommendations are then made to an investment committee comprising at least three MJPEL directors.

Long term relationships with our investee companies are important to us. Where we are a major investor in a company, we often like to appoint an independent and experienced chairman to the board - someone acceptable to the management team who can not only bring credibility but also can add value. We usually appoint one of our senior executives to the board as a non-executive director - we know from experience that this valuable link with Murray Johnstone is not only welcomed by management teams but also that it works. Obviously agreeing an exit at the beginning of the relationship is key - we are in the business of making sure that those investors who invest in us, see a return.

If you think our investment and management style is for you and you are thinking of raising finance, now or perhaps in the future, please ring the Murray Johnstone office nearest to you. We will talk to you in confidence and hopefully we can work together to our mutual benefit.

PRIVATE EQUITY of £500,000 - £20 million could be on your doorstep.

If your company is looking for between £500,000 and £20 million of equity capital, it may be closer than you think. Murray Johnstone specialises in investing in small to medium-sized companies that are set for rapid expansion, acquisition or a management buy-out/management buy-in. With offices across the country, we have a better understanding of your business environment which means that we can often do the deal faster. Timing can sometimes mean make or break. We have already backed over 500 UK companies including Greater Manchester Buses North, New World Domestic Appliances and Ferranti Technologies and we are looking for more. If you think we can help, call your nearest Murray Johnstone office on the number below.

Glasgow, Neil MacFadyen, **0141 226 3131**	**Manchester**, Gary Tipper, **0161 236 2288**
Sheffield, Sarah Pullan, **0114 242 1200**	**Birmingham**, David Sankey, **0121 236 1222**
London, Arvinder Walia, **0171 606 6969**	

MURRAY JOHNSTONE

INVESTING ACROSS THE UK

Murray Johnstone Limited (Regulated by IMRO) 7 West Nile Street, Glasgow G1 2PX. Tel. 0141 226 3131 Fax. 0141 248 5420 e-mail: info@murrayj.com

PPM Ventures

PPM Ventures is a leading international source of private equity finance, specialising in medium and large management buy-outs and institutional purchases, with offices in London, Hong Kong and Sydney.

It has a particular interest in companies with strong strategic plans for growth through further acquisition.

PPM Ventures is part of Prudential, one of the UK's largest institutional investors, with managed funds of £130 bn. Funds available for private equity investment exceed £1bn. Since 1993, PPM Ventures has invested some £545m in 48 European deals with a total transaction size of £5bn. Recent investments include the public to private acquisition of Fired Earth and the £279m management buy-in of Gala Clubs.

Although Europe remains its principal focus at present, PPM Ventures established an Asian private equity operation in Hong Kong in 1997, and in 1998 acquired Catalyst Investment Managers, the Australian buy-out specialist. Since 1990, Catalyst has raised some A$150m from institutional investors and has a dominant position in the developing Australian buy-out market.

For further information,
please contact:

PPM Ventures
1 Waterhouse Square
Holborn Bars
London EC1N 2ST

Tel: 0171 831 7747
Fax: 0171 831 9528

Regulated in UK by IMRO

Want to stand out from the crowd? We can help you make all the right moves.

- Third most active venture capitalist in the UK*

- Targeting companies worth up to £35m

- Equity of £0.5m - £12m for MBO's, MBI's, IBO's and growing businesses

- Long-term investment approach

- Active support post investment

Call one of our offices below to discuss how Lloyds Development Capital can help your business move in the right direction.

Patrick Sellers	Darryl Eales	Bernard Dale	Stuart Rhodes	Stuart Veale
London	Birmingham	East Midlands	Leeds	Thames Valley
0171 499 1500	0121 200 1787	0115 947 1280	0113 244 1001	0118 925 3292

Visit our web site: http://www.ldc.co.uk **Or E Mail:** info@ldc.co.uk

LLOYDS DEVELOPMENT CAPITAL LIMITED

9
Trends in Private Equity

Michael Joseph
Lloyds Development Capital

New sources of money

Over the past decade there has been increasing acceptance of private equity as an asset class for fund managers. Although UK fund managers have yet to commit as much as US fund managers to private equity (private equity is 0.5 per cent of asset allocation in the UK versus 2 per cent in the US), this recognition has created enormous growth in the sector. It has been driven primarily by the very strong returns made by private equity investors, particularly as a result of seeing private equity funds buying cheap as the economy came out of the last recession, then make fabulous returns on flotation or trade sale at the top of the market. There is now £41bn worth of investment under management in the private equity sector (according to the British Venture Capital Association).

This growth has a number of implications:

1. There has been a tremendous swing towards managing money for other people, as opposed to own-balance sheet finance. The difference between own-balance sheet funds and managed funds is that managed funds have to be returned to their owners at some stage. If a portfolio has to be liquidated according to a fixed timetable, then those managing the investment will naturally want to pursue opportunities which offer short-term gains rather than long-term gains, and gains which can be easily realised.

2. Funds are getting bigger. The natural response to this is to look for bigger opportunities. The result has been that competition for the largest buy-outs is very tight.
3. Funds are looking to Europe for opportunities. As the UK private equity market has become more competitive, the European market has begun to look very attractive.

The result of these three trends is that the sources of capital available to you if you are running a small to medium-sized enterprise (ie up to £30m value) have probably declined.

Furthermore, within the SME sector the trend has been towards management buy-outs and buy-ins, because there is a perception that the returns are great and the risks are small. It is also easier to engineer an exit from a buy-out within a short timescale. The result is that most of the venture capital funds available have been going towards restructuring ownership rather than enabling entrepreneurs to grow their businesses.

Less money is invested in development or expansion in the UK than in the US. This has meant that the willingness of quality management to go into start-ups and developing the potential of SMEs is very much less than it is on the other side of the Atlantic. The British venture capitalist is not a venture capitalist in the true sense of the word.

While the big funds in the UK market have been concentrating on big deals and looking to Europe, this has not necessarily been a total success for all concerned.

The unanswered question about the current European environment is whether the deals that have been done will generate liquidity within the time frame of the funds. It is still doubtful whether funds devoted to France and Germany are making an adequate return on capital now, ten years or more after the market was first opened up. If there are any winners they will be in the big ticket deals.

But even the big private equity deals have not performed as well as big public companies in the last three years. The returns from investing in the FTSE 100 share index over the past three years are greater than some of the private equity funds.

The market shock in late 1998 will have a knock-on effect on the private equity sector. In times of financial turmoil, people launching new funds will find it harder to make their targets. It should be remembered that historically a down-turn has been a very good time to invest in private equity. The three to five year time horizon means that one is buying at the bottom of the cycle and selling at the top.

The tax environment is now very much more favourable to venture capital investment, both at the institutional level and the individual level, than it was 10 years ago. This alone may be enough to ensure that private equity does not return to its pre-1990 level.

It is unlikely that fund managers will reduce the assets allocated to private equity because of short-term conditions in the public markets. There is now an awareness of entrepreneurialism. Most people now want to work for themselves. There is no longer any security in a big company. There is a wide appreciation of the benefits of equity ownership. It has been a quiet entrepreneurial revolution. It is not going to turn back.

Case study

Lloyds Development Capital and SMEs

Lloyds Development Capital's view of the market is different from many of its competitors. It has concentrated on the UK and on the SME market within the UK. It has no intention of raising outside funds, so it can take a slightly longer-term view of its investments than it would have to if it were operating a closed end fund.

As part of its strategy of supporting SMEs, it has been diversifying its activity outside London. It now has offices in Nottingham, Reading, Leeds and Birmingham, as well as the capital.

Over the last few years, LDC has become one of the largest and most active venture capitalists in the UK (it is currently ranked third most active in the UK, behind 3i and NatWest Equity Partners). It has invested in over 250 businesses in its 17 year history, recently investing £46 million in 20 deals in 1997 and £23m in 12 transactions in the first half of 1998.

Typical of the type of deal it gets involved in is ENCON.

The Encon story

In 1987, LDC led an equity syndicate of five members which invested £2 million of risk capital in the Encon Group. Encon, a private company, was then a distributor of insulation materials with a small number of depots in the UK and a contracting/installation subsidiary.

Encon's trading track record, pre the equity investment, was as follows:

£ million

y/e 31 August	1985	1986	1987
Sales	1.5	4.0	12.2
PBT	0.06	0.2	0.37

The equity funding of £2 million, along with £5 million of overdraft and loan funding provided by Bank of Scotland, enabled Encon to purchase the assets of two moribund insulation manufacturing plants in Scotland. The plants were acquired for a knock-down price of £850,000 (the full replacement costs of the assets would have been many millions) and the balance of the total £7 million of funding was used to cover:

i) re-start of the plants, including additional engineering capital expenditure;
ii) working capital to cover the planned growth of stock and debtors for the expansion in group trading activities.

The equity investors obtained an equity stake of 22.5% in the Encon Group.

The next three years (1988–90) were years of real achievement. The manufacturing businesses produced quality products and won market share in a tough sector. The Group also made a number of acquisitions with the assistance of additional bank funding. The largest of these helped to double the size of its distribution business to 20 depots. Encon's first overseas depot was also opened in France.

The business then grew rapidly:

£ million

y/e 31 August	1988	1989	1990
Sales	19.0	31.0	60.0
PBT	0.232	2.0	2.7

The benefits from rationalisation of the cost base following the acquisitions were still to come through. The business looked to be on track to achieve a full stock exchange listing in line with the aspirations of Encon's senior management and the investing institutions.

By 31 August 1990, Bank of Scotland had increased its support to £12 million (split equally between Overdraft and Term Loan) secured primarily by good book debts of £17 million.

To strengthen the balance sheet, the equity investors 'followed' their initial stake with a second stage capital injection of £3 million in December 1990, which was used to reduce some of the bank debt. The investors increased their equity stake to 32.5% in the process.

The trading year 1990–91 proved to be the most difficult one in the Group's relatively short history. The UK economy weakened, moving from 'slowdown' status to an ever deepening and seemingly endless recession. The building construction sector suffered enormously. Housing starts fell rapidly, new commercial builds halted and, not surprisingly, the price of building materials fell.

Encon fought hard to maintain its market share, but with prices falling and bad debts increasing it soon became impossible to make sufficient earnings to cover fixed overheads. A programme of rationalisation was begun during the trading year, but this involved closure costs of circa £1 million. In the y/e 31 August 1991 the following trading result ensued:

Sales £71.0m
Loss (£3.1m)

The compounding effect of very high interest rates on a highly geared business dependent on the construction sector during an economic recession was graphically illustrated in that result.

LDC, as lead investor, maintained its belief that Encon, by now a sizeable player in its market, still had considerable unrealised potential. With hindsight, Encon's management had made some strategic errors during the previous growth phase. But the team were intelligent, receptive, hardworking and motivated to restore company performance – though it was recognised that any turnaround would take two to three years.

A series of meetings took place between management/investors/Bank of Scotland and it became clear that Encon required a further capital injection to see it through the recession. The Bank of Scotland exposure had, by now, increased to £13 million (split equally between Overdraft and Term Loan) but Encon's debtor book had fallen to £16 million, and the Bank's cover was reducing.

LDC succeeded in arranging third-round funding of £3.5 million from the syndicate (although at this stage one investor dropped out). The total equity from the investors increased to £8.5 million, and their equity stake rose to 85%. It was also acknowledged that Encon was unlikely to be in a position to pay any dividends for at least another two years.

Bank of Scotland agreed to suspend its scheduled loan capital repayments and also agreed to reduce its interest rate to a fixed charge of 5% for one year to assist cash flow.

As a condition of the new equity funding, the investors appointed a new non-executive Chairman with turnaround experience to assist the management team.

The trading year 1991–92 was another year of mixed fortunes. The programme of rationalisation continued and exceptional costs that year from redundancies and closures totalled £1.8 million. Bad debt write-offs rose to £1 million as numerous customers 'went under'.

In terms of the bottom line, the year ended 31 August 1992 was the nadir in Encon's history:

Sales	£67.0m
Operating Profit	(£1.1m)
Exceptionals	(£1.8m)
Bank Interest	(£1.9m)
Trading Loss for Year	(£4.8m)

The reliance on Bank funding had increased to circa £15 million (£8 million on Overdraft, £7 million on Term Loan). This was secured by debtors £12 million, stock £4 million, freehold £1 million, plant and machinery £6 million. On a forced sale basis, it was unlikely that Bank of Scotland would have fully recovered their lending and any shareholder value had gone completely.

Despite the trading results, the fundamental operations of the business were sound and improving all the time. Working capital was under firm control, stocks had been reduced, credit control tightened and the product sales mix improved. The simple things were all being done well and it was possible to envisage a picture where rising sales and improved margins – as the UK moved out of recession – would restore profit to the bottom line.

LDC and two of the remaining four co-investors agreed upon a capital restructuring, and the management and Bank of Scotland were involved at every stage in the negotiations. The bank debt reduced by £5 million, and the balance sheet picture improved. The investors injected a further £2.5 million of equity and retained a 60% equity stake. Bank of Scotland agreed to convert £2.5 million of debt to preference share capital, and also obtained a 15% equity stake.

Management were incentivised by seeing their equity stake increase from 15% to 25%.

Between 1993–97, Encon continued its recovery and the results speak for themselves:

£ million

y/e 31 August	1993	1994	1995	1996	1997
Sales	60.0	60.0	69.0	74.0	78.0
PBT	(1.4)	0.4	2.3	3.6	4.2

No magic wand was involved – simply a combination of hard graft, innovation, and determination from a totally focused and dedicated management team. For their part, the investors and Bank of Scotland had kept their nerve in strengthening the Group's capital base. As the economy in the UK improved, Encon's board was able to focus more on future strategies rather than on fire fighting, which had been a feature for so long in the past.

Towards the end of 1996, the shareholders discussed the possibility of seeking an exit, probably by way of a trade sale. At this stage the company's auditors, KPMG, were also brought into play through their corporate finance specialists and they indicated that Encon might be valued somewhere between £30 million to £40 million. A discreet selling process was then begun.

In November 1997, the shareholders sold out their stakes to another institutional investor. Encon was valued at £35 million – not a bad result compared to the situation in 1992! The result was a good one for all classes of shareholder:

- The management team made a substantial capital gain.
- Those investing institutions which kept faith with the Group recovered all the cost of their investment plus a substantial capital gain.
- Bank of Scotland recovered all their debt, preference shares, and made a substantial capital gain.

At one stage, it had looked as if everyone might be a loser. By working together and understanding each other's needs, the pain was shared by all the interested parties during Encon's most difficult trading period. Ultimately, all the shareholders enjoyed the satisfaction and reward of a successful turnaround which had depended upon all round co-operation.

Michael Joseph is managing director of Lloyds Development Capital.

10

The Private Equity Market

Christopher Gasson
Bertoli Mitchell

Types of investor

The private equity market is divided according to where the money comes from and where it goes. There are two main types of private equity investment funds:

- *Open ended funds*: investment funds which invest from a continuous stream of money, whether from unit trust sales, pension fund contributions, insurance premiums or from their own balance sheet.
- *Closed end funds*: investment funds which raise all their capital on launch, then invest their capital to maximise the value of their portfolio without taking on new money.

There are a number of different ways in which funds are managed:

- *Captive funds*: an investment fund that invests money on behalf of a single client – usually its parent company.
- *Semi-captive funds*: those that invest on behalf of their parent company as well as third party clients.
- *Independent funds*: an investment fund that invests money on behalf of a wider range of investors.

- *Venture capital trust*: a closed end fund that has raised its capital through a stock exchange flotation. There are certain tax advantages to investing in them.

Market sectors

Private equity investment goes towards a wide variety of different sorts of deal. The British Venture Capital Association lists them as follows:

Start-up

Financing provided to companies for use in product development and initial marketing. Companies may be in the process of being set up or may have been in the business for a short time, but have not yet sold their product commercially.

Other early stage

Financing provided to companies that have completed the product development stage and require further funds to initiate commercial manufacturing and sales. They may not yet be generating profits.

Expansion

Capital provided for growth and expansion of an established company (also known as development capital). Funds may be used to finance increased production capacity, product development, provide additional working capital, and/or marketing. Capital provided for rescue/turnaround situations is also included in this category.

Refinancing bank debt

Equity investment that is used to replace debt when a company restructures its capital.

Secondary purchase

Purchase of existing shares in a company from another venture capital firm or another shareholder or shareholders.

Management buy-out (MBO)

Funds provided to enable current operating management and investors to acquire an existing product line or business.

Management buy-in (MBI)

Funds provided to enable an external manager or group of managers to buy into a company.

Most private equity funds will invest across a number of these categories. The best way of distinguishing between them is to see which of the following market sectors they fit into:

- investors willing to back start-ups;
- SME funds;
- large buy-out funds.

Investors willing to back start-ups

Start-ups are by far the most risky propositions for investors. They require people to stake their money on untried people, untried processes and untried products, a triple chance that can only be justified by very high returns.

Although businesses which are past the start-up stage but have yet to generate profits are significantly less risky than total green field start-ups, from the point of view of most institutional investors they are still too risky.

Start-ups and other early stage investments in growing businesses are usually too small for most institutional investors. In many cases the overhead involved in overseeing a £300,000 investment in a start-up is the same as the overhead involved in overseeing a £30m buy-out.

A third reason why most institutional investors tend to avoid start-ups and early stage investment is that they require specialist knowledge, and most institutional investors are generalists. Specialist knowledge is the only way in which an investor can minimise the risk involved in untried people, processes and products.

Despite these drawbacks, many institutional investors do appreciate the fact that start-up operations can offer very good returns. To take advantage of this, many of them choose to invest a tiny proportion of the funds allocated to private equity in specialist start-up funds.

These funds, often referred to as the 'true venture capitalists', usually specialise in high-growth sectors such as bio-technology or high tech. The fund managers are able to develop knowledge of the people, processes and products and therefore make a more informed investment judgement.

Outside the 'high growth' sectors, institutional funding is very much more scarce. Instead, investors have to rely on individuals or business angels.

Business angels are high net worth individuals who invest in private companies, often in response to the tax breaks offered under the Enterprise Investment Scheme (which offers tax relief at 20 per cent, but only for investments in private companies which have been trading for three years). They often specialise in particular sectors, reflecting their own knowledge and contacts.

Most business angel finance comes through informal contacts. As a rule, people give to people they know. Without personal contacts, raising finance from business angels either takes a very long time or turns out to be impossible. There are established networks and syndicates: the British Venture Capital Association will supply a list. Additionally, there are a number of brokers that specialise in introductions to business angels. Typically they might charge a fee equal to five per cent of the cash invested plus five per cent of the equity.

SME funds

SME funds make investments in buy-outs and development capital opportunities of between £250,000 and £20m.

The risks in this sector are not as great as they are in the start-up and early stage sector on the grounds that the businesses are already established: they have proven people, processes and products. However, it is often difficult to find an exit from such investments within a short timescale. The businesses are usually too small for a quick flotation, and it is often difficult to engineer a trade sale which maximises the value of the investment within three years, the favoured exit horizon of the large funds.

The result is that SME investment tends to be longer term – fund managers have to be prepared to commit themselves to five to ten year horizons rather than the three to five years that are considered to be industry standard. If an investor is going to be tied in to a business for such a long period, the dividend streams earned along the way start to become important in assessing investment opportunities.

The longer time frame mitigates against closed end funds becoming involved in this sector of the market. As they do not enjoy a constant supply of new cash to invest and often need to be able to liquidate their assets within a fixed timetable, they prefer a faster turnaround on their investments.

The other drawback of the SME sector is the size of individual investments. Again, they are usually too small to justify the overhead for many City institutions.

In these conditions it is not surprising that the main players (besides 3i) in the SME sector are the clearing banks. They have good regional networks to reach SME *in situ*, and there are obvious synergies with banking.

Most of the investments made in the SME sector are in management buy-outs and buy-ins. This reflects the attractiveness of buy-outs and buy-ins *vis à vis* any other form of venture capital. However, a significant minority of investments in the SME sector is in the form of development capital.

Development capital

Development capital provides additional equity for growing businesses. It exists to provide a return for its investors by helping companies launch new products, enter new markets, make acquisitions or otherwise seize opportunities that require additional capital.

It tends to be used by smaller companies – typically those with sales of less than £10m. This reflects the fact that larger companies are more likely to have the option of flotation or have further debt options open to them to finance their growth.

Typically a company will turn to development capital because it has exhausted its capacity to take on more debt. Strengthening the equity base of a company not only provides additional risk capital, but it will also increase the debt capacity of a business. A development capital investment is usually accompanied by new debt finance.

Development capital investors do not expect to take control of a business. They will take a minority stake in a business in exchange for their equity investment. The size of this stake will be in proportion to the value that they place on the business. This valuation is the main area of disagreement between the management of the company and the venture capitalist.

Venture capitalists complain that managers focus too much on the price that the investor is paying for the equity now and not enough on how this will boost the value of the business when it really matters, i.e. when they decide to sell out to a third party in future. The result is that they end up with 100 per cent of a small cake rather than 80 per cent of a very much larger one, the venture capitalists say.

In turn, managers of companies that are seeking development capital complain that the venture capitalists want to make a paper profit on day one. They accuse venture capitalists of valuing the business at a fraction of its real worth so that they can be sure of making a profit regardless of whether the additional capital is well spent.

The solution to this kind of dispute is the introduction of a ratchet (these are also discussed in Chapter 11). This is an agreement to dis-agree, whereby the management's stake is increased if the manage-ment's valuation of the business turns out to be correct on exit.

For example the management might contend that their business is worth £8m now, and that the venture capitalist should be accorded 20 per cent of the equity in exchange for a £2m investment. The venture capitalist might say the business was only worth £4m in its current state, and that £2m should translate to a 33 per cent stake. The dispute is settled by the venture capitalist saying: 'If you are right that the business is worth £8m now, then it should be worth £30m or more when at exit in five years' time. We will put in a ratchet so that if you are right and the business does fetch £30m, then you can have 80 per cent of the proceeds. Otherwise the split will be based on our valua-tion, which is two thirds/one third.'

Given that most development capital investors restrict their invest-ment to profitable businesses, and profitable businesses often have other means of finance open to them, the development capital market is actually quite small.

SMEs and buy-outs

The unique feature of small buy-outs and buy-ins is that they can be structured to enable the management to maintain control of the business.

In large buy-outs the management's contribution to the equity is negligible in comparison to the total value of the deal. A deal struc-tured to give the management control would require unsustainable levels of leverage.

Small buy-outs (i.e. those requiring a consideration of less than £10m) can be structured to give control because the management's contribution is likely to be more meaningful in comparison with the total equity investment required. By building a capital structure which makes full use of debt and preference shares, the management team can acquire a majority shareholding in a company for an investment that could be just one twentieth of the total value of the business.

The ratio between what the management pays for its equity and what the private equity investor pays for its equity is known as the envy ratio. The higher the ratio, the better the deal for the management.

Where the management does retain control after a buy-out, there will usually be covenants and clauses in the articles of association of the company to protect the venture capitalist. In particular, the venture capitalist will want to be protected against being forced to sell out for less than the full value of the shares.

Large buy-out funds

The greatest growth in the private equity sector in the past decade has been at the top end, among the large buy-out funds. These look at investment opportunities of above £20m. Most of them are more interested in opportunities that are very much larger than that. Historically, it has been in the largest deal that the greatest profits are to be had.

Many of the funds in this sector invest on behalf of third parties, and are expected to return their gains to their investors within a certain timeframe. This, together with concerns about getting tied to illiquid investments, has meant that the large buy-out fund sector is increasingly short term. While SME funds are often prepared to stay in an investment for up to ten years, the large buy-out funds tend to look for an exit within three years.

The following chapter outlines how the large buy-out funds operate.

11

Management Buy-outs and Buy-ins

Christopher Gasson
Bertoli Mitchell

Introduction

The trend towards tighter strategic focus has been one of the themes of management in the 1980s and 1990s. Diversified conglomerates have fallen out of favour with investors, and have been forced to restructure their portfolios to focus on the areas in which they offer clear benefits to shareholders. This trend has had two implications: first it has meant that the subsidiaries of large groups are coming onto the market regularly. Second it has meant that the diversified conglomerates which might have bought such assets in the past are no longer such aggressive acquirers. Venture capitalists have stepped into the gap.

They now play a role that has been compared to the corporate raiders who built up the great conglomerates of the past: spotting under-valued and under-managed businesses, buying them and, with either existing or new management, turning them round.

Unlike the corporate raiders of the past, they have no interest in asset stripping. They aim to grow businesses to maximise their value on flotation or trade sale.

Private equity funds have made very attractive returns for their shareholders, but they have also made an important contribution to the growth of the British economy. The private equity industry has allowed managers of businesses to acquire ownership of the businesses they have helped to build. This has assisted greatly in creating a more entrepreneurial climate in this country than existed 10 or 15 years ago.

The majority of venture capitalists typically seek an exit within three to five years of initial investment. During this time, their investment is effectively locked in. This ensures a commitment to the companies in which they invest which is not always present where shares are easily tradable, and management is free from the pressure to deliver short-term earnings growth at the expense of developing longer-term shareholder value.

It is fair to say that some funds are in it for the short term – to buy an undervalued asset and to sell it on at a profit as quickly as possible. Typically these funds are closed end funds (i.e. funds which do not have a regular supply of new money). They tend not to have long-term liabilities and to focus on the current value of funds invested. However, it is becoming more difficult for fund managers to make a quick return on their investments, as the opportunities to acquire under-priced assets are becoming scarcer.

This is because an efficient process for selling businesses has developed. Auctions are now widely used, making it very difficult for private equity funds to find bargains. The key to successful private equity investment is therefore the added value that can be developed through management and capital investment.

There are still cases where a venture capitalist will make two or three times its money in the space of a couple of years, but this is usually because they have been able to bring in management who give it a clear focus. They have been able to introduce a clear commitment to a business that had been neglected by its previous owners and they have given the business access to the capital it needs to grow. It tends not to be because the business was sold below market price.

Many funds, particularly those invested by pension funds or insurance companies, often have a much longer time horizon than the typical three to five year exit, and may be prepared to invest to build the business. Although they will still want to see an early flotation, they will be prepared to hold onto their shares once they become tradable on the stock exchange rather than distribute them among institutional investors. This gives a far greater level of involvement in the long-term prospects of a company than would be offered anywhere else.

Initiating a buy-out/buy-in

Buy-outs and buy-ins take place in a number of different circumstances. The most common situations are as follows:

- a subsidiary/division of a large group that has been identified as potentially non-core;
- an owner manager wishing to bring in new investment and/or management because of succession issues or because he or she is unwilling to take the business forward on his or her own;
- a venture capitalist may wish to sell on its interest in a business to another private equity investor who may bring with him a new management team – it may also reflect a failure to agree an exit with the management;
- a group that has run into financial difficulties and may be required to realise its assets to meet its obligations to creditors;
- a business that is peripheral to the activities/strategy of a new owner following the acquisition of its parent company;
- a business that is in receivership but the existing management or a new management team believes that the problems which brought it to such a situation can be solved.

Increasingly, managers are not given the freedom to approach venture capitalists ahead of a sale. This is because vendors have come to realise that if managers are allowed to negotiate with venture capitalists, there is a risk of upsetting the level playing field.

This means that financial buyers are increasingly bidding on the basis of the information memorandum produced by the vendor alone. They will be advised on the bid by someone who knows the sector. In some circumstances that person will join the business after the acquisition, and in other circumstances the financial buyer will strike a deal with the existing management once the sale has gone through.

Despite the financial arguments for auctioning a business, some vendors choose not to invite outside bids. There are several good reasons for this. Confidentiality, speed, and continuity are often important. In many cases the vendor may wish to continue to hold a stake in the business or to introduce conditions to the sale which may not fit in with other buyers. The management is also likely to have the best idea of the potential of the business, and will therefore be prepared to pay a competitive price for the business, as long as the vendor has a realistic alternative.

If the vendor encourages the management to work on a buy-out bid themselves, their first step will usually be to appoint an adviser who will approach two or three venture capital businesses on their behalf. The adviser will then work with the management to decide which backer is most appropriate. In general, managers should choose the people who they feel most comfortable working with. There is a lot of personal chemistry involved.

Depending on the size of the deal relative to the private equity house, the lead investor may wish to syndicate the equity among a number of private equity houses. This may happen either before or after the completion of a transaction. This again will be a function of the size of the equity requirement relative to the profile of the provider and its existing portfolio.

Besides an equity provider, the management team will also need to find a bank who will provide debt, and a law firm to represent them in the contract negotiations.

The decision to invest

Venture capitalists are interested in all sectors of the economy – including some very mature industries. However, they will only buy into situations where they can see an opportunity for growth. If the industry is mature, then growth is a matter of being better than the competition, which depends on the quality of the management, or the ability to improve efficiencies in the long term.

Their aim is to deliver an above average return on their portfolio to reflect the risk of investing equity in a small number of highly leveraged deals. Typically for funds investing in financial purchases a target of between 25 and 30 per cent internal rate of return (ie averaged over the life of the investment) is required. Individual investments may be expected to generate a higher or a lower rate of return, depending on their risk profile.

Besides growth, private equity investors are looking for four main things:

1. people who have a clear vision and understanding of where their business should be;
2. a well thought out strategy;
3. a balanced team with firm leadership;
4. a method by which exit might be achieved at some (unspecified) date in future.

The common theme is the quality of management. The venture capitalist will take references on management teams and make background checks, but their main consideration is their assessment of the team's abilities and track record. The real judgement is made during the time the private equity investor spends with the management team in the run up to the buy-out.

The buy-out timetable

The process of arranging a buy-out will take anything from six weeks to two years. It may cost more to push a deal through quickly, as the professional fees will be higher. The main delays are usually caused by difficulties in getting agreement with the vendor.

All buy-outs will happen in a different way: a buy-out resulting from the sale of a division of a public company by way of an auction might run as follows:

Week(s)	Action
1	Circulation of Information Memorandum to potential purchasers. Venture capitalist to contact bank for view of debt capacity and structure.
2	Submission of indicative offers for business.
3–6	Selection of second round bidders (possible exclusivity). Provision of Vendor-commissioned accounting due diligence. Data room of legal documents made available including draft sale & purchase contract. Management presentations and site visits to take place.
7	Submission of revised offer and marked up sale & purchase contract.
8	Grant of exclusivity to single purchaser.
9–12	Discussions with management over terms of investment and future strategy. Preparation of detailed budget for banking purposes.
	Final due diligence covering commercial, legal, accounting, pensions, insurance issues.
	Negotiation of legal documents including sale & purchase contract, banking agreement and equity documents for Newco.
13	Exchange of contracts.

During the deal process it is tough on them. They have got to run their own business as well as put the deal together. It is a short period but it is an intensive one.

Structuring a deal

Venture capital deals tend to be structured on the basis of the following considerations:

1. Debt capacity – the amount of debt that can be put into a business will give broad shape to the deal. This is determined by the level of cash flow generated, the quality of the cash flow (i.e. how regular or predictable it is), and the assets available for securing the debt. The bank providing the debt will usually have guidelines for the level of debt it is prepared to lend, based primarily on the cash flows of the business, with a view also to the balance sheet and profit and loss ratios such as asset cover and interest cover.
2. Risk profile – if the risks are high then a higher proportion of equity will be required, but the equity provider will want to protect itself and will therefore prefer to use prior ranking instruments such as preference shares or loan stock, which reduce their up-side but give them a prior claim on the value of the business in a sale.
3. Management incentive – the amount of equity the venture capitalist will need to make available to the management and the terms on which the equity is provided is negotiated. Management will be required to subscribe cash for such shares.
4. Tax – there are a number of tax considerations for the venture capitalist investor as well as the management, which may shape a deal. For example, interest payments on loan stock may be tax deductible but dividends on preference shares are not.

Besides the overall amount of debt required, there are a number of other important debt issues which are part of the overall financial structure.

1. The repayment profile – usually debt will have to be repaid within a defined period, typically five to seven years (and certainly on exit).
2. The interest rate – may be fixed or floating, but will usually be set between x and y percentage points above the bank rate for senior

amortising debt. Non-amortising debt would typically involve a significantly higher coupon (or interest rate).

3. The security required – the management would not normally be required to offer personal guarantees. The security would reflect the level of assets in the business being acquired.

4. The financial covenants – these are very much performance related and will usually refer to cash flow cover and interest cover.

Equity

The equity requirement is in the form of common shares and prior ranking investment such as preference shares and loan stock.

Preference shares and loan stock (they amount to the same thing) are equity instruments because they are risk-sharing capital. They are typically subscribed to by the venture capital buyer. They are more flexible than bank debt, but less flexible than a common share. They earn a fixed dividend (usually one to two percentage points higher than the prevailing interest rate) and are redeemed at par on sale of the business. In some cases, particularly where the business is not immediately cash flow generative, the dividend payments can be rolled up, so the principal plus all the interest is paid in a lump sum on exit. Banks will prevent repayments of preference share capital or loan stock to the venture capital investor until all senior debt has been repaid.

Preference shares or loan stock can be arranged so that they can be exchanged (converted) for common shares after a certain date or in certain circumstances. These are called convertible preference shares (loan stock), and are generally used in ratchet arrangements (see below).

Common shares give the greatest potential to benefit from any increase in the value of the business, but also carry the most risk: if the business does not perform, they can be worth nothing after all bank debt and prior ranking instruments have been paid off.

Venture capitalists will usually want to invest in a mix of both common equity and prior ranking instruments. This enables them to benefit from the upside of a profitable sale, while protecting themselves in the event of poor performance.

The following example illustrates how a £50m deal involving bank debt, preference shares and common equity might be structured, and how it might pay out on sale in different circumstances:

1. Newco issues 200,000 £1 Ordinary Shares at par (ie £1 each) to management team representing 10 per cent of the equity. Management pays £200,000.
2. Newco issues 1.8 million £1 'A' Ordinary Shares at par each to Venture Capital investor, who pays £1.8 million for a 90 per cent stake.
3. Newco issues 25 million £1, 8.5 per cent redeemable loan stock, at par to Venture Capital investor, who pays £25 million.
4. Total equity investment amounts to £27 million.
5. Newco arranges £25 million secured loan (maturing over 7 years) with interest payable at 2 per cent over LIBOR.
6. Total long-term acquisition finance raised: £52 million.

After five years the business is sold for £235 million in cash, net of expenses. In the intervening period, Newco has paid interest on the bank debt and the interest on the loan stock. It has also repaid £15 million of the bank loan.

The remaining £10 million of bank debt is paid off.

1. £25 million loan stock is redeemed at par.
2. Remaining consideration cash of £200 million is divided among the Ordinary Shareholders.
3. Venture Capital investor receives 90 per cent (ie £180 million), whilst management receives £20 million in respect of their ordinary shares.
4. Venture capital investor receives a return of £205 million for its £27 million investment, while management receive a return of £20 million for its £200,000 investment.

Suppose the business had not performed to plan and is sold for only £55 million, net of expenses after five years. A recession has hit the market, and sales have been so poor that the business has failed to meet its obligations on the loan stock: the interest payments on them have been rolled up. The business has been able, however, to meet interest and the majority of the required debt repayments under the bank facility. Under a refinancing deal with the banks in the third year of the investment, the banks agreed to postpone certain repayments in return for an increased margin on its debt. At completion, £15 million of the bank loan remains outstanding.

1. The remaining £15 million of bank debt is paid off.
2. £25 million loan stock is redeemed at par, together with approximately £12 million in rolled up interest.

3. Remaining consideration cash of £3 million is divided among the Ordinary Shareholders.
4. Venture Capital investor receives 90 per cent (i.e. £2.7 million), whilst management receives £300,000 in respect of its ordinary shares.
5. Venture capital investor receives a capital return of £27.7 million for its £27 million investment, while management receive a return of £300,000 for their £200,000 investment.

Should the business have been sold for £55m or less, the common equity would have been essentially worthless, wiping out the management's investment, but preserving at least some of the venture capitalist's investment in as much as the business was sold for more than the value of the bank debt.

Management equity

In almost all circumstances venture capitalists will look for a financial commitment from the management, but the level of financial commitment is very much geared to their personal circumstances and the nature of management's overall commitment to the business. Their commitment must be meaningful, but it should not be a case of creating an unnecessary distraction for the management.

The general expectation is that management should invest a sum equal to a year's salary. They may be required to mortgage their homes to achieve this.

The percentage of the equity that goes to the management will depend on the size of the deal and price paid. On deals of up to £50m, it would be reasonable for the management to receive between 10 per cent and 20 per cent of the equity in exchange for their investment. Above £50m there is less scope to give away such a large percentage of the value. Similarly, if a business has been acquired at the top end of the valuation scale, there will be less scope to give the management a share of the up-side.

If the venture capitalist is controlling the purchase of the assets and it is negotiating with the management team, it will put to the team what it considers to be a sensible percentage. If the management is controlling the process, then they will see where they can come up with the best offer.

Ratchets

Some venture capitalists prefer to introduce additional incentives for good performance. These are known as ratchets. They enable the management to increase the proportion of the common equity it holds on exit if a certain return on the initial investment has been achieved. Conversely, they can also be used to punish management if it has failed to achieve the projected return.

There are a number of different mechanisms through which a ratchet can work. Typically they involve convertible preference shares. These give the venture capitalists the option to dilute the management's shareholding or not. They can be timed to become convertible after a certain preferred exit date, so that the management is under pressure to provide an exit within an agreed timetable. Alternatively, an agreement can be reached through which the venture capitalist agrees not to convert them if a certain level of performance is achieved.

Unlike development capital investments, where they are often the only way to get the two sides to agree on an investment, ratchets are often seen as potentially damaging to the relationship between the investor and the management in straightforward buy-out situations. It is considered more important to have a deal that ensures that the management and the equity are working on the same targets. Furthermore, ratchets add a further layer of complication to a capital structure, particularly if further equity issues take place (e.g. for acquisition or refinancing).

Points of contention

The most important negotiation is between the venture capitalist and the vendor of the business. Unless it is successful, everything else becomes irrelevant. There are, however, a number of issues which need to be negotiated between the venture capitalist and the management team it is backing. These will include:

- *management equity*: often the most contentious area of negotiation;
- *warranties*: if the management team is in place, then the venture capitalist may require warranties that information given about the business is true;
- *service agreements*: where relevant, the service agreements will usually be rolled forward. Otherwise, new service agreements will be introduced.

Putting the plan into action

After the purchase of the business has been agreed and due diligence is complete, the first step for the management is to establish the management and financial reporting structure of the newly independent business. It is likely that, in the run up to a buy-out, the management will have been deeply involved in negotiations and will have been unable to give the management of the business their full attention. Management teams that have bought in to a business will face a different kind of challenge. The implications of the change of ownership will have to be spelled out to the employees.

When things go wrong

Inevitably, not all venture capital backed purchases go according to plan. Sometimes they will be blown off course by external factors such as an unanticipated change in market conditions, new regulations or a downwards revaluation of all companies in a sector. If the problems are caused by external factors, there is not a great deal that the venture capitalist can do, apart from sit tight and back the management.

It may be necessary to refinance the business in these circumstances. The terms on which the investor agrees to refinance the business can become a major cause of friction between venture capitalist and management. The management often has little choice but to accept the dilution of their shareholding proposed by the investor.

When things start going wrong for reasons which might be associated with the management team itself, most venture capitalists will be inclined to give the management the benefit of the doubt for as long as possible. It is only when things have gone so wrong that the value of the business is probably in jeopardy that an investor would move to replace the management.

Exits

The most common exit route for a venture capitalist is a trade sale – it accounts for around half of all venture capital divestments according to the British Venture Capital Association. Although flotations are often most popular with the management on grounds that a Stock Market quotation gives them continued independence, only ten per cent of venture capital investments end in that way. A quarter end in a partial sale such as a secondary purchase by another venture capitalist or a private share placing. The rest (the majority of which are investments in start-ups) are written off.

The timing of the exit is usually left to the management, who will want to maximise the value of their equity stake. It is only when the business is clearly not going anywhere, and therefore unlikely to benefit from putting off an exit, that the venture capitalist may put pressure on the management to sell the business.

12

Public-to-private Transactions

Brian Phillips
NatWest Equity Partners

Introduction

The venture capital business has come a long way since the ICFC – the forebear of today's 3i – was founded after the Second World War by the Bank of England and the UK clearing banks with the aim of providing long-term funding for developing businesses. For the first 30 years or more, venture capitalists concentrated on just that, with occasional forays into start-up capital, but during the 1980s a whole new type of transaction was invented: the management buy-out or MBO. With it came an explosion in the number of venture capitalists, the amount of money they had to invest (and the number of advisers they used), and the modern industry was born.

The catalyst for change in the 1980s was the development of the use of 'financial assistance', which allowed transactions to be financed where the target company assets secured the debt raised by the acquirer. This enabled large sums of money to be raised in loan finance, secured on the assets of the company to be acquired, and meant that managers, with the help of venture capitalists, could buy their companies for the investment of a relatively modest sum of personal equity. Equally important to the development of the highly geared MBO was the economic climate of the time: the recession of the early 1980s meant that large companies were keen to unload poorly-performing subsidiaries at keen prices, but also gave those subsidiaries great upside potential for their new owners. Relatively high inflation had a very positive effect on the equity value of these highly leveraged companies. A combination of earnings growth and an arbitrage on the exit price earnings multiple, further improved equity returns. Both venture capitalists and bankers made high profits and deals grew in number and value. At the same time, the level of debt being raised for these deals was increasing to a remarkable extent.

Something had to give. Sure enough, the high profile failures of the leveraged buy-outs of Magnet and Gateway proved the harbinger of doom for the excesses of the 1980s MBO market. The recession of 1989–91 and beyond changed the face of the venture capital business. Out went excessively high gearing and management equity stakes of as much as 60 per cent; in came a more realistic distribution of the equity between managers and venture capitalists, a much lower level of debt (crucial in an era of low inflation and high real interest rates), and a concentration on improved performance as a means of extracting value from the investment.

As part of the shift in power between managers and backers, new buy-out vehicles were invented: first the management buy-in or MBI, where the venture capitalists identified the deal and put together a management team to run it, rather than working with existing managers. Then came the logical extension of this – the institutional buy-out or IBO – where the venture capitalists bought the company and worried afterwards about who was going to run it. This latter development followed established practice in the US and was made possible by the increasing size of deals being done.

The latest turn of the wheel has brought in the public-to-private (PTP) transaction, where, instead of buying a public company subsidiary (an entirely private deal from the purchaser's point of view), the venture capitalist bids openly for a public company with a stockmarket quote, with all that this involves in terms of offers to all shareholders.

Why public-to-private?

The main catalyst for the development of PTP deals in the UK has been increasing levels of capital allocated to venture capital. This has increased competition for private deals to such a point that better value can often be found among smaller quoted companies. It is the function of a capital market to allocate deals efficiently to the more deserving cases. The development of PTP transactions is an example of this process in action, although the enormous costs of doing PTP deals has deterred many potential participants. Despite the costs and the difficulties imposed by the takeover rules, some venture capitalists have become very active in the PTP market.

A logical consequence of this activity must be that, after an initial flurry of deals, the valuation of smaller UK quoted companies should rise as investors spot the next PTP targets. These deals are, of necessity, self-limiting.

In a market where the 'typical' company is almost impossible to define, it is refreshingly easy to identify a typical candidate for a public-to-private deal. There are perhaps three categories of candidates. The first of these comprises companies probably capitalised at between £50m and £300m. At that level, these companies find that their stock is fairly illiquid. This may be exacerbated by a large controlling shareholding, or it may simply be that the company is under-researched and therefore attracts little trading interest. There are implications here for both the company and its shareholders.

From the company's point of view, much of the point of a stock-market quotation is lost, since access to the capital markets is effectively constrained by the lack of liquidity and, probably, a below average share rating. In addition, many funds simply can't or won't invest in smaller companies, thus reducing still further the pool of potential providers of capital. These companies have none of the benefits of a quote, and all the disadvantages in terms of expense and onerous reporting duties.

For shareholders, whether small or large, the situation can be equally difficult. Institutional investors with sizeable holdings are unable to sell their stake in the market, and when this happens, those shares cause an overhang which depresses the price and further reduces the company's ability to raise funds. Private shareholders, too, find it hard to sell their shares at a sensible price, and end up locked in to a poorly performing investment.

The second category of companies that are candidates for PTP deals include companies that may have short-term trading problems but sound medium to long-term investment plans that will pay off handsomely in, say, five years' time. The pressure on institutional investors to perform in the short term means that most funds investing in the stockmarket only take a 6–12 month view, at best, of a company's prospects. Companies with longer-term prospects are clearly less likely to be in favour with fund managers: what is needed are backers who will take a longer-term view and be prepared to wait for their returns. A PTP deal with a venture capital house could well be the answer.

There is a small number of companies which fall into a third category – those whose business or management are such that they should never really have come to the market in the first place. Obvious examples are Virgin and Really Useful, both of which quickly realised they had made a mistake and were bought out by their founders.

Who benefits?

Having established some of the reasons for going private, who benefits and how? First and foremost, existing shareholders achieve an exit at a price that is almost certainly ahead of the prevailing market value. Not only that, but they may find that an auction commences for their company once it has been 'put in play' by an offer from a venture capital house.

One often-voiced fear about public-to-private deals is that the managers and venture capitalists are somehow stealing a march on existing investors and buying the company cheaply. Takeover Panel rules, which insist that any information given to the purchasers must also be made available to any other potential bidders, mean that the scope for unfair advantage is very limited. Add to that the role of independent directors of the target company (who will not be included in the new management team), plus the part played by their own independent advisers, and protection for ordinary shareholders looks comprehensive. Given that venture capitalists are currently eschewing hostile bids, the requirement to obtain a recommendation from the independent directors ensures that bid prices are, at the least, fair.

A common criticism levelled at management is that they intend to profit at the expense of shareholders. It is true that they will typically get an opportunity to purchase shares in Newco and those shares have the potential to generate large gains. It is equally true, though, that the transaction carries increased risk (due to higher debt levels) and the shares have often been bought for a significant amount of money, whereas a senior public company executive can anticipate a stream of executive share options and bonuses for no cost and little or no risk.

What of the venture capital house and the people behind it – the investors in its funds? Some of them may be the very same institutions that have sold their shares in the target company, but by investing in the funds run by the likes of NatWest Equity Partners (NWEP), they have taken the decision to put a certain amount of their money into longer-term prospects. And 'longer-term' is the key here. NWEP is typically looking at a timescale for investments of three to five years or even longer, giving ample time for a company's growth plans to come to fruition or for market conditions to move in its favour. Compare this to the stockmarket's much vaunted short-termism and it's easy to see the attractions of going private.

Given that venture capitalists are prepared to invest for the long term, how do they expect to generate their eventual return? In the 1980s, this came primarily through price arbitrage – companies were often bought on the basis of recession-depressed earnings and very low PE ratios, and the backers made their exit a few years later at a higher price/earnings rating and on earnings boosted by inflation, recovery from recession and the impact of high initial gearing.

Currently, though, venture capitalists are not looking to make much on the difference between buying and selling prices. In some cases, venture capitalists are assuming that their exit multiple could be less than their entry multiple. The venture capitalist still expects to enjoy some benefit gearing but, increasingly, above average returns are dependent on the challenge of identifying companies with above-average growth prospects. This has always been the venture capitalist's most valuable skill and its importance in deal-making has never been higher than in PTP deals where there is very little scope to buy cheaply.

How does a public-to-private deal work?

NatWest Equity Partners has certain criteria when looking at a potential PTP deal. A company with a very fragmented shareholder base is never going to be easy to target; ideally NWEP would like to see an identifiable block of shares, maybe as much as 25 per cent, which can be targeted as a starting point. Next, ready access to the management and board is crucial. Thus far, at least, all PTP deals have been on an agreed basis, so friendly relations with the board are vital.

Thirdly, there must be a good and logical reason for the proposed deal, one that will be appreciated by shareholders, analysts and the media. Problems such as: shortage of capital; management succession gaps; family shareholders seeking an exit; or the need for acquisitions in order to advance, can all contribute here, but need to be properly communicated if the deal is to gain wide acceptance and if shareholder suspicion is to be allayed.

Finally, there needs to be a cogent plan for the eventual exit from venture capital ownership. Will going private now damage the company's chances of returning to the market in, say, five years' time? If so, perhaps going private is not such a good idea after all. The UK is not yet quite so ready as the US to accept a two-way street between public and private, and British perceptions and sensitivities need to be taken into account.

When it comes to the mechanics of a PTP, they are very similar to a normal corporate recommended takeover bid. The only fundamental difference is that the bid will not generally become unconditional until acceptances reach 75 per cent, rather than the 50 per cent that is usual in corporate takeovers. The reason for this is very simple: the rules governing financial assistance (i.e. the securing of loans on the assets of the company being acquired) only apply to private companies, and 75 per cent is the level at which the acquirer can de-list the target and re-register it as a private company. That is the point at which the lending banks can be given security, and therefore the level at which they are happy for the bid to go unconditional. It remains to be seen whether this requirement will be relaxed as the banks get more used to this type of transaction.

In most other respects, these deals are just like any other bid. Despite the recommendation of the board, there is no guarantee that they will succeed – shareholders outside that magic block of 25 per cent or more could vote against, or there could be a rival bidder offering more money. On the whole, though, once the company has been put into play, its days as a quoted company are numbered.

Where does the venture capital market go next?

Developments in the venture capital market come thick and fast. Already we have seen Nomura introduce the idea of securitisation of

Case studies

Betterware

NatWest Equity Partners has completed four public-to-private deals in the past year or so, and of these two are particularly interesting – Betterware and Healthcall.

Betterware plc specialises in household products sold from mini-catalogues that are delivered door-to-door, and following its flotation in 1986, it became one of the stockmarket's best-performing companies. In the early 1990s, however, trading problems led to three profit warnings in the space of five months in 1994, and the share price has suffered ever since.

By the mid-1990s, Betterware had developed a strategy for overseas expansion, centred around joint ventures with Avon Cosmetics involving a push into the growing markets of South America and Eastern Europe. The stockmarket was not convinced by this strategy, given that the new ventures are unlikely to make any significant contribution to profits until 2000 at the earliest, and it became apparent to the principal Betterware shareholder that the company would be better off in the private arena while the investment was developed and carried through. The transaction was ideal for NWEP and after a full due diligence exercise, a deal was agreed. This involved a commitment to backing management for three to five years, and an understanding of the long-term potential of the overseas expansion. The £127 million acquisition was completed in January 1998.

Healthcall

The acquisition of Healthcall plc was a little less straightforward. The core business of this company, which was floated in 1994, is the provision of out-of-hours GP cover services. The uncertainty surrounding healthcare reforms meant that the shares had fallen badly out of favour with investors. The management team, together with NWEP, put together an offer at 90p per share, valuing the company at around £50 million.

This time a rival bidder was attracted – in this case Transworld Healthcare, a NASDAQ-quoted company that already owns

Omnicare and Allied Medicare in the UK. Transworld indicated that it was interested in offering 105p a share for Healthcall, but the offer never materialised, as Transworld realised that the NWEP offer was a full offer which it did not wish to increase. The deal was completed in April 1998, and Rob Moores, the Director concerned at NWEP, commented: 'We have taken a long-term view on the prospects for Healthcall and believe that, current short-term uncertainty as a result of healthcare reforms apart, the company has a strong market position, good management and excellent long-term prospects. The difference between our investment horizon, and that of the stockmarket, means that the company will be better placed to invest and develop its services as a private company.'

revenue stream into its acquisition of Thorn. How long will it be before the first billion pound plus public-to-private deal? And the first hostile bid by a venture capitalist? The amount of money raised by venture capital funds, often on a pan-European basis, means that prices are being driven higher, inevitably adding to the overheating of the entire stockmarket.

Some say it will all end in tears. Others, more sanguine, believe that new, even more creative, uses for these long-term funds will be dreamt up by the venture capitalists and the whole industry will move on. In the meantime, though, any management team struggling with an unsympathetic stockmarket and disgruntled shareholders could do worse than to contact some venture capitalists who may well have the perfect solution – a public-to-private deal.

Brian Phillips is a Director of NatWest Equity Partners.

Specialist expertise, proven performance

£36,000,000
Management Buy-In
of 40 Beefeater Pubs
from Whitbread plc

Led, structured and arranged by
NatWest Equity Partners

£65,400,000
Public to Private:
Management Buy-Out
from Healthcall plc

Led, structured and arranged by
NatWest Equity Partners

£49,000,000
Acquisition with
Management
from First Leisure plc

Led, structured and arranged by
NatWest Equity Partners

£127,000,000
Public to Private:
Institutional Buy-Out
from Betterware plc

Led, structured and arranged by
NatWest Equity Partners

NatWest Equity Partners is a leading European provider of private equity, specialising in structuring and leading UK and Continental European buy-out transactions.

For further information, please contact
David Shaw or one of his team on 0171 374 3505.

NatWest Equity Partners Limited Regulated by IMRO

NatWest Equity Partners

13

Legal and Taxation Aspects of Private Equity Transactions

Roger Fink, Susan Biddle, and
Mark Cawthron
Biddle

Introduction

The common thread running through all private equity transactions is the existence of a management team backed by an institutional investor (commonly referred to as a 'venture capitalist').

This chapter concentrates on certain key legal and taxation aspects of a typical management buy-out (MBO) or management buy-in (MBI) involving the acquisition of a private company. These issues are considered from the perspective of the management team and institutional investor, whether in dealing with each other or with third parties. An increasingly common type of transaction involves an offer for a public company financed by an institutional investor – this is known as a 'go-private' or 'public-to-private' since the target company will generally be converted back to private company status following completion. All of the issues dealt with in this chapter will be relevant to 'go private' deals but the constraints of space do not permit any analysis of the issues that are unique to these types of deal, such as the implications of The City Code on Take-overs and Mergers or the potential conflicts of interest for management which often arise.

Although this chapter is specifically focused on MBOs/MBIs, some or all of the issues discussed will be relevant to any private equity transaction.

Preliminary considerations

Members of the management team should obtain legal advice at the earliest possible opportunity, particularly in the areas of disclosing or receiving confidential information relating to the company/business being acquired (the 'Target'), and personal taxation.

It is common practice in an MBO/MBI for the management and institutional investor to negotiate with the seller a period during which Target's owners will not negotiate with anyone else (known as an 'exclusivity period'). Such an agreement will commonly be included in the same agreement in which the management and institution agree to keep information on the Target disclosed by its owners confidential.

A legal due diligence report on Target will be required and will usually be prepared by the lawyers acting for the institutional investors.

Establishment of Newco

A newly incorporated company will invariably be set up ('Newco'), which will usually be financed by a mixture of the proceeds of shares (and quite often loan stock) issued to the institution and management, bank loans and possibly mezzanine loans.

At the time Newco is established the following main tax questions arise for management, and need to be dealt with:

- If they are borrowing money to fund their investment, will they obtain tax relief on the interest payments?
- As an alternative to relief for payments of loan interest, can the management's share subscriptions qualify for relief under the Enterprise Investment Scheme (EIS)? Where an individual's investment does qualify, he or she will initially obtain income tax relief at 20% on the amount invested, up to a maximum of £150,000; in addition, capital gains realised on other assets can be deferred by investing in new EIS shares. The subsequent sale of shares will be free of capital gains tax (CGT), although this exemption does not extend to the deferred gains above, which then come back into charge. Crucially, however, in

order to retain the income tax relief and to enjoy the CGT exemption, the individual must generally retain the shares for at least five years, and the institution may have in mind an exit within that period.

- Interest relief on loans and EIS relief are mutually exclusive – they cannot be claimed on the same investment.
- Should management members take steps to transfer some shares to or for the benefit of members of his or her family or others, possibly within a trust structure? There may be potential CGT and inheritance tax benefits from doing so. In particular, as a result of the introduction of the new CGT taper relief in Finance Act 1998, it may sometimes be more attractive for some of a manager's shares to be held for the benefit of family members from the outset, rather than, as has often happened in the past, such shares being transferred at a later date at a time when an exit is very much in prospect.

It should be noted however that tax relief for loan interest ceases to be available to the extent that shares acquired with the aid of the loan are subsequently transferred to family members or family trusts. EIS relief may also cease to be available on such share transfers.

Both Newco and management will need to be clear whether, in any particular case, the shares issued to management (or any particular members of the management team) are acquired by them because they are directors/employees of Newco or Target. If that is the case, a Schedule E tax liability could arise in the year in which the shares are acquired (although that would be unusual); more importantly, a Schedule E tax liability could arise at a later date in certain circumstances, by reference to the growth in value of the shares. In particular, there are new rules in Finance Act 1998 intended to catch increases in value on shares which convert into a different class. These new rules need to be watched in the context of drafting the terms of any 'equity ratchet' providing for the managers' equity stake to be increased depending on future trading results.

Funding of Newco
Institutional/management

Funding by the institution and management will be in the form of an issue to them by Newco of shares and, possibly, loan stock. The institution will normally subscribe for a mixture of:

- redeemable preference shares with a prior right, before all other shares, to a fixed dividend and which will be redeemable by Newco on specific dates;
- 'preferred' ordinary shares which, after the dividends on the redeemable preference shares, carry a prior right, before all other shares, to a dividend normally calculated as a percentage of Target's net profits and then ranking for dividends with the managers' ordinary shares;
- loan stock carrying an agreed rate of interest and redeemable by Newco on specific dates.

In working out the form and terms of the investment by the institution, the tax consequences of such investment by way of (preference) shares or loans should be understood. Interest payments by Newco should be deductible for tax purposes; dividend payments by Newco will not be. Where the management's forecasts indicate that the business will not pay corporation tax for some time, the value of tax relief on payments of interest is reduced and it may be worth reducing the cash cost of borrowing at the expense of obtaining a deduction. In addition, where there are substantial payments or accruals of interest by Newco in the early years, there may be insufficient taxable profits in Target against which to set the interest (by way of 'group relief'), and the excess interest could then effectively be locked into Newco and only be relievable in future years against profits of Newco (rather than profits of Target). In certain circumstances it may be possible to overcome these potential tax difficulties and nevertheless still maintain the desired level of loans within the financing structure.

Looking at the position of the investing institution, this will often be a nominee for its pension fund clients and those pension funds will be exempt from tax on both interest and dividend payments received out of Newco. A significant difference though, since July 1997, is that cash dividends received by a pension fund no longer carry a repayable tax credit, whereas tax withheld on payments of interest by Newco is reclaimable.

The managers will invest in ordinary shares ranking for dividends with the preferred ordinary shares after all prior rights to dividends. These shares, together with the preferred ordinary shares of the institutions, comprise Newco's 'equity'. On a sale of Target or other form of exit, after repayment of bank and mezzanine debt and redemption of the preference shares, the proceeds realised will be paid to the holders of these shares. In other words, they share in the 'upside' of a successful exit. A 'ratchet' is sometimes negotiated between the managers and institution whereby, dependent on results, the managers' equity stake can be increased or decreased.

The terms of the investment by the managers and institution will be documented in:

- a Subscription Agreement;
- Articles of Association regulating Newco's share rights and constitution;
- a Loan Stock Deed (if loan stock is issued).

The key issues that commonly arise in the course of negotiating these documents include:

Good Leaver/Bad Leaver

Managers will be required to sell their shares on leaving employment. How those shares are valued will depend on whether the manager in question is a 'good leaver' or a 'bad leaver'. If a 'bad leaver', which essentially covers fault-based dismissals and leaving employment within a certain period after the acquisition, the manager will usually receive the lower of the amount paid for the shares and their market value. If a 'good leaver', the manager will usually receive the higher of the amount paid for the shares and their market value. The method of valuing the shares will be set out in Newco's Articles of Association.

These provisions benefit both the institution and the remaining members of the management team in keeping ownership of the equity in the hands of shareholders involved in Newco's management. A shareholder not involved in Newco's management could present an obstacle to a successful exit.

Drag-along/Tag-along

These provisions will almost invariably be included in Newco's Articles of Association. A 'drag-along' provision will require all shareholders to join in a sale if holders of more than a certain percentage (the figure to be negotiated but likely to be between 51% and 90%) of preferred ordinary and ordinary shares have negotiated a sale to a third party. Conversely, a 'tag-along' provision gives the right to minority shareholders to join in a sale that has been negotiated by more than a certain percentage of preferred ordinary and ordinary shareholders.

Restrictions on transferring shares

Transfers of shares will generally be prohibited, subject to certain limited exceptions which will be defined in Newco's Articles. Transfers normally permitted are:

- transfers by the institution within its own group of investors or to other funds under common management. In addition, the institution may be able to syndicate to another venture capital institution;
- transfers by managers, in carefully described circumstances, to family trusts for tax planning purposes.

The rationale for restricting transfers is, again, so that the institution and managers can control ownership of Newco's shares, thereby avoiding obstacles (because, for example, a shareholder cannot be traced or will not consent) to a successful exit.

Where managers are required to sell their shares on leaving employment, the Articles will provide for these shares to be offered first to remaining members of the management team. These shares will only be offered outside the management if they are not taken up in full under the 'offer-round' procedure.

Warranties

The managers will give warranties to the institution in the Subscription Agreement. These will cover:

- in relation to those managers who were managers of Target before the acquisition, Target's business. This is particularly important for the institution where liability of Target's owners for breach of warranty in the Share Sale Agreement for Target is excluded on the grounds of the knowledge of the management team;
- the business plan which the management team will have prepared;
- parts of the accountants' report;
- answers to the personal questionnaires which will have been provided by the institution;
- ownership of their shares and, in particular, that they are not subject to any third party rights.

Restrictions on the operation of Target

The Subscription Agreement will provide that certain matters relating to Target's on-going business will require the institution's prior consent. Typical examples of these are:

- acquisitions of other businesses or disposals of any part of Newco's business;
- capital expenditure above certain limits;
- hiring, firing and remuneration of senior staff;
- borrowing;
- approval of budgets.

Restrictive covenants from management

The Subscription Agreement will include undertakings from the managers not to compete with the Newco Group's business or solicit its customers or employees within an agreed period after leaving Newco.

Other safeguards for the institution

Other provisions will be included in the Subscription Agreement to enable the institution to 'keep an eye' on Target's business. These include:

- a right to appoint a director to Newco's and Target's Board or, alternatively, an observer to attend board meetings;
- reasonable notice to be given of board and committee meetings;
- a regular flow of information within agreed time periods, including forecasts, budgets, management accounts and annual accounts.

Senior debt

The majority of the funding, comprising finance both for the acquisition and for Target's on-going capital requirements, will come from banks and will be secured by charges over Newco's and Target's assets. The terms of the funding will be contained in a Facility Agreement and Security Documents and will be negotiated by the institution and management, acting together on behalf of Newco, with the banks. This form of funding is known as 'senior debt' because it ranks ahead of any other form of finance such as mezzanine funding (see below) and subordinated loan stock issued to the equity provider.

Issues that will arise in negotiating the terms of the senior debt include:

- permitted payments of dividends and redemptions of Newco's shares and loan stock before the senior debt is repaid. The banks will seek to restrict these as much as possible to preserve their priority;

- negotiation of financial covenants given by Newco, which the institution and managers will seek to make achievable and reasonable;
- matters requiring the bank's consent and circumstances in which the debt is repayable.

The charges given by Target will need to be 'whitewashed' to avoid breaching the statutory prohibitions on financial assistance. This will require a declaration from Newco's and Target's directors, backed by an auditor's report, that Newco and Target are solvent and will remain so over the next 12 months.

Mezzanine finance

This comprises additional finance, usually in the form of a secured loan (although occasionally in the form of shares), ranking behind the senior debt, which often carries enhanced interest and/or the right (in the form of a warrant or option) to subscribe for shares in Newco in recognition of the greater risk it bears.

Assuming the finance takes the form of debt, the documentation and issues will be similar to those relating to the senior debt. In addition:

- the mezzanine and bank lenders will negotiate an 'inter-creditor agreement' setting out their respective rights of priority and enforcement;
- the mezzanine lenders will negotiate an agreement with the managers and institution setting out the terms on which they will be able to subscribe for shares in Newco.

Acquisition

This chapter will not discuss in any detail the steps involved in acquiring Target, which is explained elsewhere in this book. The acquisition will be by Newco and the terms will be negotiated by the institution and management with Target's sellers. Amongst the issues that will arise in the course of negotiations with the sellers are:

- the warranties relating to Target and its business to be given by the sellers. As previously mentioned in this chapter, the sellers may ask for a carve-out from the warranties for matters within the knowledge of managers of Target pre-acquisition. To the extent that any carve-out is agreed, the institution will seek to 'plug the gap' by strengthening the warranties in the Subscription Agreement;

- the terms of the indemnity from the sellers in relation to Target's tax liabilities. In the case of an MBO, the sellers may seek to argue that the management are best placed to know whether Target has complied with its tax obligations (particularly on PAYE/VAT matters) and that the sellers' liability should be limited accordingly. Management, and their institutional backer, are unlikely to be sympathetic to this argument;
- the terms of undertakings from the sellers not, for an agreed period, to compete with Target's business or solicit employees or customers;
- the disclosure letter which is written by the sellers, disclosing exceptions to the statements made in the warranties.

Management

Service contracts will be entered into between Newco and the managers and will be negotiated by the institution on behalf of Newco. These are essential for the protection of both the individual managers and Newco's and Target's business. Issues that will arise include:

- the term of employment and the length of notice required on either side;
- undertakings from the managers not to compete with the business or solicit customers or employees for an agreed period after leaving employment.

The institution and banks will also require Newco or Target to take out keyman life insurance (over which the banks will take security) for all or most of the management team.

Roger Fink and Susan Biddle are partners in Biddle's Corporate Department with particular expertise in private equity, having acted for institutional investors and management teams on numerous private equity transactions.

Mark Cawthron is a partner in Biddle's Tax Department and has experience of advising both institutions and managers on the tax implications of a wide range of private equity transactions.

Section Four
Public Equity

Solomon Hare: Signalling success for the entrepreneur

Stephen Toole from Solomon Hare reflects on the success of one of the firm's major clients, Prism Rail. The company operates four of the passenger rail franchises made available by the UK Government during the recent rail privatisation process. In the space of three years, Solomon Hare assisted in Prism's growth from the seed of an idea to a fully fledged business quoted on the UK's main market with a capitalisation of over £100 million.

Prism Rail was founded in early 1994 by the proprietors of four bus companies and a fifth member, Ken Irvine, who introduced Solomon Hare as advisers to the founder shareholders. The company was formed specifically to bid for the British Rail passenger franchises. Bidding for BR franchises at that time was a risky business, since nobody knew for certain that the privatisation programme would be achieved or that it would have continuing political support. The founders needed a sound bidding strategy before the formal privatisation process got under way, together with a plan for raising the necessary finance.

Solomon Hare advised the founding shareholders to develop a strategy based around building a balanced portfolio of franchises. In the early days of the bidding process, the founders faced many problems, not least the tight timetable and limited in-house resources at Prism's disposal. It also became clear from the outset that a flexible funding structure was necessary. Stephen Toole recalls "We quickly identified that the main competition would come from the UK's major quoted transport groups and large corporations. We advised the Prism directors that they would need suitably priced finance to enable them to compete with other likely bidders."

On 26 May 1996 the determination of the team paid off when Prism was awarded its first franchise for the London Tilbury and Southend line. Although Prism's management had a track record in terms of their experience and expertise in the bus industry, the company could not qualify for the UK's main market since it was a new enterprise. Solomon Hare came up with the idea of floating the business on the UK's market for smaller and developing companies, known as the Alternative Investment Market or AIM, which was becoming established at the time. "We quickly determined that AIM was a suitable source for raising finance since it was cheaper than venture capital. A flotation was possible due to the more relaxed entry requirements compared with the full list" continues Stephen Toole.

Solomon Hare also had to convince the Government's financial advisers, HSBC Investment Bank, that such an innovative funding proposal could be achieved. Patricia Hudson, the director responsible at HSBC, recalls: "the Solomon Hare team's clarity of thought on the technical requirements and their determination that the AIM route would succeed won the day".

The idea was introduced by Solomon Hare to London stockbrokers Williams de Broë, also known for their innovative approach to developing financing solutions for smaller companies. Within six weeks the £8 million needed to fund the acquisition had been raised on the back of an AIM flotation. Tim Worlledge from Williams de Broë comments "We were delighted to support this innovative and well-researched proposal, particularly as it made good use of the AIM market. As a consequence, it brought a rapid and positive response from our institutional clients."

The scale of work that followed was significant. During the next few months, Solomon Hare helped Prism with its bidding strategy, reviewing the detailed information for every franchise offered for sale, advising on which ones to bid for and how to structure the finance for a successful bid. In all, Prism submitted bids for 17 of the 25 rail franchises that were privatised, and were shortlisted on 12 occasions.

The process yielded further successes, as Prism and its advisory team were successful in their bids for three other franchises. By the end of January 1997, the West Anglia Great Northern, South Wales and West Regional Railways and Cardiff Railway Company franchises were operating under Prism ownership. The company returned to the market for fresh capital to fund each new franchise, raising a further £25 million in the process. This innovative financing route was recognised by the market when Prism was awarded the "Best Use of AIM" award for 1996. Its four franchises ended up as the second highest number for a single bidder throughout the entire privatisation process.

Three years down the line from the original concept, Prism is now a very substantial transport business in its own right, with annual turnover of over £450 million. In July 1998, the company joined the UK's main market, its shares having been one of the top ten AIM performers since flotation, and is now quoted with a market capitalisation in excess of £100 million. Prism's transfer to the main market was made via an Introduction under the Stock Exchange's exempt listing provisions, a simplified route available to companies with two years' trading history on AIM.

It is clear that the original imaginative method of financing has enabled Prism to take advantage of the opportunities available along the way. At the same time, the founder shareholders were able to retain over 30% of the business, demonstrating Solomon Hare's ability to convert a vision and ambition into commercial reality. Giles Fearnley, Prism's Chief Executive and one of the original founders, comments "Right from the outset we knew their total dedication would deliver a result. Our challenge now is to continue to improve the quality of service to our passengers whilst at the same time meeting the demands of our public shareholders".

On 25 June 1998, the week before the move up to the main market, Prism announced profits of £16.5 million for the year to 31 March 1998, the first full year of ownership and operation of the four franchises. Given that this has been achieved on a capital base of a little over £30 million, it is not surprising to note that shareholders have benefited from a four fold increase in the value of their investment. Prism's challenge is to continue this success as it enters the next stage of development as a substantial transport group.

Stephen Toole is a corporate finance partner at Bristol-based accountants, Solomon Hare.

Solomon Hare Corporate Finance has established a national reputation as one of the leading bespoke financial advisory units outside London and, with over 20 highly experienced and motivated professional staff, undertakes work all around the UK and overseas. Solomon Hare Corporate Finance is a registered sponsor on the main market and approved by the Stock Exchange as a nominated advisor to AIM companies, acting for two of the top ten share price performers on AIM.

GREIG MIDDLETON
~ *Corporate Finance*

GM

Guidance Matters.

Currently over 65 quoted companies turn to Greig Middleton for advice on corporate finance matters. Our professional team has the expertise to guide you or your companies through the maze of flotations, secondary equity issues, acquisitions and disposals, and to advise on all aspects of small and medium sized company activity. To find out how to secure guidance for your business, call Robert Clinton on 0171 655 4000.

30 Lombard Street, London EC3V 9EN Tel: 0171 655 4000 Fax: 0171 655 4100
155 St. Vincent Street, Glasgow G2 5NN Tel: 0141 221 6578 Fax: 0141 221 6578

14

Flotation

Ralph Catto
Greig Middleton

Part 1: The public equity market

The public equity markets offer significant access to risk capital. The amounts invested have been very large, with over £4 billion raised in new issues (i.e. flotations) on the London Stock Exchange in 1998. It is also arguably the cheapest source of external equity funding, largely because of the reduction in an investor's risk, due to there being a market in the shares. If public equity investors believe that the risk/return profile of an investment is no longer attractive to them they can seek to exit from that investment through the stock market. This is not usually an option for private equity investors and, as their investments are less liquid (i.e. tradable), they will require a larger share of the company relative to their investment to compensate for the risk of illiquidity.

There are, however, various drawbacks to being 'quoted'. Shareholders of public companies have an expectation of continuous growth in value and this puts management under greater pressure than would generally be the case in private companies. There are also increased regulatory and reporting requirements. For owner managers, flotation will lead to some loss of control, initially to outside shareholders and potentially to a predatory bid. Risks associated with flotation are considered more fully in Part 4.

The decision whether to float or not will be driven largely by financial considerations. The principal consideration will normally be whether the cost of quoted equity is appropriate relative to alternative sources of funding. If debt funding is available then this may be attractive, but before making the decision to take it, the additional risk of debt funding to existing equity shareholders should be considered. If debt funding is not available then sources of equity funding should be considered (i.e. flotation, venture capital, development capital, etc).

Reasons for flotation that are not purely to do with funding the company at the time of flotation, include:

- providing an exit or partial exit for existing shareholders;
- providing quoted shares within incentive schemes for employees;
- improving the company's profile with customers, suppliers, landlords, etc;
- having the additional resource of quoted shares in negotiating acquisitions; and
- raising further equity at some later date from the public equity market.

Part 2: Suitability for flotation

There are a number of technical requirements a company has to meet to qualify for admission to public markets. In addition to those there is the equally important requirement that the company must be attractive to potential investors.

The principal technical requirements and the general profiles of the Official List (the main market of the London Stock Exchange), AIM (the second market of the London Stock Exchange) and EASDAQ (a Brussels based market affiliated to NASDAQ in the USA) are as follows:

	Official List	AIM	EASDAQ
Minimum proportion of shares in "public" hands	25 per cent	no minimum	20 per cent (suggested)
Minimum financial track record	3 years*	no minimum	no minimum
Minimum track record of management within the business	3 years*	no minimum	no minimum
Last audit	within 6 months	no requirement	no requirement
Minimum total asset value at flotation	no minimum	no minimum	ECU 3.5 million
Minimum capital and reserves at flotation	no minimum	no minimum	ECU 2 million
Minimum aggregate share value at flotation	£700,000	no minimum	no minimum
Number of companies on the market**	2,296	312	39
Aggregate value of market**	£2,299 billion	£4.415 billion	£10.15 billion
Number of flotations in 1998 calendar year	124	75	17
Funds raised on flotations in 1998 calendar year	£4.196 billion	£267.5 million	£629.3 million
Aggregate value of flotations in 1998 calendar year	£47.46 billion	£1.178 billion	£2.246 billion

*   There are certain limited circumstances where an applicant to the Official List will not need to meet these requirements.

**   Derived from the most recently published information for each market.

The criteria of investors are somewhat different. They are seeking a sufficient return to balance the risk of the equity investment. There is no such thing as a typical flotation candidate, but core traits that investors will be looking for are:

- a business with a defined, realistic strategy which will achieve increased returns for both existing and new equity shareholders;
- a capable management team to implement and control that strategy; and
- a historic demonstration of the quality of the business and management – most likely demonstrated through historic financial growth.

Investors will prefer to see a track record for both the flotation candidate and its management. If investors are being asked to pay a high price for shares because of an expectation of substantial growth over the next few years, it helps credibility if the company has demonstrated substantial growth over the previous few years. Similarly, if growth is largely to come from acquisition, then investors will consider whether the management team has a proven record of making successful acquisitions. In both these scenarios, history lends credibility to the likelihood of future outcomes and in doing so potentially reduces the risk in the eyes of the investor.

Most companies going to the market are valued at below £100m (in terms of market capitalisation) at the time of flotation and the principal institutional investors will therefore be the 'small company' funds. Small company funds are generalists in the main – i.e. not limited to any particular sector specialisation. They are able to invest in a wide range of potential flotation candidates provided they believe that the growth prospects of their investment are suitable to meet their particular risk/reward requirements.

There are, at any one time, certain business sectors that are viewed by investors as being able to provide excess returns and are consequently more popular with investors. By way of an example, a sector that has been affected in such a way over recent years is the restaurant sector. The potential for rapid growth is possible where companies with proven dining concepts replicate these into new areas. Additionally, this sector benefited from a rising trend in the number of times people eat out in the UK. However, with a forecast economic downturn in recent months, this sector has become less popular due to the concern that people will eat out less often as they cut back on 'luxury' items.

Although there is a vast amount of money invested in public equity markets, it must be remembered that the supply of cash is not infinite and investors will always search out the best returns. The laws of supply and demand apply and it is easier to market the flotation of a company if it is in a sector that is popular with investors than if it is in a sector which is in the doldrums.

All this is not to say that companies with a complex or difficult to understand product, or diversified range of business do not make successful flotations, but it may be harder to achieve, and that fact may ultimately be reflected in the valuation.

What the investors like least is uncertainty. With certainty of return and certainty of risk, an accurate assessment can be made of what the appropriate price would be to deliver the investors' required return. Unfortunately, we do not live in an environment where certainty is stock in trade. The art of investment is based on uncertainty. However, the lesson here is to deliver to the investor as much certainty as possible in preparing a company for flotation. A period of 'grooming' prior to flotation is very wise. The grooming period may vary between three months and two years, dependent on the circumstances of the company. Typical areas that might require attention in a growth company prior to flotation would be:

- strengthening the management team, which may be a reflection of the growth of the business or to reduce dependence on key personnel;
- prioritisation of business growth;
- improvement in financial controls and reporting – often in a fast growing company this vital aspect lags behind the growth in the company; and
- identification of knowledge gaps and sourcing of appropriate non-executive directors to fill these.

It is best to present an investment opportunity in a focused business to potential investors. The more focused a company is about what it is seeking to achieve and how it plans to achieve it, the simpler it is for the investor to assess the potential likelihood of success and hence the risk and return. Typically, institutional investors will mitigate the risk of any particular investment going wrong by way of holding a portfolio of stocks. There is, therefore, arguably no reason for any one company to diversify its risk by investing in unrelated areas and it should instead focus on core activities. Although there is a converse argument to this, the low stock market rating of companies which have heavily diversified and are described as 'conglomerates' reflects the investment community's view of which is correct.

Additionally, the simpler and more focused the opportunity that the company represents, the easier it is to get that across to potential investors. In considering the amount of time that an institution will have to consider a potential flotation candidate, one must look at how many other flotation candidates an institution may be reviewing, as well as the number of already quoted companies that they are looking after in their portfolio; their time is limited. Typically, the marketing of a flotation candidate to institutions will comprise of a short analytical document, which will give the stockbroker's view of prospects and value; the prospectus, which is a legal document that forms the basis of the investment; and a number of meetings with institutional investors which may last as little as 20 minutes. The marketing of a flotation candidate is considered more fully in Part 6.

Part 3: The flotation timetable

Within reason, the more time there is to organise a flotation the better. Management involvement in the flotation process can be planned and spread over a reasonable period, creating more opportunity to continue the smooth day-to-day running of the business. This, it is hoped, then avoids the necessary distraction of the flotation process damaging the business.

A reasonable period over which a flotation process could be drawn would be six months, as demonstrated by the bar chart overleaf. However, ideally, a company will have sought advice earlier than that as to the best way to groom itself for the flotation process and make it as attractive as possible to potential investors. A company seriously considering flotation should seek to interview a number of potential financial advisers and/or stockbrokers to identify those that the management or existing shareholders wish to work with towards the goal of flotation. Such a 'beauty parade' might be held as early as 12 to 18 months prior to the proposed flotation date. The adviser(s) would seek to understand more about the business of the flotation candidate over the months following appointment, to assist in grooming the company's business before the more intensive pre-flotation work begins.

Week No.	1	2	3	4	5	6	7	8	9	10	11	12	13	14	15	16	17	18	19	20	21	22	23	24	25	26
Appoint advisers																										
Business issues																										
Tax advice																										
Long form report																										
Legal due dilligence																										
Specialists reports																										
Insurance review																										
Audit																										
Prospectus																										
Short form report																										
Working capital report																										
Research note																										
Placing agreement																										
Verification																										
Marketing																										
Public relations																										

Flotation complete and dealings commence

The above chart shows an example of a flotation timetable of 26 weeks and the activities at each stage are explained briefly below.

Appoint advisers.   At this early stage it is important to decide which firm will be the financial adviser, as it will lead the advisory team. This will most likely be the first appointment specifically related to the flotation. If the stockbroker is to be independent of the financial adviser, this is also an appointment to be made at an early stage in order to assess value, stockmarket sentiment and the likelihood of a successful flotation. The financial adviser will assess the company's existing relationships with solicitors and accountants and advise if there is a necessity to appoint new firms for the flotation; as flotation is a new stage in the development of a company, it may be that current advisers' strengths are not in areas required for flotation.

Business issues.   During this period, the financial adviser will seek to attain a clear understanding of the business of the flotation candidate. This then allows early identification of business areas that require attention prior to flotation and thereby maximises the time available to address them. The appointment of appropriate non-executive directors will also be driven to some extent by this. The appointments are most often made from the end of the overall timetable.

Tax advice.   There are a number of areas where tax advice may be necessary or advisable. These may relate to the company or the position of existing shareholders. They may be the resolution of historic tax issues or may relate to the structuring of the company pre-flotation for tax efficiencies in the future. Where the advice relates to the company, it is most likely to be the accountants to the company who will provide this. Where issues relate to existing shareholders these may be dealt with by a separate adviser to the shareholder(s).

Long form report.   'Long form report' is the name given to the document which most completely describes the business of the flotation candidate. This document is prepared by the accountants to the flotation. The document will provide a considerable level of detail on all aspects of the business and will be the foundation for much of the rest of the preparation. As well as considering the prospects of the business, the long form report will also highlight areas of weakness that will require rectifying as much as possible and which potentially will be reported in the flotation prospectus. The financial adviser and/or stockbroker will review this report carefully and may, as a consequence, require further work to be undertaken on certain areas of the business. This report will be produced by the reporting accountants to the flotation which may be a separate firm to the company's accountants.

Legal due diligence.   In a similar way to the investigation in the long form report, the solicitors will be instructed to examine the legal aspects of the business. This will range from checking that all required information has been properly registered with the Registrar of Companies to a critique of the company's terms of trade. The financial adviser and stockbroker will, again, review this report carefully and may require further work to be undertaken in certain areas.

Specialist reports.   If the activities of the company are such that a specialist could provide an insight to risk or return by providing a report, then such a specialist may be engaged (e.g. a property report where property is an integral part of the business or a minerals report for a mining company). Depending on the stockmarket that the flotation is to be on, a specialist report may be a requirement in certain circumstances.

Insurance review.   This is another part of the due diligence process and seeks to confirm that the company has an appropriate level of insurance cover to provide for all aspects of its business.

Audit.   This may not be a requirement for every flotation but a recent audit is preferable, regardless of whether it is a specific stock market requirement. This will be undertaken by the accountants to the company. Where this falls within the timetable will depend on the company's accounting period end.

Prospectus.   This is the legal document which is published and on which an investor will rely to make their investment decision. Consequently, it is a legal requirement that the prospectus presents the business of the flotation candidate in a balanced way, covering both the potential returns and the risks associated with them. The preparation of the prospectus is co-ordinated by the financial adviser but will require input from almost all of the advisory team. The prospectus should be complete prior to the marketing commencing, in order that a 'pathfinder' prospectus can be produced. This is a version of the final prospectus which omits the price of the issue and information that is calculated from that.

Short form report.   This is not an abbreviated version of the long form report as may be implied by the title. Instead, it is a summary of the financial history of the company over the most recent years and this is included in the prospectus. Preparation of this report is the responsibility of the reporting accountants to the flotation.

Working capital report.   The working capital is considered as part of the flotation process in order to assess whether the company will have sufficient funds to sustain it for a reasonable period, typically 12 to 24 months, once floated. The document concerning working capital typically takes the form of a board paper, compiled by the company under the guidance of the reporting accountants to the flotation and with the input of the financial adviser and stockbroker.

Research note.   An analyst from the stockbroker will undertake a review of the company and publish a background research note in advance of marketing commencing. The purpose of this is to provide potential investors with information from an analytical perspective at an early stage in order to aid their assessment of the risk and reward potential from the flotation candidate.

Placing agreement.   This is the legal document prepared by the solicitors engaged by the financial adviser and/or stockbroker (the solicitors to the issue) which sets out the mechanism under which the company engages the financial adviser and/or stockbroker to place shares with investors to raise money for the company and/or for existing shareholders. This will typically require the management and vendors to enter into warranties (covering commercial issues associated with the business as well as title over securities and other such mechanical issues) and an indemnity. If the financial adviser or stockbroker is guaranteeing to buy shares it cannot find investors for, then this 'underwriting' arrangement will be included in the placing agreement.

Verification.   It is a requirement of law that the information provided to investors is accurate and not misleading and the directors of the company are personally liable if this is not the case. Consequently, all information that is published will require verification. The principal verification exercise will revolve around the prospectus but, in addition, the marketing material, press releases and other published material will also require verification.

Marketing.   Marketing will typically be in the form of a number of meetings with potential investors, which will be arranged by the stockbroker. The potential investors will have seen the research note and pathfinder prospectus prior to the meeting. During a meeting the company will make a presentation on its business, typically followed by a question and answer session.

Public relations (PR).   Towards the end of the flotation timetable, coverage in the press of the flotation should prove useful. Often, just prior to marketing commencing, the PR adviser will seek to place an article in the business section of a major Sunday newspaper and the additional recognition that that might bring will assist the stockbroker when setting up meetings with potential investors. From that time on, a positive newsflow will assist in marketing to potential investors, pre- or post-flotation. An additional benefit may be to raise the company's profile with customers or suppliers.

Flotations can be achieved in less than 26 weeks but there are risks to the company. The intensive involvement of key management in the flotation process may cause the business to suffer; the cost to the company may increase and, if there is something untoward identified in due diligence, it may not be possible to deal with it within such a short timetable. All these topics are examined further in Part 4.

Part 4: Risks of flotation

At all stages, the primary risk to a flotation is the state of the stock market and investor sentiment towards the sector that a company is seeking to join. If the stock market as a whole, or if the sector specifically, is weak then this may cause downward pressure on the price at which the flotation can be achieved, or halt the flotation altogether.

Pulling out of a flotation is very much the last resort. However, market conditions do change over time, sometimes quickly and sometimes slowly. Given that the flotation exercise can be a protracted one, it must be accepted as a commercial risk that there is potential for such a change to take effect at some time in that process. The important factor here is an on-going dialogue between the existing shareholders and management of the flotation candidate and the stockbrokers to the float. From the perspective of the existing shareholders and management, they will wish to know on a regular basis what the chance of a successful flotation is in order that they can plan the company's future. It is no good for the stockbroker to be then appointed at the beginning of the process, only to be brought in at the end to market the shares if, during the flotation process, had the stockbroker been asked, it would have said that the flotation was no longer a realistic alternative. In that scenario, significant costs would have been incurred which might not have been incurred had there been an on-going dialogue with the stockbroker. However, if a flotation is to be halted at all, it is best to happen prior to any marketing or any press coverage of the potential flotation. This way the company can seek to float at a later time and not be seen by potential investors as having failed earlier.

Another area that may halt a flotation, regardless of the state of the market, is 'due diligence'. It is in the company's best interests and, therefore, the interests of both existing shareholders and management, for the advisers to be fully conversant with both the prospects and the risks, comprised within the business. This will allow them to formulate a realistic and balanced marketing strategy prior to seeking new investors at flotation, and, additionally, investors will be comforted by the knowledge that the company has been examined in detail.

In order to attain a position where the company's advisers are in possession of the relevant facts to assess the prospects and risks, there must be a considerable due diligence exercise undertaken as described in Part 3. It may be that, at this stage, something is discovered which makes the company inappropriate for flotation in the short term and the problem needs to be addressed prior to a delayed flotation date. This delay may mean that the company misses out on the opportunity it was seeking to access by attaining the flotation. The likelihood of this happening can be lessened by working with the company's advisers from an early stage and informing them that flotation is a real prospect in the view of management and existing shareholders. Advice can then be given with a possible flotation in mind.

A less documented risk of flotation is the detrimental effect it may have on the business. This may occur where either management's attention is distracted by the flotation process away from the running of the business, or management see flotation as an end in itself and relax their efforts following flotation because of this. Either way, the business may suffer or slow down as a function of management's 'eye being off the ball'. The first year as a quoted company is arguably the most important year. It is the year in which the company has to prove that it can sustain its historic growth, prove that the prospects against which it persuaded new investors to invest are there, or the acquisitions that it said were available are delivered. If a company does not perform to expectations in its first year and falls out of favour with investors then it may take some time to regain credibility in the eyes of the investors. It is important not to promise too much about the company's prospects in the future or to play down the risks attached to such prospects, and therefore not to be greedy in pricing an issue thus leaving little for new investors to benefit from in the future. Instead, it is vital to be realistic in order to establish the company as having a credible perception with investors, with the goal of establishing a profitable relationship in the future for all investors, new and old. After all, it should be remembered that a key advantage of a flotation is the future use of quoted equity to make acquisitions and to raise money.

A further risk, which may well befall a company with a disappointing performance in their early years, is the risk of the company itself being taken over. As a quoted company, there is an increased requirement to publish information about results, trading, prospects, etc. and therefore competitors will be more easily aware of the performance of a quoted company over that of an unquoted company. How widely the equity of a company is owned will also affect the risk of a take-over. If, for example, management have retained more than half of the equity, a bid is unlikely, but if the equity is widely spread, a hostile approach may become reality.

The final risk covered here again relates to the requirements on a quoted company to publish more information and more often than an unquoted company. This might lead to competitors taking commercial advantage of that position without resorting to make a take-over.

What happens then if the flotation has to be halted? Depending on the other factors influencing a company, there are a number of alternative routes open to the company if a flotation is halted. There are a number of companies that have successfully floated at the second attempt, so to wait for better market conditions is a very real alternative. If the company does require equity in the shorter term, a private placing may be an option or indeed venture or development capital. If an exit for existing shareholders was one of the primary driving forces behind flotation, then the sale of the entire company may be an appropriate alternative route.

Part 5: The costs of flotation

Although the return required by investors in the public equity markets is low, relative to unquoted sources of equity, the initial costs of tapping into the quoted equity sector may exceed those of unquoted equity. The costs are largely those paid to the advisers, and the need for the advisory team is considered below.

The advisory team is used for a number of reasons:

- There are some advisers that are commercially required (e.g. the stockbroker will physically raise the money required), and some that are commercially preferred (e.g. the PR) in order to maximise any beneficial effect there may be for the company associated with becoming a quoted company.
- There are few company directors who have gone through the flotation process more than once. Consequently, it is logical to hire expertise from a source which has greater experience of such matters to co-ordinate the process. This expertise will come in the form of the firm acting as financial adviser.
- Investors require assurance that they have been given a thorough and balanced view of the company's prospects. The knowledge that there has been a comprehensive due diligence exercise performed by the advisory team will assist in providing that assurance. In this regard, an investor may also consider who was in the advisory team and review the quality of the advisers.
- Legal requirements which affect a company seeking investment from public equity sources will most typically be different and more stringent than those that applied in equity raising in the company's past. With such legal responsibility ultimately resting with the directors, good advice to avoid mistakes in this regard is plainly appropriate.

The costs associated with a flotation will depend on a number of factors, including onto which market or stock exchange flotation is sought, the complexity of the business of the flotation candidate, the need for expert reports and the time available to achieve the flotation. Additionally, there is an economy of scale relative to the amount of money to be raised as, typically, the commission associated with the fund raising will be percentage based but other fees will be set amounts. Consequently, the more money raised, the lower the aggregate costs are as a percentage of funds raised.

As a guide to flotation costs, set out below are estimates of fees and commissions associated with the flotation of a company, valued at £25 million before new money raised at the flotation, onto the Official List of the London Stock Exchange (these fees do not include value added tax).

Fees
Adviser

Financial adviser	£150,000	to	£250,000
Stockbroker	£50,000	to	£100,000
Accountants	£50,000	to	£100,000
Solicitor to company	£50,000	to	£100,000
Insurance adviser	£5,000	to	£20,000
Solicitor to issue	£15,000	to	£50,000
PR	£15,000	to	£30,000
Stock Exchange	£15,000	to	£15,000
Printing	£15,000	to	£30,000

Commissions
Adviser

Stockbroker	1%	to	3%

Therefore, assuming that £5 million new money was raised for the company, the aggregate cost range is £415,000 to £845,000 before the cost of any specialist reports. Although this may seem a very wide spread, it is impossible to define the 'typical' flotation candidate and therefore equally impossible to define the costs associated with it. However, taking the average of these two figures may prove a fair working assumption for a company of that value, as differing aspects of a company will mean that the flotation process is expensive in some areas and not in others. A method of cost saving often used in the flotation market is to merge the role of financial adviser with either the firm of stockbrokers, who have been acting in this dual role for some time, or accountants, some of whom have more recently marketed themselves as being able to undertake both roles. This will normally result in a lower aggregate fee for the two roles. Although the total costs as a percentage of funds raised is high, it must be remembered that these are one-off costs and, once floated, a company will typically be able to raise additional equity at a later stage at a lower relative percentage cost. Although there is typically a lower required return to public equity investors compared with private equity investors, the cost of accessing each type of equity must be included when considering the cost of equity. For small amounts of money, the quoted equity market may not prove an economic option.

Part 6: The placement process

There are a number of ways in which a company can raise equity on flotation, the most common of which is a placing. The mechanism works by the stockbroker placing shares, either new shares issued by the company or existing shares being sold by vendor shareholders, with investors. These investors may include insurance companies, pension funds, investment trusts, unit trusts and private client stock-brokers. The rules that cover the sale of shares to such 'sophisticated' investors are easier and cheaper to comply with than a general offer to the public and allow for the exercise to be completed more speedily, all of which make the placing route an attractive option.

Although the placing will be effected on a single day, the impact day, there is a considerable build-up to that point. This starts approximately six weeks prior to the impact day with the publication of the stockbro-ker's research note referred to in Part 3. This will cover a range of areas and most likely include background on the business, the management team, prospects and risks, comparison with quoted companies and comment on valuation. This research note is sent out by the stockbroker to sophisticated investors who are known to be interested in flotations in order to provide background to potential investors.

In the fourth week prior to impact day the prospectus will be veri-fied and complete, save only for information dependent on price. This document is then made up as a 'pathfinder' prospectus. The final ver-sion of the prospectus is the document that an investor will rely on in making their investment decision and, as this will not be available until impact day (i.e. when the price is known and the document can be completed), this pathfinder prospectus is provided. The pathfinder prospectus will be sent by the stockbroker to the same potential investors who received the research note.

Three weeks from impact day the physical marketing begins. As referred to in Part 3 this will take the form of a timetable of meetings with potential investors, either one at a time or in small groups depending on the preference of the investor. There may be as many as five meetings in one day and the meetings will stretch up to impact day. At these meetings, investors will want to meet the key members of the management team who would be responsible for providing them with a return on their investment. The first part of the meeting will typically be a well-rehearsed presentation by the company's man-agement, which is then followed by a question and answer session that allows the potential investors to ask questions arising from the research note, pathfinder or the presentation itself.

A representative of the stockbroker will attend each meeting and will follow-up after the meeting to get an indication of whether the investor wants to buy shares and, if so, how much. At this stage most declarations of interest are indicative as, with the impact day being some time away, the price is not set. Additionally, the investor will not wish to commit in case there is a change in the market or sector sentiment or indeed in case they see another investment which is preferred.

As the marketing period draws to a close, the stockbroker will seek to clarify potential investors' declarations of interest in order that a final view on price can be given to the flotation candidate. Typically, the marketing will have been done against the background of a range of valuations and, although the stockbroker will have discussed pricing with the flotation candidate from the outset of the flotation process, now is the time for fine tuning the valuation and deciding the price.

In the final days prior to impact day, the placing agreement is signed and this sets out the mechanism under which the placing is to be effected. A day or two before impact day a copy of the prospectus called the 'placing proof', is sent to each of the investors participating in the placing, along with a letter detailing the price and the number of shares they have been offered. They are required to confirm their commitment orally to the stockbroker with a written commitment to follow.

On impact day the successful placing of shares and intention to join the relevant stock market is announced. The prospectus is registered with the Registrar of Companies and the application is formally made to the stock exchange concerned for admission of the company. This application process will take approximately one week, even though the stock exchange will have been involved at a much earlier stage. The process is not a rubber stamping exercise but it is unlikely that a company would be turned down at this stage.

Approximately one week after impact day the shares of the company will be admitted to the stock exchange and dealings commence. The company and any vendor shareholders will then receive the money from the placing as investors receive their shares.

A placing is the most frequently used method of selling equity at the time of flotation. Other mechanisms are an 'intermediaries offer', where shares are marketed to financial intermediaries who in turn allocate the shares to their own clients, or an 'offer for sale/ subscription', where shares are offered to the general public (in the way of most of the government privatisations). Both of the mechanisms can be effective in the appropriate circumstances but are not covered here as they are typically more expensive than the placing route and consequently used far less for smaller and medium-sized company flotations.

Part 7: Pricing an offer

The price at which a company is floated is determined by the advice of the stockbroker who, in turn, will assess the likely level of interest from potential investors and draw comparisons between the flotation candidate and currently quoted companies. Potential investors will also make such comparisons. This may allow them more quickly and accurately to understand the business of the flotation candidate, whilst at the same time provide a basis for valuation comparison. Therefore, the easiest and arguably the best measure of a company is to look at the nearest quoted alternative, or the valuation of the sector into which a flotation candidate is entering.

Assuming a situation where there is a comparable quoted company with a very similar business profile to a flotation candidate, then the flotation pricing would be derived by calculating an appropriate discount or premium to the valuation of the existing quoted company based on the appropriate valuation method of the quoted company, i.e. price earnings ratio, cash flow analysis or asset-based valuation. The discount or premium will seek to reflect:

- the quality of the flotation candidate relative to the quoted comparable(s);
- the fact that the quoted company has a track record on the market already; and
- the flotation will be priced to increase by between ten and fifteen per cent when dealings commence, to encourage investors to participate.

In determining the flotation price, it is not a question of getting the highest possible price but of getting the right price. It is neither to the company's advantage to be over-priced nor to be under-priced. If it is over-priced, then it runs the risk of its share price going below the flotation price in the early stages of its stock market career and once it has done so it may prove difficult to re-establish the shares above the flotation price. If the price does not perform, the 'currency' of the company's shares is less attractive both to investors and to potential acquisition targets. If it is under-priced, then the question of there being a premium to the flotation price is not an issue. Instead the question is whether the company sold too much equity to attain the required funds and whether existing shareholders were disadvantaged either by selling too cheaply or by being diluted through an excessive issue of shares.

One perception is that stockbrokers will sell an issue as cheaply as possible in order to advantage their own investor clients. There is, however, a flaw in the logic to this argument. If a stockbroking firm establishes itself as only selling flotations cheaply, it will not attract new flotations and therefore its business in that area will dry up. The stockbrokers will typically be looking for the pricing to achieve an appropriate upward movement of the share price in the days following flotation of some 10–15 per cent. (The US market would be looking for a premium of circa 20 per cent.) At such a premium the vendors and the company issuing new shares should be content that they have not given away too much and new investors should be content that they have had an appropriate initial profit to assist in making their participation attractive.

In terms of how a company can ensure that it gets the 'right' price, it should seek to have a clear understanding of how its stockbroker has arrived at the valuation suggested at the very outset. The company, should also examine the stockbroker's track record in flotations during the selection process and continue a dialogue on the stockbroker's views on valuation throughout the period of flotation preparation.

With the right price and appropriate post-flotation support by the stockbroker, and subject always to market conditions, the flotation candidate should not see their share price fall below the flotation price. It may well trade on a plateau for a period and the end of that period may be marked by the announcement of the maiden set of results. The logic is that the market is waiting to see the company's results before it adjusts the share price significantly from the flotation price.

Poor share price performance post-flotation does matter because the company will typically be floating to increase its access to further equity capital in the future, as well as the equity it raises at the time of flotation. Such future equity might be in the form of a rights issue or placing, or may be in the form of issuing quoted shares to acquire another company (the fact that they are quoted will make them considerably more attractive to a vendor than if they were unquoted and therefore not marketable). Therefore, if the share price goes up, then for the company to raise further money in the future or pay for an acquisition it will need to issue less new shares and therefore existing shareholders will suffer less dilution. If the share price stagnates or declines, the level of dilution will be greater – or worse, it may not be attractive to investors to put up more money or for vendors of acquisition targets to accept shares as consideration.

Low liquidity (i.e. where shares are traded infrequently) is another problem that affects some companies. Illiquid shares are particularly sensitive to relatively small share transactions and the rises and falls in share price may be pronounced. Many investors prefer to avoid such companies because of the difficulty in buying and selling shares without affecting the price. Liquidity is affected by a number of factors, including the number of shareholders, size of shareholdings and the effectiveness of the company's stockbrokers.

Illiquidity should be taken seriously by a company. An illiquid share will be an unattractive share to new investors and will therefore limit the potential use of new equity in terms of raising further money and the use of a company's shares in making acquisitions – i.e. if the recipients under either of those scenarios believe that to sell their shares would prove difficult, then they will not be attracted to them in the first place.

Illiquidity may arise from a tightly held shareholder list. Possibly the original founding equity holders (family or partners) perceive that to release more equity would be to lose control. It may be that they cannot be persuaded otherwise, but most often a single shareholder, or group of shareholders, can exercise control despite holding below 50 per cent, particularly if it is a widely held shareholder base. The Panel on Takeovers and Mergers have, in setting the requirements for any individual, or group of individuals acting in concert, to make a bid at above 30 per cent, indicated their opinion that effective control may be exercised at or above 30 per cent.

Part 8: Life as a quoted company

A mistake that can be made by management in seeking a flotation is to see the flotation itself as the end, whereas flotation should be just the beginning. Investors in the quoted market are looking for growth and are seeking to identify the companies that will achieve that growth. Also, the market provides some liquidity in their investments so they are able to swap from one company into another if a better opportunity is presented to them. This should therefore force management of a company to perform to the best of its abilities at all times in order to ensure that existing investors stay with the company, and indeed that the company attracts new investors. In an unquoted environment, if a company has a poor year the investors may be forced to stick with their investment as there is no option to liquidate their shareholding. In the quoted market they are able to sell out of their investment and return in a year's time, thereby creating a period of weakness in the company's share price and therefore vulnerability.

Another difference in being a quoted company is the amount of information a company is required to place in the public environment. It is required both to place more information and to provide such information more quickly than if it were a private company. This, therefore, provides more information to competitors, customers, suppliers, etc. This may be good or bad. For example, a customer might feel more comfortable with the company being quoted and more information being available and therefore provide more business to the quoted company. Alternatively, a competitor may be able to take advantage of the information or indeed may mount a take-over bid.

Ongoing communication with investors and potential investors, once floated, is key. As has been emphasised already in this chapter, an investor is looking at two things in considering any investment: risk and return. Once they have made an investment, this does not change and they will wish to receive a flow of relevant information in order that they can update their view on both risk and return on a regular basis. It is easy to see why companies wish to trumpet their successes to investors and the press at large, which is great for investors in making their ongoing risk/return assessment as they have information readily available. However, companies often fall into the trap of having an information blackout when there is bad news. Faced with this scenario, an investor will often assume the worst in order not to get caught out. This might therefore push them into making an investment decision, i.e. a selling decision, which they might not have made had they been in possession of all the facts.

It must be borne in mind that an investor buying shares in a company does accept that the company's prospects, relative to the risks, offer a good investment. The investor wants the company to succeed as they will then benefit from it financially. It is certainly not in their interests to see the company fail and therefore institutional investors should be seen as an asset to a company both in times of success and distress.

It is both correct and incorrect to say that institutions take a short-term view on their investments. It is correct in that they have quarterly or half-yearly meetings at which they have to justify their performance. In this way they are interested in the short-term performance of the portfolio. However, a fund manager will not be likely to invest in a company that only has a short-term strategy. Fund managers are interested in seeing a business that has real growth prospects over a long term, has a defined strategy to optimise its prospects and has the management to execute the strategy. Fund managers are therefore vitally interested in the long-term strategies of companies.

15

Legal and Taxation Aspects of the Flotation Process

Martin Lane, Peter McLoughlin
and Mark Cawthron
Biddle

Introduction

The procedure for obtaining a full London listing and the documentary requirements are set out in the London Stock Exchange's Listing Rules (also known as the Yellow Book for obvious reasons). To guide it through these rules, a company seeking a listing must appoint a *sponsor* who is on the Stock Exchange's approved list (normally a corporate broker or investment bank) who will also usually act as underwriter.

The sponsor will be required to confirm to the Stock Exchange that all the requirements of the Listing Rules have been satisfied in connection with the application for listing and that the directors of the applicant company have had explained to them the nature of their responsibilities and obligations.

This section describes briefly the key documents that are relevant to the legal aspects of the listing application process itself, and to life as a listed company afterwards.

The prospectus

Any company seeking a new listing must produce a *prospectus* or, more rarely, listing particulars (the distinction is of limited importance for most purposes). This is the document upon which investment decisions ought to be based and it must be approved by the Stock Exchange in advance.

Contents

There are detailed contents requirements in the Listing Rules for the prospectus which include:

- financial information (in the form of an accountants' report or a comparative table) for the last three financial years and a statement of the company's current borrowings and other indebtedness;
- a statement that the company has sufficient working capital for its present requirements (made on the basis of a board memorandum produced in conjunction with the company's accountants);
- a description of any significant changes in the company's financial or trading position since the end of the last financial period;
- summaries of all material contracts;
- a description of the company's current trading and prospects;
- where a profit forecast or estimate appears, a list of the principal assumptions upon which it has been based, together with an accountants' or auditors' report on the forecast or estimate;
- a statement that the directors of the company accept responsibility for the contents of the prospectus;
- in certain sectors, e.g. for property companies, an independent valuer's report.

In addition, there is a general statutory requirement that the prospectus contains all such information that investors and their professional advisers would reasonably require, and reasonably expect to find, in order to make an informed assessment of the assets and liabilities, financial position, profits and losses, and prospects of the company and the rights attached to the company's shares.

Responsibility and liability

The persons who are responsible for a prospectus which, as well as the directors, include the company itself and any selling shareholders, will be jointly liable to pay compensation to any person who has acquired shares on the flotation and suffered loss in respect of them as a result of any untrue or misleading statement in the prospectus or the omission of any matter required to be included.

Liability may also arise under a number of other heads, including negligent mis-statement, breach of the duty owed by directors to the company and breach of warranties given to the sponsor in the underwriting agreement.

Furthermore, persons connected with the process, particularly directors, may incur criminal liability if, for example, they knowingly make any misleading, false or deceptive statements or dishonestly conceal any material facts, or deliberately engage in any act or course of conduct which creates a false or misleading impression as to the market in, or the price, or value of a company's shares.

In order to minimise the risk of potential liability, the directors will need to review the prospectus carefully as it is being prepared. In addition, a detailed verification exercise will be carried out, involving the solicitors and management, in which the accuracy of all statements of fact and opinion in the prospectus is tested and back-up documentation is collated. This process results ultimately in a set of *Verification Notes*, containing a complete set of questions and answers, which are signed by the directors. Although verification is a lengthy procedure which many directors consider absorbs an undue amount of valuable management time, it is in their interest to ensure that full attention is devoted to it.

The directors will also be asked to sign *Responsibility Letters* addressed to the company and the sponsor, confirming their understanding of the duties and liabilities imposed on them and authorising the issue of the prospectus on their behalf.

The underwriting agreement

The *underwriting agreement* (depending on the method of listing used, also known as the placing agreement or offer agreement) formalises the relationship between the company, its directors and any selling shareholders on the one hand and the sponsor on the other. It would normally be signed the day before Impact Day (the day on which the prospectus is issued and the pricing of the issue is fixed and announced) but does not become effective until Impact Day itself following an early morning telephone conversation between the company and the sponsor. The agreement will usually cover the following matters:

- *Setting out the underwriting obligation* – namely, an obligation on the sponsor to use reasonable endeavours to find subscribers/purchasers for the shares to be issued or sold and, to the extent that it fails to find such persons, itself to purchase or subscribe to the shares.

  On a placing, the sponsor would expect to have obtained (informal) expressions of interest in the issue from potential 'placees' prior to Impact Day (possibly on the back of a draft of the prospectus known as the 'pathfinder') and, in practice, the sponsor would only usually commit itself once it was reasonably confident of being able to sign up placees for the full amount of the placing on Impact Day itself. For a flotation involving a public offer, the sponsor would expect to sub-underwrite the risk of a shortfall in public demand on the first day. The period between Impact Day and listing, and hence the risk period, is typically a couple of weeks longer than for a placing and this is reflected in the commission payable.
- *Termination* – the sponsor will wish to reserve for itself the ability to terminate its underwriting obligations in various circumstances, including a breach of any of the warranties given to it or if a *force majeure* event occurs, i.e. a national or international event which would have a significant adverse effect on the flotation such as a stock market crash. Whilst there is an argument that the underwriting commissions are being paid to compensate for some of these risks, it is common practice for such a right to be reserved, although this is frequently only extended until the close of business on Impact Day.
- *Fees* – the agreement will specify the fees and commissions payable. This should just be confirming the terms agreed at an earlier stage and normally recorded in the engagement letter. In this context, it is important for the company to have a clear understanding upfront as to which payments are success-related and which are not, and indeed what constitutes 'success' – the sponsor will usually argue that the success-based commissions should be payable once the underwriting agreement has become effective, even if the listing is not subsequently achieved, although an exception may be made if the reason for this is a *force majeure* event.

- *Warranties and indemnities* – the sponsor will expect to have the benefit of a set of warranties/indemnities relating to the prospectus and the company's business. The purpose of the warranties may be regarded as threefold:
  - to enable the sponsor to recover any loss it may suffer in carrying out its duties as sponsor/ underwriter;
  - to elicit information about the company and focus the minds of those giving the warranties; and
  - to enable the agreement to be terminated if the warranties were untrue when given or subsequently become untrue as a consequence of subsequent events. (This enables the sponsor to get out of its underwriting commitment if there is a material change in the company's position between Impact Day and the listing date.)

  The sponsor would look for these warranties to come from the company, the directors and any selling shareholders, although it would be usual for differing limits on liability to be agreed and/or the scope of warranties to vary for the different warrantors. As an example, a new non-executive director could well baulk at having to give extensive warranties about the business of a company with which he or she has only just become associated and may therefore only be prepared to give limited warranties based on his or her actual knowledge.

  A tax indemnity will normally be entered into by the executive directors, under which they covenant to make payments to the company in certain circumstances. These are where the company has suffered, but not provided for, a tax liability on dealings between the company and the relevant director – broadly where such dealings either take place in his personal capacity or arise as a result of the company having been a company in narrow ownership (a 'close company' for tax purposes) rather than the more widely owned listed company it is about to become on flotation.
- *Ongoing Obligations* – partly to protect their own reputation by association and partly to ensure an orderly market in the company's shares, the sponsor will include various undertakings and controls in the underwriting agreement covering the short to medium term after listing, for instance that:
  - the company will comply with the Listing Rules and not take any steps which are inconsistent with its policy or intention as expressed in the prospectus;

> – the company's directors will not sell their shares in the company without the sponsor's consent.

Other documentation

Whilst the prospectus and underwriting agreement are probably the two most important documents, there is a host of other documentation which will or may be produced in conjunction with the flotation including:

- reporting accountants' long form report on the company and its business;
- the company's solicitors' legal due diligence report on the Group;
- new service agreements for executive directors and letters of appointment for non-executive directors;
- share option schemes: in this context, regard must be had to the guidelines laid down by institutional investor committees (primarily those of the Association of British Insurers and the National Association of Pension Funds) as to the maximum number of options which should be granted to individual directors/employees and by the company as a whole, as well as the nature of performance conditions which ought to be set. If the options are to be 'approved', it will also be necessary to reach agreement with the Inland Revenue on the terms of the scheme and the exercise price for the options (usually the float price);
- new Articles of Association: the company's existing articles may need to change to comply with the Listing Rules (most particularly to allow free transferability of shares) or to enable shares to be held through CREST;
- numerous declarations, confirmations and comfort letters required by the Stock Exchange and the sponsor from the parties involved.

Continuing regulation

The Listing Rules lay down various continuing obligations and restrictions for listed companies and, as such, they represent an additional tier of regulation. The following aspects are particularly of note:

- *Model Code*: In addition to the statutory insider dealing laws which will apply (possibly for the first time) to the company once listed, the company must adopt a share dealing code for its directors and

key employees which is no less exacting than the Stock Exchange's Model Code. This prohibits dealings by directors and certain employees in the company's shares, *inter alia*:
- on considerations of a short-term nature;
- in the two-month period preceding the preliminary announce-ment of the company's annual results and the publication of its half-yearly report;
- if the person concerned is in possession of unpublished price sensitive information.
- *Disclosure obligations*: In order to ensure 'the maintenance of an orderly market in securities and to ensure that users of the market have simultaneous access to the same information', the Listing Rules contain detailed requirements as to the information which a company must disclose to the market through the Stock Exchange about its activities. Overlying this is a general obligation on the company to disclose, without delay, any major development in its sphere of activity which is not public knowledge or any change in the company's financial condition or the expectation of the per-formance of its business which is likely to lead to a substantial movement in the price of the company's shares.
- *Corporate governance*: The directors will come under pressure to comply with the various codes of best practice relating to corporate governance and, in certain respects, would have to justify any devi-ations from these codes in the company's annual report. In this con-text, the company will usually establish, in advance of flotation:
  - an audit committee to review the company's financial state-ments and the underlying accounting policies and to liaise with the auditors; and
  - a remuneration committee to review the pay and other benefits of the executive directors.
  Both committees are expected to be made up of non-executive directors to demonstrate their independence.
  In addition, there would typically be a list of reserved matters drawn up (e.g. significant acquisitions or disposals, capital expendi-ture, new share issues) for which the approval of the full board would be required.

- *Transactions*: Information on material acquisitions, disposals or other transactions proposed by the company must be disclosed. Furthermore, if the transaction is of a sufficient size (broadly 25% of the size of company calculated by reference to any one of a number of financial ratios) or involves a 'related party' (broadly, a director of a Group company or a 10% plus shareholder), a circular must usually be sent to shareholders and the transaction must be conditional upon their approval in general meeting.

The Alternative Investment Market

The entry requirements for AIM differ from those for a full listing in a number of key respects. For example:

- there is no requirement for a three year trading record;
- there is no need for three year continuity of management;
- there is no minimum percentage of shares which must be 'in public hands' following flotation.

The absence of these qualifying requirements is consistent with the Stock Exchange's vision of AIM as a market for small and growing companies. From a legal perspective, however, the documentation is very similar to that needed for a full listing. The key document is known as the AIM Admission Document (often constituting a prospectus) – its contents will be similar to a prospectus or listing particulars on a full listing, although they are governed by the AIM Rules and the Public Offers of Securities Regulations (rather than by the Listing Rules and the Financial Services Act).

Taxation

When planning for a flotation, particularly where a full listing is involved, shareholders should review their personal tax circumstances (and perhaps their wills as well). For example, certain tax reliefs are available in relation to transfers or gifts of shares in unquoted companies (this will include shares on AIM) which are not normally available for shares in a company quoted on the main London market:

- capital gains tax hold-over relief is available for transfers of unquoted shares in a trading company or the holding company of a trading group (there is an alternative form of hold-over relief which applies to shares generally, but this is broadly restricted to transfers of shares which are chargeable transfers for inheritance tax purposes);

- capital gains tax retirement relief may not be available after the flotation, bearing in mind that family interests may be diluted and certain individuals may cease to qualify for retirement relief (though note that retirement relief is in any event being phased out over the period to April 2003);
- the relief from inheritance tax, known as 'business property relief', applies to all holdings of unquoted shares in trading companies.

Whether or not taking advantage of these reliefs is attractive will depend very much on personal circumstances, and may well also be influenced (particularly bearing in mind the new capital gains tax 'taper relief' for assets held long term) by whether it is intended that shares should be retained going forward after the flotation, or sold in order to realise cash.

Another important area, in the run up to a flotation, relates to employee share or bonus schemes. It will be necessary to consider both the impact of a flotation on existing schemes and the possible introduction of a new scheme or schemes. There may be tax consequences (partly as a result of recent changes to the PAYE and NIC regimes) for the company, as well as for employees, arising on the exercise of share options; and these may be different depending on precisely when the relevant options are exercised.

Martin Lane is a partner and Peter McLoughlin is a solicitor in Biddle's Corporate Department with particular expertise in corporate finance. Recent deals include the flotation of City North Group plc on the Official List and related scheme of arrangement, Kier Group plc's recommended offer for Bellwinch and Fairplace Consulting plc's admission to AIM.

Mark Cawthron is a partner in Biddle's Tax Department advising on the tax implications of a wide range of corporate finance and commercial transactions.

Section Five

Mergers and Acquisitions

Whose guide to disposals is priceless, and free?

the answer is **Deloitte & Touche**

focusing **only** on clients

For your free copy of 'Disposals – A Practical Guide' please contact Alice Marshall or Louise Lauchlan at: Deloitte & Touche Corporate Finance, Stonecutter Court, 1 Stonecutter Street, London EC4A 4TR. Tel: 0171 303 6928 Fax: 0171 303 5920. e-mail: corporate.finance.uk@deloitte.co.uk **www.deloitte.co.uk**

Deloitte & Touche Corporate Finance is a division of Deloitte & Touche, which is authorised by the Institute of Chartered Accountants in England and Wales to carry on Investment Business. This announcement appears as a matter of record only.

16

Buying a Business

Eileen Walker and Mark Golding
Deloitte & Touche Corporate Finance

Introduction

Acquisitions have always been an important part of the business world. In recent years a number of factors have boosted the level of corporate acquisitions still further. Principal amongst these has been strong stock market performance and strategic issues such as globalisation. Strong stock markets provide access to more capital whilst global coverage has become a necessity for many businesses and cross-border acquisitions are seen as an effective way of achieving this.

In this chapter we explore the strategies which companies may adopt in acquiring a company, how to get the acquisition right, appointing advisers and a typical acquisition process.

Acquisition strategy

The underlying reason for all acquisitions should be as a means of enhancing shareholder value. Although companies may be able to improve shareholder wealth by internal organic growth, there may be opportunities to grow earnings and shareholder wealth more rapidly through acquisitions.

There are six main ways in which businesses seek to enhance shareholder value through acquisition:

- synergy;
- geographical spread;
- improved focus;
- competitive position;
- operational improvements;
- building critical mass.

Synergy

Synergy is defined as a situation in which the combined effect of two or more actions exceeds the effect of the individual actions. There are two main ways in which acquirers hope to achieve a synergy: either through an activity sharing relationship (e.g. joint procurement, joint production, cross selling, shared development), or through skills transfer (e.g. acquiring a new technology, applying marketing skills learned in one sector in another sector).

Synergy is also the most problematic area of acquisition strategy. It has become associated with numerous failed acquisitions, either because the expected synergies have failed to materialise, or because the costs associated with achieving them have outweighed their benefit. Activity sharing relationships almost always have a hidden cost. For example, shared branding or cross selling will often lead to inconsistent product images and buyer reluctance to purchase too much from one firm. Shared production will often run into problems because of different standards of quality and performance. The problem with skills transfer synergies is that they are often difficult to identify and quantify. Firstly the skills to be transferred should be the ones which add value or give a competitive advantage to the business. Secondly, the skills must be transferable if the expected synergy is to occur.

As well as the difficulty of achieving synergies, there is also the problem that synergies may not last long enough to repay the investment. Competitors may be able to undermine the advantages of any synergies achieved. For this reason the best sort of synergies are those which cannot be easily replicated by competitors.

Geographical spread

Globalisation has been one of the management buzzwords of the 1990s. As trade barriers have come down, companies focused on purely national markets are finding new competitors taking market share from them. Some have responded to the challenge and become global players, buying companies overseas to guarantee the necessary geographical reach.

It is a high-risk strategy. The rewards for those who have achieved the transition from domestic to global market leadership are enormous. The downside is that cross-border acquisitions are notoriously difficult to get right. The linguistic barriers often conceal a much greater cultural divide that works to undermine shareholder value.

Improved focus

Focus is usually considered a strategic justification for breaking up a diversified company rather than a reason to make an acquisition. However the process of divesting unconnected businesses generates cash for reinvestment. Managers face the choice of returning this money to shareholders to reinvest themselves, or spending it developing the core business through acquisitions. The management will have developed expertise within the sector they have chosen to invest in, which will mean that they are better placed to make acquisitions in that sector than a non-specialist investor. Shareholders may respond well to acquisitions that sharpen the focus of a business, but the danger is that the synergies will not be there to ensure that their expectations are met.

Competitive position

Acquisitions that develop the competitive position of a business aim to generate shareholder value by defending or enhancing the competitive position of existing businesses, or altering the market environment to disadvantage competitors. This might be achieved either by acquiring competitors to build a stronger market position or by acquiring a customer or supplier to secure access to raw materials or markets.

The pitfall here is that the acquirer may have to pay a premium to take over the business, which is not justified by improvements in operating performance. Such acquisitions are often justified on defensive grounds, arguing, for example, that there was a danger that shareholder value would have been forgone had the acquisition not gone ahead. In these circumstances management needs to be certain that the strategic premium payable is justified.

Operational improvement

Operational improvement often offers the clearest means of enhancing shareholder value through acquisition. If the acquirer can provide better management of the business so that it satisfies customer needs more effectively or reduces operating costs, then the returns from acquiring the business may justify the price paid. An improvement that is often overlooked is the improved management motivation that an acquirer may be able to bring to a company. The incumbent management may achieve greater results because they prefer their new parent.

Some buyers, particularly financial buyers, will rely on operational improvements alone to justify their acquisitions. The risk is that the price paid to acquire the business will be based on achieving a whole range of operational improvements, from the straightforward to some that are considerably harder to achieve. This is particularly the case in auctions, where a number of financial buyers are competing.

These operational improvements must then be delivered. There are two aspects to this. First, the acquirer must have the management resources to achieve these improvements and, second, the improvements must be made in such a way that does not destroy the asset that has been acquired. For example, operational improvements in service-based companies, where the people are the most important asset, often alienate the staff to the extent that they walk out the door.

Building critical mass

Many companies acquire simply because they need to get bigger. Size alone can contribute to shareholder value in two specific ways. First, a business with high fixed costs may need to boost its turnover significantly before it can maximise its profitability. For example, a company with a national brand may only have a regional distribution network. In order to maximise the returns from its brand it might consider acquiring distributors to improve its network.

The other way in which size can contribute to shareholder value is in advance of a flotation on the stock exchange. Small companies tend to achieve low ratings on the grounds that the market in their shares is illiquid; many fund managers are prohibited from investing in companies below a certain size, and there is less research data available. The result is that companies approaching a stock market flotation may be encouraged to increase their size in order to improve their rating on flotation.

Naturally, buying companies for their size alone has risks attached. An acquisition strategy based on building sales to cover fixed costs can go wrong when it turns out that it is more difficult than expected to integrate the cost base of the two companies. An acquisition strategy based on building sales in advance of a stock market flotation can go wrong when a company with a good business acquires several weak companies that then become the driver of the valuation of the enlarged group.

Getting it right

There is a flip side to every positive reason for making an acquisition. Even if the strategy is right, there is also a danger that the price will be wrong. Paying too much for an acquisition can destroy shareholder value as effectively as buying the wrong company. Here it is worth making the distinction between the price of a business and its value to shareholders. The price is a function of competing bids. The value to shareholders is a function of the future earnings or cash flow that the business will generate. As long as the value to shareholders is greater than the price paid, then an acquisition will be in the shareholders' interests.

The problem is that it is very difficult to calculate the value to shareholders accurately. The correct method is to project all future cash flows from the business, and then calculate their net present value discounted for risk. Without a crystal ball it is impossible to calculate these cash flows accurately. This means that estimates will always have to be made which will lead to a risk of overpayment if rose-tinted spectacles prevail.

Companies must therefore ensure that they do not pay a price that is against their better judgement. There are five main reasons why they might find it difficult to resist this temptation:

- *Buying for glory*: A company may find itself in a situation in which it will buy at any cost. It might do this for valid strategic reasons, but these have been allowed to over-ride the financial issues. Another common problem is for a deal to become ego driven, with an executive driving through a deal simply because it will enhance their status.
- *Scarcity value*: a company may be tempted to pay too much because it has over estimated the scarcity value of an asset. The fear that it

will not be able to acquire a similar asset in future makes it difficult to focus on the value of the earnings stream that is being acquired.

- *Buying the best*: when a company decides to buy the best performing business in a sector, the price paid is likely to reflect its full potential, leaving very little room for developing shareholder value.
- *Underestimating competitors*: a business might appear correctly priced on the basis of past performance, but after acquisition loses value because of the action of competitors. For example, a company that buys a company without contracts may find it difficult to keep the business post-acquisition, particularly if the business relied on personalities as well as products.
- *Financial engineering*: many companies are attracted to acquisitions that help them meet short-term performance targets. For example, an acquisition that is structured to increase earnings per share strongly in year one, might look very attractive to a publicly quoted company. However, the longer-term earnings generated by the acquisition might not justify the price paid.

Choosing advisers

In order to minimise the risks associated with making acquisitions, many companies prefer to involve professional advisers right from the beginning. This helps to ensure that an independent view of the potential opportunity is received as well as providing a number of skills which the acquirer may not possess in its own personnel. The principal advisers for an acquirer would be as follows:

Financial Advisers: These might typically be one of a Corporate Finance division of a large accountancy firm, merchant bank or a boutique which would have respective deal sizes of >£250m, £10–250m and <£10m. These advisers will help identify acquisition targets, act as an intermediary to approach these targets, advise on valuation and financing the bid. Most important of all, in most cases, is their ability to guide managers through the bid process and tactics. If external equity or debt finance (beyond normal bank facilities) is required, then they will be responsible for arranging this. The Takeover Panel regulates M&A activity among publicly quoted companies. If this is relevant to the acquisition being considered it is essential that the financial adviser appointed has expertise in this area. The details of the code are beyond the scope of this book. They are paid primarily on the basis of a success fee, which is usually a percentage of the value of the deal.

Most advisers will expect an element of fixed fee up-front, with the majority only payable on completion of the deal.

Consultants: Strategic consultants are used at the beginning and the end of the acquisition process. At the beginning they help define the strategic goals and assess how these might be achieved through different acquisition targets. At the end of the process they help bed down the acquisition to ensure that these objectives can be achieved. Some consultants also offer specialist due diligence services. They are paid according to the time spent on advisory work.

Lawyers: An acquirer will appoint a law firm to work on the contractual side of the deal. In most cases, an acquirer might also require legal due diligence to investigate the legal status of the assets to be acquired, litigation, pensions etc. They are usually paid a fee in accordance with the amount of work done.

Accountants: Accountants are involved at the due diligence stage. Their role is to investigate and report on the financial statements provided in the information memorandum, the data room and any other sources. They may also offer commercial due diligence services and market report services (see due diligence, below). They are usually paid a fee in accordance with the amount of work done.

Funding acquisitions

It is impossible to separate acquisition strategy from acquisition finance. The finance available will dictate the size of acquisition that can be made, and the business that is acquired will also have an impact on the type of finance which is available. A company interested in making an acquisition will therefore have to review the finance available at an early stage.

Aside from cash balances, there are two principal sources of new money to finance acquisitions: debt and equity, although financial instruments, such as mezzanine capital, will fall between these two layers, having characteristics of both. Debt issues are examined in more depth in section two and equity is covered in sections three and four of this book. Different sources of capital have different prices attached and different conditions imposed. A financial adviser will structure the package which is most appropriate to the circumstances, taking into account the risk profile, the cash flow forecasts, and the shareholders' interests.

The purchase process

The purchase process will usually consist of the six main stages outlined below. Many of these stages will run concurrently, creating time pressures that can be alleviated by the use of professional advisers.

Identifying targets

After the strategic and financial issues have been covered, the next stage is to identify possible targets. In many cases the company making the acquisition will already know of all the businesses that would make strategically sound and financially deliverable acquisitions. Sometimes there might be opportunities that the acquirer will not have considered, or will not have come across. One of the important roles of a financial adviser is to ensure that all potential acquisition opportunities have been considered. Getting the best results, particularly with international searches, is usually a matter of giving refined search criteria, together with an element of lateral thinking to try to ensure that all potential opportunities are considered. In most cases there will be a number of opportunities that are right for the acquirer. The next decision will be which ones to approach and how.

Making an approach

Most businesses are not immediately available for sale. Their owners need to be brought round to the idea. It is usually difficult for a potential acquirer to discuss this issue directly with the target, particularly where both are competing in the same market. Most companies will employ advisers in these circumstances. They have a reputation for integrity that will enable them to discuss options with the target company in a way that a potential acquirer could not. Most people see that they have nothing to lose by agreeing to discuss this issue with an intermediary.

The adviser's initial approach will normally be anonymous, so that the target does not learn the identity of the acquirer. In general, the best deals will come out of situations where the adviser already has an established contact in the business who can be approached to discuss the opportunity in principle.

In order to ensure that the adviser secures the acquisition for its client, rather than risk losing it in an auction, the adviser has to give the vendor confidence that it will be receiving a fair price. The vendor may also be prepared to accept an offer if:

- the operational disruption to the business caused by an auction would be greater than the financial benefits that may arise from an auction;
- there are no other potential acquirers who would be serious competition in an auction;
- there would be large risks associated with circulating confidential information to a large number of competitors.

These arguments carry more weight if an adviser makes them. Advisers have to maintain their reputation for integrity. If they have a good name, the vendor may trust them to offer reasonable advice, even when they are acting for the acquirer.

Although auctions do take time, and increase the possibility that the business will be bought by a rival, there are some positive aspects from the acquirer's point of view.

- Bids at auction are based on a full information memorandum. Private offers often have to be made on the basis of less than perfect information (although there is still the opportunity for due diligence).
- If a company is being auctioned, the vendor will have taken a deliberate decision to sell. It is only necessary for the acquirer to pay a premium to encourage the vendor to part with the business if they are convinced they are genuinely in competition with other bidders.
- Acquirers at auction have the confidence that they have paid a market price.
- If an acquirer has strong strategic reasons for making the acquisition, then they are likely to offer the best price at auction.

Taking these factors into account, if an auction is the only circumstances in which a vendor will be prepared to sell, an acquirer has little choice other than to take part in the process. This will keep their options open; they can always withdraw from the process at a later stage if the opportunity ceases to be attractive.

Valuation

Valuation is central to the acquisition process. A number of different 'values' are important: the value of the business to the acquirer, the value of the business to competitors at auction, and the value of the business to the vendor. These should all be considered with as objective a view as possible. Valuation issues are covered in Chapter 18.

Non-financial considerations

It is too simplistic to say that vendors are only motivated by the amount they receive on completion. There are a number of other considerations that may include the following:

- *Tax planning*: the amount received net of tax is more relevant to the vendor than the gross price paid for the business. Imaginative tax planning may save money for both sides.
- *Timing and certainty*: confidence in a bidder's intention to complete will undoubtedly increase the chances of being awarded exclusivity.
- *Continuing involvement*: often the principal shareholder may wish to carry on in the business. Agreeing to this may help to compensate for a lower offer for the business.
- *Commitment to staff*: owner managers who have built up businesses over a number of years often like to know that their employees will be looked after.
- *Warranties*: many vendors, particularly venture capitalists, will not want to give warranties about operations. An acquirer who does not require them may be able to offer a higher price.
- *Restrictive covenants*: another non-financial consideration that should be taken into account in making an offer. They may be applied to both the vendor (preventing them from re-entering the market) and to key staff in the business. It is up to the acquirer (or its advisers) to identify which staff are essential to the future of the business, and to investigate what steps can be taken to tie them in.

Due diligence

At some stage the vendor will award exclusivity to the acquirer who has made the most satisfactory offer. The vendor will agree not to negotiate with anybody else for a period of three to four weeks. This will give the acquirer the opportunity to carry out any due diligence. It is at this stage that the acquirer will start incurring significant costs in terms of professional fees.

The scope of the due diligence will depend on the acquirer's knowledge of the business and the market in which it operates. In addition to basic due diligence to ensure that the facts are as stated in the information memorandum, an acquirer may also undertake the following processes:

- *Commercial due diligence*: research into the products, markets and customers of the business and the markets in which it operates, often carried out by financial buyers and others who do not have direct knowledge of the markets.
- *Market report*: the commercial due diligence may be reinforced and amplified by a marketing study carried out by external consultants.
- *Accountants' report*: the contents will vary, but will generally include a review of the historic trading record, the net asset and taxation position and the assumptions underlying the acquirer's projections for the business.
- *Legal due diligence*: this will tend to focus on the implications of litigation, title to assets (especially property) and intellectual property issues.

The objective of the due diligence can also vary. It can either be set up to give the acquirer the comfort that the price is correct, or to enable the acquirer to negotiate a lower price.

There are risks attached to the latter course of action. All deals depend on good faith. A buyer who reduces its offer after due diligence because it has 'discovered' facts which were contained in the information memorandum risks losing this good faith. Furthermore such buyers are likely to gain a reputation for dropping their offers, and may find them discounted in future auctions. Such tactics are unlikely to work in tight markets, when high quality assets are for sale. In slack markets, or with assets of poorer quality, reducing the offer after due diligence may be more successful.

The general rule is that if your original assumptions about the business were correct, then you should be prepared to pay the agreed price.

Completion

Once due diligence is under way, lawyers will be instructed to prepare the legal agreements concerning the transaction. The primary document is the sale and purchase agreement that will be negotiated by your advisers to ensure that the lawyers draft commercial points appropriately. Usually exchange and completion will occur at the same time, but where the transaction requires shareholder approval, or there are delays with property conveyancing or the consideration is subject to revision according to audited accounts, completion will be later than exchange.

Summary

As this chapter shows, the decisions involved in making acquisitions are complex and the process itself can be extremely complicated. Many acquisitions are successful and the success is usually due to a combination of good planning and execution, both of the deal itself and the integration of the company post acquisition. As with all business transactions, acquisitions should neither be rushed into, nor carried out on a whim. To make them succeed will take both time, effort and no little patience. However, the potential rewards can be extremely large if carried out correctly.

Eileen Walker is head of Mergers and Acquisitions and Mark Golding is Assistant Director in Deloitte & Touche Corporate Finance.

17
Selling a Business

Eileen Walker and Mark Golding
Deloitte & Touche Corporate Finance

Introduction

Divestment is becoming an increasingly important part of business strategy. It is now widely recognised as a crucial step in developing shareholder value. How it is handled often becomes the key determinant of the success or failure of a company. All sales therefore justify good preparation, clear objectives and an understanding of the market place.

This chapter sets out aspects of the disposal decision process, some potential pre-sale activities and also an outline disposal timetable. Finally, a list of 'dos' and 'don'ts' of disposals is provided.

The decision to sell

The decision to sell or retain a business is rarely straightforward. A company will have to consider a whole range of issues in deciding its strategy. Some of the objectives of selling a business are as follows:

- *Developing focus*: current management theory suggests that shareholders are best served if businesses focus their investment in related markets or activities. One of the most frequent reasons for a divestment is that the business has been identified as non-core.

- *Raising capital*: a business may be sold to raise money for other projects that will generate higher returns or to return to shareholders.
- *Market consolidation*: Marketplaces undergo structural changes from time to time that polarise the competition between a limited number of very large players and a large number of niche players. In these circumstances the businesses in the mid-market have to ask themselves whether they want to stay in and buy, or sell and exit.
- *Portfolio management*: Maximising shareholder value should involve the regular review of a portfolio of assets to ensure that the value attributed to them by shareholders is greater than the value which could be realised in a sale.
- *Technological change*: these can make a sale advantageous at a particular moment.
- *Investment requirements*: a business may need additional investment in order to develop. The parent company or the shareholders may be reluctant to provide that investment themselves.
- *Handing on the baton*: the present management may have developed the business as far as they are able to or want to.
- *Loss of key staff*: the retirement of an owner manager is an obvious example. The departure of the driving force behind a business will always raise questions about the future of that business.

On the other hand there may be reasons why one might choose to hold onto a business:

- *A cash cow*: a non-core business providing regular profits and cash still scores over a core business which does not.
- *Development potential*: there may be opportunities to grow the business, building value which can be realised at a later date.
- *Weakness in the market*: the market conditions may not be right for a sale at the present moment.
- *Founding a dynasty*: the business may provide the opportunity for a successful transfer of management and eventually ownership to a succeeding generation of the owner's family.

Once the decision to sell has been made, the next step is to begin the grooming process and work out a timetable for the sale.

Grooming and timing

Planning for a sale can begin as much as three years before the event. However, flexibility is required and, in such a timeframe, external conditions are unpredictable. For example, current conditions in the marketplace may be favourable but within three years the economy may have changed. It could, therefore, be more profitable to sell a business now even though it has not been prepared for sale rather than wait three years. Flexibility will always be important in these situations together with the ability to move quickly to exploit any opportunities.

Matters to be considered at the initial planning stage are:

- *Reasons for the sale*: since buyers are often cautious, understanding the reasons for a sale may be important to a buyer.
- *Profit patterns*: such as trends in turnover, gross profit and pre-tax profit are crucial. Ideally, purchasers look for consistent, balanced and steady growth in the pre-sale period. Risky projects should be avoided, as should long-term or onerous commitments; capacity should be planned carefully and non-business expenses minimised. Unprofitable contracts should be dropped if they are likely to influence valuation.
- *Accounting presentation and policies*: potential buyers may expect accounts to be presented in a certain way, so that they can be easily compared to other companies.
- *Management structure*: there may be historic idiosyncrasies in the management structure that no longer make financial or operational sense. These should be straightened out ahead of a sale.
- *Business composition*: maximise value by considering the mix of business and consider piecemeal sales of separate businesses.
- *Confidentiality*: employees, customers and suppliers will undoubtedly be unsettled by a prospective sale and confidentiality is essential. However, a communications plan for staff, customers and suppliers to be told at the right time should be drawn up.

When you are selling a company it is much easier to sell it based on facts than promises. If you say to an acquirer that they can improve the performance of the business by selling off part of the business, improving the margins or improving the purchasing power, the acquirer will always ask why have you not done it already.

You may not have the resources or you may not have the distribution network. It may be something that the acquirer can bring to the business. If, however, there is no real reason why action has not been taken to improve the sustainable profitability of the business, then that action should be part of the grooming process.

It is a very risky attitude to cut costs to the bone at the expense of future profitability on an assumption that the business will be sold. If, for some reason, the company does not find a buyer immediately, then you have a major problem on your hands. It is a very much less attractive proposition to hold onto the business, and if you try to sell it again, it may attract a fire-sale price. For this reason, information memoranda usually balance the suggestion that costs might be cut with the fact that there may be some drawbacks.

It is worth remembering that an acquirer will always place more reliance on audited accounts than management forecasts, whatever the quality of the business. Where management forecasts are projecting a significant improvement in profitability it will always be useful if the management accounts for recent periods are able to support this improvement. If the improvement is anticipated to occur in a few months it may be worth delaying the disposal process until this improvement is seen, or is, at least, beginning.

Despite this natural scepticism about forecasts, most acquirers do put faith in historic trends. If sales have risen two years in a row, they will usually accept that, on the balance of probabilities, they will rise for a third year. Conversely, if the trend is downwards, it is very difficult for a buyer to believe that the business has growth potential and should be valued accordingly. If the fall-off in sales has been too steep, it can become difficult to sell a business at any price.

The final element in grooming and planning prior to sale is effective tax planning. This is critical to ensure that the net cash realised from a sale is maximised. The issues involved are discussed in more detail in Chapter 19.

Professional advisers

Using a third party to arrange the sale formalises the process. Some executives feel that managing a divestment themselves will enhance their standing, but there is the risk that potential buyers will not take the sale seriously unless a third party has been appointed. Acquirers will recognise that it is a proper process and they are going to have to prepare a serious offer for the business or miss the opportunity.

The most important quality in an adviser is trustworthiness. They would also be expected to have good knowledge of the marketplace, practical experience of transactions of a comparable size, a thorough knowledge of the tax and financial aspects of selling a business, and, on the personal level, an eye for detail, excellent negotiating skills and the ability to spread calm over very tense situations.

The first thing that an adviser will do is to offer an initial evaluation of the sale, including an assessment of the likely sale price. The adviser may suggest a formal valuation of the business to be sold which will provide a better estimate of the potential sale proceeds. If this valuation is unattractive from a vendor's point of view a delay or cancellation of the disposal can save both time and money.

Having reached a view that there may be a willing vendor at a price the market is willing to pay, the adviser will offer a realistic appraisal of how this price might be obtained, offering advice on pre-sale grooming, timing, prospective acquirers and other market conditions.

The financial adviser's fees will usually have two elements. The first is a fixed fee which will be payable at a certain stage of the disposal – usually the production of the information memorandum. This will usually be a small element of the overall fee. The second element will be a success fee which will only be payable on a successful completion. In order to align the interests of the vendor and their advisers, the success fee will often be on a ratchet basis where larger disposal proceeds result in larger fees payable to advisers.

The sale process

The sale process will usually consist of the following seven stages:

1. Preparing an information memorandum

The information memorandum is a selling document. It is, however, covered by the Financial Services Act, which places limits on what can and can't be said. However this is not the only reason why an information memorandum should aim to tell the whole truth about a business. Later in the sale process, and during due diligence especially, the acquirer is likely to uncover all material facts about the business. Any evidence that the vendor has not acted in good faith may be used to either reduce the offer for the business, or as a reason to pull out of the sale altogether.

An information memorandum should therefore aim to set out the key facts in such a way as to make clear the virtues of the business and try to deal with obvious concerns about its problems. It will include a review of the operations, details of the organisation, management and staff, competitive position, prospects for growth and financial details and forecasts.

Besides giving an accurate reflection of the present, it should also offer the acquirer some ideas of how the business could be developed. It is the future potential of a business that may make a price at the top end of the vendor's expectations look like a bargain from the point of view of the acquirer.

The information memorandum may contain confidential information about the business that one would not want to show to a third party unless they were likely to be seriously interested in acquiring it. For this reason, a one-page, no-names summary is often produced to test potential acquirers' interest. If they are keen to proceed, they will then have to sign a confidentiality agreement before receiving a copy of the information memorandum. Note that the most sensitive commercial information is not revealed until very close to completion of the deal.

The purpose of the information memorandum is to draw out indicative bids for the company from prospective purchasers.

2. Identifying prospective purchasers

The objective is to maximise the potential interest in the business, whilst maintaining confidentiality. The list of potential purchasers will always be discussed between the vendor and the financial adviser before any approaches are made.

The vendor will often have a list of names, and the adviser should be able to add to that. The list might include competitors, companies seeking vertical integration or others seeking synergy. The adviser should also be able to identify which financial buyers are likely to be interested and know which contacts to approach.

Financial buyers will usually be attractive potential purchasers if the retention of key management and maintenance of confidentiality are important in securing a premium value for the business.

3. Approaching potential purchasers

Often a letter or telephone call to the chairman or chief executive is best, but there may be matters of commercial sensitivity that will require a different approach. The one-page business summary is often used as an initial marketing tool. This summary may describe the business in general without naming it in particular, although this approach may fail to keep the vendor's identity secret due to the market knowledge of trade buyers approached.

In practice, stages one, two and three will run concurrently in order to keep the disposal timetable relatively short.

4. The bid process

The potential purchasers will be given up to six weeks to come up with an indicative bid. Not surprisingly it is quite common for a pro- portion of those approached to decide against pursuing the purchase after receiving the information memorandum. Others may submit unsatisfactory bids, so that if ten companies are approached, four might submit a serious bid worth taking further.

The second stage will usually involve the release of more informa- tion to the acquirer, for example, a meeting with the management, visits to plants, handing over more detailed financial information and in some cases meetings with the principal customers or suppliers. The current trend is towards vendor due diligence. The vendor's account- ant can either carry this out, or if the vendors prefer, a third party auditor can be introduced. It involves providing a long form report, the scope of which is decided by the vendor. This report will go into greater detail than the information memorandum, and will often take a more investigative stance, aiming to clarify areas of uncertainty and raising the prospect of risks or problems not identified in the first set of information provided to acquirers.

On the basis of the additional information provided at the second stage, the potential purchasers will then be asked for formal bids, which will be subject only to confirmatory due diligence.

The first round bids will be confidential. However, it is possible to tell the prospective purchasers how their bids are positioned in rela- tion to the other bids. This gives lower bidders the opportunity to reposition themselves for the second round.

In order to help distinguish between the second round bids, the prospective purchasers might be asked to prepare a mark-up of the sale and purchase agreement. This will highlight areas of disagreement so the vendor knows the amount of extra protection (such as warranties) the acquirers are seeking.

5. Assessing final bids

Unless the vendor has indicated that all bids should be in cash, and payable on completion, it is likely that the different prospective acquirers will have structured their bids in different ways, using any combination of cash, shares, deferred considerations, earn-outs and debt instruments. It can be like comparing apples and oranges, when in fact the vendor wants a strawberry.

The professional adviser will be expected to help evaluate the different bids, as well as help negotiate with the different bidders to encourage them to restructure their bids in a more favourable way where necessary.

As well as the sale price, the vendor will need to know as much as possible about the basis on which the company has been valued (this will make it more difficult for the purchaser to reduce the price after due diligence). Additional information required may include the official clearances which would be necessary for the bid to go ahead, the time scale for completion and the level of additional due diligence which will be required. Another issue that affects how a bid is perceived is whether the prospective purchaser can satisfy the vendor that it has access to the necessary funds.

The professional adviser will have a confirmatory discussion with the various bidders to clarify their terms and to inform those whose bids are considered to be less valuable that an improvement will be necessary if they wish to acquire the business.

6. Awarding exclusivity

Once the vendor is satisfied that the prospective purchasers have each put forward their best offer, it will be necessary to take a decision as to which party should be allowed a period of exclusivity for further due diligence work.

The prospective purchaser will be responsible for paying for the due diligence work, although the vendor may be able to decide the limits of their investigation.

The due diligence process may throw up issues that the prospective purchaser may wish to exploit to reduce the offer. The vendor then has to decide whether to accept the new offer or to invite another buyer to begin due diligence.

The decision to accept or reject a revised offer is always difficult and will usually depend on two factors. First, the size of the price reduction, set against the original offer, offers received from other acquirers and the additional costs and inconvenience of reopening discussions with an alternative acquirer. Second, whether the revision is due to factors which are genuinely new to the acquirer and which would affect other acquirers similarly, e.g. where recent performance has fallen below that forecast in the budget.

The vendor will often feel in a weak position in these circumstances. It is for this reason that the adviser will do everything possible to ensure that the prospective purchaser is in full possession of all the facts before due diligence starts, and that the basis of the valuation is fully explained and understood.

The best way of keeping pressure on the prospective purchaser is to ensure that he or she is aware of the continuing interest of rival bidders. In certain circumstances the vendors can protect themselves by taking more than one prospective buyer through to due diligence, but this is usually difficult to manage on the grounds that prospective purchasers have to meet the costs of due diligence whether the deal completes or not. Furthermore, good faith on both sides is an essential ingredient of any sale, and this may not be achieved without the award of exclusivity.

The final decision as to whether an offer is accepted or rejected is always made by the vendor and its shareholders. Theoretically, there can be a conflict of interest between the vendor and the professional adviser at this stage, because the professional adviser will usually receive much greater remuneration if there is a sale rather than no sale. However, a good professional adviser should offer the best advice in every circumstance.

7. The sale contract

The sale contract marks the culmination of the sales process and will involve lengthy and complex documents, and protracted and painful negotiation, particularly on the question of the extent of the vendor's warranties. During this final stage, there remains a constant risk that the deal will fall apart, especially if the differences between the two sides become personal. Both the vendor and the purchaser will probably be exhausted by the whole process, and may be unwilling to handle last minute problems with the patience they require.

Professional advisers are expected to take as much of the stress out of this process as possible and to ensure that personalities do not come to blows. In most cases there will be a solution to every problem. The professional adviser's ability to provide suggestions and solutions to these problems will be essential to ensure completion.

Eileen Walker is head of Mergers and Acquisitions and Mark Golding is Assistant Director in Deloitte & Touche Corporate Finance.

18

Valuation

Christopher Gasson
Bertoli Mitchell

Introduction

There is only one way to value a company accurately: sell it. All other methods involve a degree of subjectivity not least because they involve taking a view of the future – who is to say that there is a buyer in the market who shares that view?

Of course nobody wants to go as far as selling a business to get an idea of its value. That said, it has to be remembered that mathematical methods of valuation can be manipulated where necessary:

- An unscrupulous broker asked to value a business, as part of a beauty parade to select a firm to handle the sale, will calculate a value based on the highest figure they can quote without stretching their credibility.
- Financial advisers asked to value a business for tax reasons or for the purpose of valuing a minority shareholding may well calculate the lowest value they think they can justify.
- Venture capitalists investing in established companies can reach absurdly low valuations to ensure that they obtain the largest possible shareholding for the smallest possible investment.
- More acceptably high and low valuations can be bandied about during the sale of a business, as the buyer and seller attempt to massage the expectations of the other.

Making different valuations, based on different assumptions, is, in fact, essential to the sale process:

- They can tell an executive how much a business is worth to his or her company, and therefore inform the maximum amount he or she should be prepared to pay for it or, in different circumstances, the minimum amount he or she should accept to sell it.
- They can tell an executive how much other bidders at an auction might be prepared to bid for a business, enabling him or her to decide on a bid which is high enough to secure the asset, but still low enough to ensure there is a margin of profit from acquiring the business.
- They can tell an executive how his or her shareholders might view an acquisition: whether they would consider it to be a good investment or a bad investment.

However, it is the determination of the market price today that is the aim of most valuations.

In publicly quoted companies, whose shares are regularly traded on the Stock Exchange, this valuation can be calculated very simply by multiplying up the share price by the number of shares in issue.

Everyone else has to use one of the subjective methods: discounted cash flow, price ratios, or asset based. The only way they can ensure that the valuation they obtain is as close to being objective as possible is to make sure that the assumptions are as objectively sustainable as possible.

Even then, one has to accept that the valuation reached is going to be justified for a very short space of time. Just as share prices on the stock exchange change daily as assumptions about future earnings change, so should valuations calculated by mathematical methods.

It is also important to remember that markets are far from perfect. While the auction process has become more widespread, and the expansion of the private equity sector has meant that there are always financial buyers around to pick up under-valued assets, there are still a number of obstacles to the establishment of a free market in businesses:

- *Businesses are not alike and interchangeable*: some will command a premium because they are unique, others will be ignored because they do not fit in, regardless of the financial value they could deliver.

- *There are fashions in corporate strategy*: vertical and horizontal integration, globalisation and empowerment focus have all created waves of corporate activity which have rarely had a long-term effect on earnings, but have had significant short-term effects on valuation.
- *Auctions are often oligopolistic*: usually there will be only three or four serious buyers. If their ability is impaired for any reason (such as they are between chief executives, or they have just made a big bid for something else) then the final auction price will be affected.
- *Information is not perfect*: buying a business is always going to be something of a lucky dip. The price paid will always depend on how much of a risk the various buyers are prepared to take.
- *Management makes a difference*: it is often difficult to separate the value of a business from the value of its management. One can buy one but not always the other.
- *Auctions are not open*: the fact that most auctions have to be carried out in conditions of secrecy means that some potential buyers will be excluded.

The result is that the price that a business realises on sale is often more a matter of chance than the financial value of the business.

It is for this reason that executives regularly involved in assessing the value of businesses tend to rely on instincts and rules of thumb rather than the more intellectually sound methods of valuation recommended by valuation professionals. In fact, many valuation professionals also rely on rules of thumb (such as sales multiples) and then justify their findings using more highfalutin methods such as discounted cash flow analysis.

Valuation methods

The three main methods of valuation are:

- *Discounted cash flow* (sometimes called the Capital Asset Pricing Model or CAP-M) is based on the idea that a company is worth as much as the net present value of the cash flows generated by a company for distributing around its shareholders.
- *Price multiples* compare the price per pound of the sales or profits between companies to illustrate how a business might be priced.
- *Asset-based valuations* price the balance sheet assets of a business separately to reach the value of the whole.

Discounted cash flow (DCF) valuation is theoretically the most pure. It keeps the mind focused on the actual value of the cash benefits derived from ownership rather than what other people might pay for a business. The main weakness is that it is highly dependent on forecasts. In fact in many cases it is necessary to be able to forecast more than 10 years into the future before one has a valuation which is any more accurate than a simple price multiple method. Consequently, DCF valuation tends to be used primarily within companies for the purposes of determining strategy. Consultants recommend using it as a means of assessing which course of action is most likely to build shareholder value.

Where one does not have full information about operations it is usually very difficult to carry out a DCF accurately.

Price multiples are the most widely used method of valuation. In fact, because they are so widely used, they are often the most reliable means of predicting the market price of a business. They are easy to use, and they do not require a great deal of information about the operation to be applied. Different multiples are used in different situations. Trade buyers, who tend to have a very strong idea about the profitability of businesses within their sector, often prefer to use sales multiples, although they do rely on instinct for their accuracy.

P/e (price to earnings) ratios enable one to compare the price of a pound of profit across different businesses. On the face of it they are more rigorous than sales multiples, although they do not take different accounting treatments into account, and often fail to predict what a trade buyer, who is in a position to alter the cost base of the business, might be prepared to pay. P/e ratios are the most widely used method of valuation among stockbrokers because they make it possible to compare the financial benefits of holding different shares.

Asset-based valuations are used only where the value of a business is easily expressed in terms of its assets. Where the primary assets are intangible, such as brands, copyrights, human capital, or goodwill, then asset-based valuations are less popular (or, if they are used, it is in conjunction with another valuation method). Investment trusts, property companies, mining companies, and other businesses whose assets have a clear market value are suitable for asset-based valuation.

Capital structure

The capital structure of a business will include both debt and equity. For some purposes, such as making investment or divestment decisions within a company, it is important to obtain a value of the unlevered company (ie as if it had no debt). In other circumstances, such as when one is buying a business complete with debtors and creditors, it is necessary to value the levered company.

The difference in the value of the levered and the unlevered company is not just the value of the debt. The debt will bring with it interest tax shields which have a value in themselves, and it will also impose a different risk profile on the equity. The more debt, the more risky the equity.

It would be wrong to ignore the difference between the value of the levered company and the value of the unlevered company, even in a crude valuation. However, it may be justifiable to avoid calculating the value of the interest tax shields and the additional discount for risk if one is using a crude price multiple method.

DCF valuation

DCF models aim to value a business by calculating the net present value of the free cash flows generated by it. These free cash flows are calculated as follows:

Earnings before interest and taxes (EBIT)
+ (–) non-cash expenses (revenues) e.g. depreciation
– cash tax payments (not including any interest tax shield)
– net cash capital expenditure
– (+) increases (decreases) in required working capital
– other cash operating expenditures not in EBIT
= **free cash flows of the unlevered business**

– post-tax cash interest and preferred stock dividends
– (+) other cash payments to (from) non-equity claimholders
= **free cash flow of the common equity**

These cash flows have to be forecast out as far as accurately possible. Every human effort has to be taken to ensure that they are as accurate as possible. One should start by analysing the business to identify the drivers of sales, and then examine what factors have affected these drivers in the past, such as the business cycle, interest rates, exchange rates, demographics and so on. The relationship between sales and gross and operating profit has to be examined, and the balance sheet ratios that help predict capital expenditure and interest payments looked at too.

The next stage is to draw up a forecast of the profit and loss account and the balance sheet for each year, with the two feeding into each other through interest payments and retained profit. Ideally one would want to forecast at least five years ahead. In some cases it may be necessary to forecast even further. These can then be checked against themselves by seeing whether the balance sheet ratios have been maintained and the profit and loss account has remained within the scope of what has historically been achieved in the industry. Finally, figures for the free cash flow can be derived.

Once the free cash flows have been calculated, they need to be discounted at the relevant rate. This rate has to take into account three factors: the opportunity cost of capital, risk and capital structure. To calculate the discount rate relevant to the opportunity cost of capital, one has to find the amount of money one would be prepared to forgo today in exchange for receiving the forecast cash flow in the future. This is a function of the interest rate:

$$\text{Future cash} = \text{present cash} \times (1 + r)^n$$

Where r is the interest rate and n is the number of years before the future cash is generated. This equation can be rewritten as follows:

$$\text{Present cash} = \text{future cash}/(1 + r)^n$$

If one was 100 per cent sure of obtaining those future cash flows then $1/(1 + r)^n$ would be the only discount factor which needed to be applied. However, one is never sure of the future cash flows generated by a business and this has to be taken into account.

The way this is done is to include an additional risk discount factor. This can be calculated thanks to a modern portfolio which states that for any equity investment the:

Expected return = risk free return (ie if it were invested in treasury bonds) + βx the premium for having invested in the market,

where β is the riskiness of the equity investment relative to the market as a whole. This can also be expressed as:

Expected return = risk free return + β (market rate of return – risk free return)

The risk free return can be calculated by looking at the interest rate on long gilts. The market rate of return can be calculated from looking at long-term returns from investing in the market. For the UK, the premium for investing in the market has been variously estimated as between five per cent and six per cent. β is calculated as follows:

β_e = (covariance of return on equity e and the market return)/(variance of the market return)

This is a complex calculation, which can be easily carried out if one has access to one of the screen-based historic pricing services, but is otherwise laborious. The value of β is normally between 0 and 2.5, where a β of 0 would refer to an investment which offers the same security of a government bond, and a β of 2.5 would appropriate to some of the more questionable penny share investments.

The β calculated above is the β of the business complete with its existing level of debt. Calculating the value of the unlevered β requires two further steps. The first step is to calculate the impact that the debt has on the relative riskiness of the business. This is done by calculating the debt β or β_d:

β_d = (expected return on the business' debt – the risk free rate of return)/(expected rate of market return – the risk free rate of return)

This can then be fed into a formula for the unlevered β which is based on the weighted average of the debt β and the equity β, adjusted for the present value of the interest tax shields (calculated by discounting the value of the interest tax shields each year by the cost of the company's debt):

Let
β_u = β of the unlevered firm
β_e = β of the equity
β_d = β of the debt
E = market value of the equity*
D = market value of the debt
T = net present value of interest tax shields

$$\beta_u = \beta_e [(E/E + D - T)]/ [\beta_d (D - T/E + D - T)]$$

*because of this circularity, it is only possible to calculate the value of an unlevered β for a quoted company, or part of a quoted company, accurately. When valuing unquoted companies it is necessary to estimate the relative proportion of the debt and equity within the capital structure, and give a weighting to the debt and equity βs accordingly.

The relevant β can then be used to determine the correct rate of return by which the cash flows have to be discounted:

Rate of return e_r = risk free rate of return + β × the premium for investing in shares rather than bonds.

So if the interest rate on long gilts is five per cent, and one is dealing with a business which is slightly more risky than the market as a whole (i.e. β = 1.2) then the relevant interest rate to use in the discounting formula is 12.2 per cent (i.e. $1.05 + 1.2 \times 0.06$).

This interest rate is then used to discount the forecast cash flows as follows:

Present value = free cash flow/$(1 + e_r)^n$

The value of the business is equal to the sum of the net present value of the free cash flows from now until the end of time. As it is not possible to forecast them that far into the future, the normal practice is to forecast them as far as possible and then to add a terminal valuation representing the value of the business after the forecast period.

The terminal valuation has to be calculated by an alternative method, such as a price multiple method or an asset-based method. The alternative is to agree a constant level of growth that would apply after the forecast period, whose net present value can easily be calculated.

The important thing is to ensure that not too much of the value of the business is the result of the terminal value after the forecast period. If it is, one may well be better off using another valuation method in the first place.

Price multiple models

The alternative to a discounted cash flow model for valuing a firm is a price multiple model. This does not attempt to reach an absolute value for a firm with the integrity of a DCF valuation. Instead, it provides a means of comparing the price of a firm with others in the same sector. The differed multiples used include:

- price to earnings (after tax) – the p/e ratio;
- price to operating cash flow (EBITDA);
- price to free cash flow to common shareholders – the free cash flow multiple;
- price to sales – the sales multiple;
- price to operating profit;
- price to gross margin;
- price to earnings before interest and taxes;
- price to net book value;
- price to replacement cost of net book value (ie replacement cost of the assets less market value of the liabilities);
- market value of the equity plus debt to operating cash flow.

Of these, only price earnings multiples and sales multiples are used regularly. The others are used only in special circumstances. For example, when comparing companies that are subject to different tax regimes, one might look at free cash flow multiples. Price to net book value ratios are commonly used where the assets rather than the cash flows drive the value of the company, i.e. in banking.

Applying a p/e ratio involves finding a proxy, or series of proxy companies, that face similar earnings growth prospects and whose price is known (either because they are quoted or because they have been involved in a recent trade sale). This is used to obtain a relevant p/e ratio for the company being valued, which can then be multiplied by that company's earnings to reach a valuation:

Market value of a business = earnings of business × p/e ratio of proxy company

Sales multiples work in the same way but using price/sales ratios rather than price/earnings.

The main weakness is that it has no objectivity in the selection of proxies. One also has to bear in mind that sales multiples do not take the capital structure of the business being valued into account. There is also a temptation to overstate the value of a business by applying p/e ratios from last year's accounts to earnings forecasts for next year without discounting for risk, inflation or the opportunity cost of holding cash.

Asset-based valuations

In many businesses the assets on the balance sheet are the main driver of value, and the assets themselves have an easily established market value. This is particularly true of the financial services sector, but can also be applied to other areas such as property, house building, and mining. In these circumstances, asset-based valuations tend to be used.

The total value of the asset, as accounted for on the balance sheet, can be added up, and liabilities deducted to reach a value of the business. Usually this value is notional: most businesses actually trade at a discount to their net asset value because of the costs associated with assessing that value. This discount can be estimated by looking at the discounts which apply to similar businesses either on the stock exchange or in recent trade sales.

19

Legal and Taxation Aspects of Buying and Selling Private Companies or their Businesses

Hugh Gardner, Andrew Masraf
and Mark Cawthron
Biddle

Introduction

This chapter sets out certain key aspects which are usually addressed by lawyers in any UK transaction for the sale and purchase of all the shares in a private limited company (*'Target'*) or all its business and assets.

The key aspects concern:

- the preliminary structural (including tax) issues;
- the Sale and Purchase Agreement and ancillary documentation;
- the mechanics of the transaction process.

Additional considerations may arise where the transaction relates to only part of the shares or business and assets of the Target or where the purchaser or seller is a public or quoted company (in which latter case the Listing Rules of the London Stock Exchange or the AIM Rules, and the City Code on Takeovers and Mergers may also apply).

Preliminary structural issues

Both parties need to consider four main issues before the start of (or early on) in the transaction process as follows:

- shares or assets?;
- tax;
- finance;
- consents.

Shares or assets?

A business may be sold either by transferring the *shares* of the Target company or its *assets*. Subject to the tax issues raised below, the most important consequences of this distinction are that:

- a purchaser of shares will acquire the whole of the Target, including certain assets and liabilities it may not want or of which it may not be aware;
- a purchaser of assets acquires only those assets and liabilities which are specifically identified, but not any other liabilities attaching to the Target itself (save for certain statutory exceptions such as those relating to employees and the environment).

Tax issues on a share sale

There will be stamp duty, at 0.5 per cent, calculated on the amount of the purchase price. It is sometimes possible to structure the transaction so as to mitigate this stamp duty charge.

The selling company or group may be advised to strip out part of the value of the company it is selling by way of a pre-sale dividend. This will reduce the sale price (and therefore any gain) and so reduce the tax payable by the seller.

There are a variety of ways that an individual seller of shares may be able to avoid capital gains tax (CGT), or reduce or defer his liability to tax. These include:

- *Retirement relief*: This relief, which is to be progressively withdrawn between now and April 2003, currently exempts up to the first £250,000 of qualifying gains from tax, and exempts one half of up to the next £750,000 of gains. The seller will need to be over 50 to qualify, but does not have to retire.
- *Taper relief*: Shares in a Target may qualify as *business assets* qualifying for a 3 per cent reduction in the CGT rate for every year held, up to a maximum of 30 per cent after 10 years. That means that the effective CGT rate is only 10 per cent after 10 years. Taper relief is also available on shares which are not business assets, but at a lower rate.
- *Pre-sale dividend*: As described above. The rate of tax on a dividend may be lower than the rate of CGT where cash is received as sale proceeds. A *stock dividend* can have a similar effect.
- *Gifts to spouses*: By gifting shares to a spouse prior to a sale it may be possible to make use of the spouse's annual CGT allowance (each individual can currently make gains of £6,800 tax free each year) and the spouse's lower tax liability, if applicable. The spouse may also be taxable at 20 per cent or 23 per cent on any balance of gains over and above the annual exemption. Gifts may also be made to other family members.
- *Paper for paper exchanges*: Reliefs exist to defer CGT where the seller receives paper (shares or loan stock) rather than cash.
- *Going non-resident*: A seller willing to spend a period of time abroad can make use of the reliefs available in relation to paper for paper exchanges to sell the Target while he is resident in the UK and then to realise the new shares or loan stock (thereby triggering the tax charge) at a time when he is no longer resident in the UK (i.e. when he is not liable to CGT). The period of absence would normally need to be five years although, in appropriate circumstances, absence for one complete tax year may suffice.
- *Offshore trusts and companies, UK trusts, and insurance policy schemes*: Not for the faint-hearted, but for those determined to save tax by any lawful means there are a variety of complex (and expensive) tax schemes which aim to eliminate or greatly reduce the CGT charge. These schemes do not suit everybody, they are not guaranteed to work, and they can be easily invalidated by a careless move.

Tax issues on an assets sale

The way the price is allocated to the different assets transferred will be important to the purchaser and seller. For the purchaser, money paid for revenue items (e.g. stock, work-in-progress) is tax-deductible immediately. By contrast, money paid for certain capital assets (e.g. land, buildings and goodwill) will not qualify for tax relief until the business or asset is disposed of, although the acquisition of such assets (and certain other qualifying capital assets) may enable gains previously realised on the sale of qualifying business assets (e.g. a former trade) to be deferred, and 'rolled over' into the new assets. If part of the price can be allocated to depreciating capital assets such as plant, machinery, cars, furniture and equipment, the cost can be written off against tax over a number of years.

If the seller has been carrying forward trading losses in the business, the seller may want to use up those losses as part of the sale (since otherwise the seller will lose them). In that event the seller will be keen to allocate as much of the price as possible to revenue items. Another alternative would be for the seller effectively to sell the losses as an additional asset to the purchaser, but this would involve first transferring the business to a new company owned by the seller (known as a *hive-down*) and then selling the new company – i.e. a share sale rather than an assets sale.

It may be possible to avoid tax on a gain by selling the assets through another group company which has realised capital losses. Alternatively, the tax could be deferred by re-investing the proceeds of sale in further qualifying business assets (e.g. another trade).

The VAT issues are very different depending on whether the purchaser is acquiring assets only, or the assets, staff and customers as a going concern. Care is required to ensure that the right VAT treatment is applied.

The purchaser will be liable for stamp duty on such items as land and buildings, and goodwill, at rates up to three per cent of the purchase price for those items. It will sometimes be possible to avoid or reduce the stamp duty liability.

Finally, it is worth making the point that, where an individual owns the shares in a company, he or she will usually (though not necessarily in every case) wish to sell his or her shares rather than have the company sell its business/assets. This will avoid potential double taxation, firstly in the company (on selling the assets) and thereafter on the individual when the proceeds of sale are extracted from the company.

Finance

Finance for the acquisition may come from a variety of sources, each having its own legal and taxation implications. Where cash is to be used, it could come from:

- the reserves or working capital of the purchaser;
- the purchaser's bank as debt (e.g. a loan/overdraft), but note that it is generally unlawful for the Target to give *financial assistance* (including the giving of security over the Target's assets) for the acquisition of its own shares;
- a subscription in cash for further shares in the purchaser by its shareholders.

In a share acquisition where cash consideration is *financed by borrowings* it will be necessary to make sure that the Target will have a stream of income in future years against which to set off the cost of servicing those borrowings in the Purchaser, which generate a tax relief for the purchaser, otherwise this relief may be lost.

Where the consideration is to be satisfied by the purchaser *issuing new shares* or loan stock to the sellers, various tax provisions are available to defer CGT for the seller until the new shares are sold or the loan stock is redeemed.

Consents

Certain industries are highly regulated and any transfer of ownership or control of a business may require the prior approval of the appropriate regulatory authority.

Also, where two or more enterprises are brought under common ownership or control, or it is agreed that one of them will cease to be carried on in order to prevent competition between them, and either

- the enterprises each supply or acquire goods or services of a similar kind and together supply or acquire at least 25 per cent of all those goods or services supplied in the UK, or
- a substantial part of it or the gross value of the worldwide assets being acquired is more than £70,000,000

then, unless prior approval of such a transaction is obtained, there is a risk that the transaction will be investigated by the Office of Fair

Trading and ultimately referred to the Monopolies and Mergers Commission, which could require the parties to rescind the agreement or give undertakings to remedy or prevent the adverse effects to competition occurring.

European Community Merger Regulations may also apply to large mergers with a 'community dimension'.

The Sale and Purchase Agreement

In a share sale

A purchaser of a Target company buys its history. If the Target has undischarged liabilities, they will fall to be paid later in the hands of the new owner. Therefore purchasers of shares expect sellers to give *warranties and indemnities* that there are no liabilities other than those specifically disclosed and that the business is as it has been described by the seller to the purchaser. If this proves to be incorrect, the purchaser will look to the seller for compensation. A *retention* of part of the consideration may, for instance, be placed in an *escrow account* specifically created for this purpose. The seller's aim will be to limit these warranties and indemnities so far as possible, as they represent an ongoing commitment to the purchaser.

Typically, warranties will address matters such as corporate compliance, accounts, finance, tax, assets, liabilities, litigation, trading, contracts, property, environment, employment, pensions, intellectual property and information technology.

The tax warranties are invariably backed up by an indemnity (sometimes described as a *covenant for tax*) either as a separate document or as part of the main agreement. The tax warranties and indemnity together are intended to give the purchaser maximum cover for unprovided tax liabilities which do not come to light until after the sale, but which relate to the seller's period of ownership.

It is common for the purchaser to impose *restrictive covenants* on the seller to prevent it from carrying on activities after completion which compete with the business that has been sold.

Where a seller is also employed by the Target, the purchaser may require the seller either to resign or enter into a new service agreement on completion of the acquisition.

In an asset sale

Similar considerations are likely to apply, save that the warranties are likely to be limited to those assets and liabilities being transferred.

It is usual to transfer by delivery all physical assets (other than the properties included in the sale) in order to minimise stamp duty. Intangible assets, including the goodwill and intellectual property rights, may, for instance, require a *Deed of Assignment* to pass legal title.

The transaction process

The mechanics of the transaction process will largely depend on whether the transaction has been initiated by the purchaser or the seller.

Where the transaction is initiated by the purchaser, it is likely the purchaser's lawyers will draft a non-binding *Heads of Terms* setting out the main commercial points, which may include a binding *Lock-Out/Exclusivity Agreement* and a *Confidentiality Agreement*:

A Lock-Out/Exclusivity Agreement will seek to prevent the seller from selling (or negotiating to sell) the shares or assets to a third party during the exclusivity period.

A Confidentiality Agreement will oblige the purchaser and its employees, advisers and agents to maintain confidentiality in relation to all matters disclosed to them concerning the business.

Once these are agreed, the purchaser's advisers will prepare a Sale and Purchase Agreement and will carry out a legal and financial *due diligence* investigation to determine exactly what it is buying. A purchaser will, for instance, want to be aware of any key contracts which contain provisions that would be breached or triggered by the acquisition. The seller's lawyers will prepare a *Disclosure Letter* qualifying the warranties in the Sale and Purchase Agreement.

Where the transaction is initiated by the sellers, it is possible that there will be an auction process, in which case the seller's lawyers will prepare a Confidentiality Agreement which, once signed, will entitle prospective purchasers to review the *Information Memorandum* outlining the key features of the business. Serious bidders may then be given access to a *Data Room* containing further information about the Target. Once a prospective purchaser has been identified by the sellers, the purchaser is likely to require a Lock-Out/Exclusivity Agreement pending completion of the due diligence process and exchange of contracts.

Completion often occurs at the same time as exchange of contracts, although it may be conditional on the occurrence of certain events, such as receipt of any relevant regulatory or other consents.

Hugh Gardner is a partner and Andrew Masraf is a solicitor in Biddle's Corporate Department with particular expertise in the acquisition and disposal of private companies. Recent publicly announced transactions include the sale of Flying Colours Leisure Group to Thomas Cook, Lopex plc's acquisition of Fotorama, the sale of Collins and Hayes to Aquarius Group plc and Dawson Holdings PLC's acquisition of the Johnsons Newspapers wholesale distribution business.

Mark Cawthron is a partner in Biddle's Tax Department advising on the tax implications of a wide range of corporate finance and commercial transactions.

20

HR Issues Arising from Acquisitions

Judy Brown
PricewaterhouseCoopers

Introduction

Business leaders have begun to realise that deals are increasingly about people. Sometimes this is because they represent a major unexpected cost discovered in due diligence, perhaps due to an unfunded pension liability, but often the risks are more subtle. For instance, two teams of people previously worked in competitor organisations and believed – or were told – that their way of doing things was different – if not better – than the competition. They are now expected to work with the former competitor team, together as one. Difficulties are bound to arise.

In fact, management and people issues are the main reason for deals failing. Survey results show this time and again. These issues are therefore critical to the deal – and they need to be taken account of as an integral part of the merger and acquisition process.

Like all other aspects of an acquisition or merger, the HR elements flow through three basic phases:

- *Before*: identifying business strategy; assessing the target; planning the deal;
- *During*: doing the deal itself; negotiating; planning for Day 1;
- *After*: making the deal work; integrating, consolidating, harmonising.

This chapter identifies the most important HR issues that are likely to arise in a deal within this basic framework, including employee demographics, benefits, terms and conditions, and performance management. However, these issues cannot be assessed in isolation. An approach of 'Smith will do the pensions issues and Jones will assess the key people' leads to incoherent strategy and scope for unnecessary risk. Our approach identifies areas of overlap when looking at each of the issues.

> *Reshaping the workforce is not merely an exercise calculating the redundancy cost and corresponding reduction in payroll costs. It has significant effect on the pension needs, collective agreements, employee demographics and the culture of the entity. It may affect incentive plans and even performance management systems – are these people being made redundant because of inadequate past training, will re-training be introduced so potential candidates for redundancy can fill existing vacancies elsewhere in the organisation? Only by looking at the whole picture can the questions be asked and answered sensibly.*

In the HR area there is likely to be as much, if not more, time spent on post-deal issues. Holding on to key staff, the formation of new pension schemes and other benefit arrangements, the integration of two work forces (involving harmonisation of terms and conditions), reduction in staff numbers through redundancies and assessing existing relations with a trade union are all post-deal issues which a buyer may face. Evidence shows that many deals fail because one or more of these issues is mismanaged.

> *Recent surveys have focussed on lessons learnt. Post-deal feedback consistently contains the message that early planning of the post-merger stage has a significant impact on success. Without such planning, a company cannot implement necessary changes quickly enough to achieve maximum results.*

The key to success, then, is a successful HR strategy, which we start with below. HR strategy must be aligned with the overall deal objectives and must act as a constant focus for the detailed HR issues throughout – and beyond – the deal process.

> *Unfair dismissal claims, TUPE penalties, unfunded pensions, loss of certain key, but replaceable, staff will all give rise to one-off costs of varying significance, but ill-considered or 'forced' commitments on salary or pension funding, loss of critical skills and experience, or a failure to harmonise certain systems, will mean that the business plan is never met.*

Strategy

Strategy covers the ground from today's position, to the deal, and then to the desired performance.

Ideally, the HR director will be responsible for the HR issues in the deal, but not all companies have HR directors. The CEO or Finance director could take on the responsibility personally, but only if he or she has sufficient time to devote to it. If there is no one with sufficient relevant knowledge and authority internally, then external help in this area is an option.

In the area of HR strategy the role involves responsibility for aligning the calibre, retention and performance of staff with the overall business and acquisition strategy – and for the associated cost.

Although individual businesses and deals are all different, this should include:

- identification of the HR drivers in the deal;
- identification of the impact of the deal on the HR drivers;
- the extent to which the strategy requires a high or low level of integration of the businesses;
- the extent to which a fundamental change in operation is required to achieve merger/acquisition goals;
- cultural fit – the extent to which 'ways of working' and style are likely to mesh between acquirer and target businesses (see below) and;
- basic communications messages.

> *Various stakeholders, particularly employees, will expect an announcement of a deal to have credible analysis running through it from a 'people' perspective, and for the messages to be conveyed in a robust and effective way. Inconsistencies, doubts and gaps in the people dimension are likely to flow through the deal beyond integration and increase the probability of failure.*

Strategy needs to take account of:

- geographic profile – the challenge of managing or understanding cultural issues, employment law and tax impacts in the target geographies can significantly affect the cost of the deal;
- sector issues, including regulatory impact – strategically, moving into another sector can involve management control issues for the acquirer, more than usual reliance on the target management team, under-estimating or missing sector differences, exacerbated culture clash, or search and selection in unfamiliar markets; and
- demographics and size of acquirer in relation to target – there may need to be regional differences, and the impact on the culture and style of the acquirer will often be underestimated.

Cultural fit

Cultural fit is not simply an internal people issue – the integrity of the brand, and the customer's view of a business, are significantly influenced by cultural factors.

For a successful merger the culture must fit the business strategy. Culture embodies the corporate values which need to be well defined and communicated (see later under Communication and Consultation). It is also supported and moulded by tangible factors:

- employee demographics, the age, skills, motivators of management and workforce;
- contracts and agreements, written and unwritten;
- remuneration from pensions to incentive schemes; and
- performance management systems.

Cultural imbalances between the acquirer's organisation and the business it is buying should not be disregarded. Cultural issues run deep in people, and many employees leave for no reason other than the fact that they do not like the way things are being done.

Strategy can be refined as information is gathered, and it is important to refer back to the strategy throughout the deal process, and assess how the deal and the business are meeting the strategic objectives.

The three stages of a deal

Before: assessment

As with all other elements of the deal, before the buyer commits to acquiring his target he needs to know what he is getting. A thorough due diligence of the people issues is an especially vital part of the assessment process, even when the acquisition is achieved by the purchase of business assets rather than shares in a company. This is because the Transfer of Undertakings (Protection & Employment) Regulations 1981 (known as 'TUPE') will likely apply.

> *The TUPE Regulations transfer, by operation of law, the employees engaged in the target business to the acquirer. The acquirer inherits their terms and conditions of employment, their accrued periods of service and all rights and obligations relating to them. Only certain pension rights are currently excluded (although this is often quite significant).*

The prudent buyer should plan for and carry out as much due diligence as possible. HR due diligence should identify, quantify and prioritise the financial and business implications associated with people in mergers and acquisitions. These include existing liabilities, one-off costs, the need for future incentives and cultural fit. This analysis is a precursor to building a successful transaction.

HR due diligence includes all of the following areas:

- understanding hierarchy, demographics, working conditions and terms and conditions of the employees;
- identifying the key people and the key skills, understanding their 'fit' with the business strategy;
- quantifying the associated pay, benefits, pensions, training, and system costs;
- estimating the likely costs resulting from the deal;
- examining full compliance with tax, pension and legal requirements;

HR due diligence means looking at people issues in the round.

A fair amount of information is usually available early in the process as it is often in the public domain. Annual reports, press reviews, articles and in-house magazines, publicity and recruitment material all have their own story to tell.

When data are available directly from the target, a detailed and specific information request must be made. Sometimes, depending on the circumstances of the deal, and often when only general requests are made, information on people can be the most sensitive and the hardest to obtain. Partial information is useless. Press for complete information and you will probably have insights on the workforce the target never had.

Key questions to be addressed in this process are:

- What does the HR asset look like as an investment? Are there areas which affect the desirability of making an offer?
- What HR costs and risks will there be in the transaction?
- If the company is to be reshaped, how expensive will this be?
- Will the right people stay? Will people perform at the highest possible level and in line with the business strategy?
- What are the cultural issues (which can cause an ostensibly sound deal to fail)? On so-called softer issues, it is amazing what information can emerge out of simple interviews of managers which would not be apparent from written material.

During a due diligence exercise, an HR director was asked why the pay rates were less than market rates and the staff turnover rate was less than the industry norm. Had this company cracked the HR retention issue with good training, or with a supportive culture? No, she said, the people weren't very good and could not command market rates and this was why, regardless of any other excuses, the results were falling off.

This assessment provides a proper basis for determining what employees must be offered to secure their commitment in the future. It should also identify any potential ongoing cost liabilities and negative consequences that the deal could trigger (for instance the crystallisation of benefit arrangements, which have the effect of loosening handcuffs).

HR due diligence is most effective when it draws on the integrated skills of employment lawyers, actuaries, share scheme specialists, tax experts, performance management and communications experts, who are up-to-date in their area of competence. The latest cases on pension funding and transfer of value, on the effectiveness of restrictive covenants, the latest Revenue statement on PAYE and share schemes, up-to-date benchmark data, will all affect the outcome of the acquisition.

During: negotiations and transition planning

Key areas of specific negotiation at the time the deal is actually done are likely to be:

- Warranty terms and disclosures on employment, pensions and employee tax matters.
- Where TUPE applies to the transaction, a specific clause allocating (usually by way of legal indemnities) the employee liabilities, account being taken of the impact of TUPE.
- Pension arrangements (as to which, see below).
- In some cases equity and other incentive plans that are disturbed by the deal, or needed to retain key staff.

The due diligence and the warranty/disclosure process are closely linked. Communication between the people who carried out the due diligence and those who are negotiating the HR warranties and indemnities is vital, otherwise problem areas which have been identified through the hard work on due diligence may never be covered legally.

A clear example of this is pensions which, after salaries, can be the single largest employee cost. It is important to establish whether the costs currently being incurred are sustainable in the future. This includes not only reviewing the underlying assumptions used in calculating the pension costs, but also understanding how pensions are to be dealt with as part of the transaction. For example where pensions are financed through external arrangements, whether the whole scheme is being transferred or a transfer payment is to be made available; if it is the latter, negotiations will have to be undertaken to ensure that adequate funds are made available to meet liabilities taken on by the purchaser. The past should not, however, affect the future. Going forward, there should be no constraints on the freedom of the purchaser to put in place arrangements for the future which accord with its corporate objectives. Checking for pensions exposure goes far beyond the review of the formal pension schemes rules – it is also necessary to establish what individuals have been promised both in employment contracts and other communications.

Separate from the agreement, the businesses must retain key people and ensure that they perform throughout the transition to a consistent standard. It is imperative to manage the gap between the idea of the deal and completion date.

- Negotiate where possible with key people.
- Plan for day one and beyond.
- Identify 'must dos' and do them.

The communication and consultation issues (particularly those which are legally required under TUPE) must be addressed on a timely basis. The longer the time between when employees first heard about the deal and the actual time of the transition, the greater the opportunity for failure through, for example, the loss of key staff.

Keep a focus on day-to-day HR matters. Businesses need to keep a tight review of what is going on in the 'business as usual' arena, and ensure that liability risk is not introduced through loss of focus. This may suggest a particularly cautious approach to line HR matters during transition.

After: post-deal performance

After the deal has been closed there are still many tasks to be completed to achieve effective performance. The most important of these are discussed below (see The main HR issues). Whilst these should be planned for prior to acquisition, it is only after closing that the purchaser is able to implement.

Longer term, all of these steps need to be consolidated in the creation of development and performance goals in an effective performance management system. The performance management system is often the point at which many HR 'enablers' to business success come together – it is important therefore that consideration is given to 'complementarities' with other HR processes. Key factors for the development of an effective performance management system include:

- the values of the newly merged organisation;
- support for behaviours appropriate to the new culture;
- individual and team levers against the key value drivers for the business;

- clarity of links to pay review, bonus and skills development; and
- appropriate mix of operational management, and integration transition effort.

> *Plan for day 2 and beyond – as well as day 1. Focus on d-day may lead to a problem with longer term planning. Both transition and line teams need to maintain a forward looking orientation and continually move their working horizon forward, as far beyond day 1 as is feasible. Clear reporting and authority should be established to adapt and reflect the changing context.*

Systems need to support the new strategy. Different evaluation systems running in parallel can rapidly cause discontent and, potentially, statutory risk.

Much of the HR transition planning review flows through into the post-deal implementation phase. Here, the key is for fast, effective action. The notes below outline some ways in which the transition planning focus evolves into action.

> *Review HR systems in terms of integration requirements and compliance. HR systems strategy for the new business must be clearly articulated and action agreed. As part of this process, potential problems need to be identified quickly; for example Year 2000 compliance, and European Monetary Union implications.*

The main HR issues

Key appointments and organisation

The shape of the organisation and key appointments and the methods by which these are put into place send a strong signal about the kind of business a newly-integrated organisation will be. New appointments should clearly have the respect of stakeholders (staff, shareholders and colleagues), and so require early assessment and careful consideration.

Who will manage the business? Some deals have foundered embarrassingly publicly at this point – it is clearly an issue that needs to be addressed courageously and without delay. And it is not just one chief appointment that needs to be made. Retention of other key people may well be an issue.

Appointments should be made quickly and decisively in order to maintain leadership momentum. Delay to the appointment process can create risk – during hiatus there is unlikely to be effective articulation of new strategies and goals. Any hiatus gives the people who are uncertain about their future the opportunity and incentive to make mischief, putting their own contribution in the rumour mill and encouraging press speculation. Expediency in the interim will inevitably diminish the ability of new management to take a strong lead when finally appointed.

A lack of contingency succession plans for leadership and key staff who do leave, or the failure to implement such plans immediately, will risk unnecessary staff turnover and will have an immediate effect on the bottom line.

For the wider workforce, plan an industrial employee relations strategy. Where unions are recognised in relation to the target, these recognitions will normally be inherited by the buyer (including an assets acquisition under TUPE). Currently, union recognition is not a legal right, so derecognition is an option for the buyer (although this will not necessarily remain the case given government proposals on union recognition). If derecognition is considered, great care is needed given employee relations and (particularly in TUPE situations or if staff reorganisations are planned) legal considerations. If recognition is to continue, the buyer needs to prepare for dealing with the unions (within the context of its own recognition arrangements, if any).

Key skills

> 'Adverse selection', the process whereby if people have a personal choice, they make the wrong decision for the company, is symptomatic of acquisitions: the good people with valuable skills walk away, often to competitors, and the others stay. Early cash payments triggered from incentive schemes exacerbate the issue. Deferred handcuffs are sometimes used but retention without performance can be a waste of money. This needs to be explored before and during the due diligence process and action taken to minimise the waste of talent.

In some instances, sellers may be willing to give a buyer access to staff, either to meet and discuss a senior person's or team's likely future in the new organisation, or to agree and complete new employment contracts.

This approach is not risk free. Executives who recognise that they are key can set a higher price for their services if they realise the deal is dependent upon them (although a buyer may be quite willing to pay what it takes). Confidentiality issues are also raised and, whatever executives say, they might walk away anyway. But the process allows a more thorough understanding by the buyer of what he or she will (or may not) get.

With or without these commitments, a carefully planned implementation is necessary to ensure that the key assets do not walk out the day after completion. A recent survey showed that most companies underestimate the number of people with key skills they will need after a transaction, and in the event do not retain even this too low number.

> As part of its bid to acquire Orangina, Coca-Cola signed an agreement with representatives of Orangina employees, guaranteeing current staffing levels until the end of 2000 and maintaining a 35-hour working week. It was seen as a last-minute lobbying effort to win trade unions' support and regulatory approval. Europe is likely to see more of these types of arrangement.

Above all, there must be careful structuring and communication of incentive arrangements at all levels within the new organisation. It also means that the employees be given, and understand, the organisational back-up necessary for them to do their jobs.

Restructuring

Restructuring includes expansion, relocation and contractions (or any combination of these).

Where continued growth is required by the acquisition, recruitment effort must be sustained. This may mean development of market facing materials and induction training programmes which should tie in with the general external marketing strategy.

HR issues in location decisions need to be considered as part of the planning process. The merger of offices/closure/relocation could make the difference between someone staying through the transition or not. More fundamentally, the sooner people are located together, the quicker they work together and the faster the business performance should improve (or at least stop declining).

Mergers are often associated with job losses, at senior level and/or across the work force more generally. At the transition planning phase the focus is likely to be on assessing the numbers and costs involved. Some planning for the process may be undertaken. Care, again, is needed where the deal is subject to TUPE, as there are extra restrictions on carrying out dismissals at the time of a TUPE transfer and there may be an ongoing process of formal worker consultation.

If there are structural changes, the cost of any redundancies, the training needs, the likelihood of equal opportunity claims, the consultation process and, possibly most importantly, the communication process must be established very quickly. Those who remain must see that a 'no redundancy' promise is kept, or if redundancies are inevitable that redundancies are handled openly and fairly, otherwise they will not perform for the business. Badly handled redundancies not only increase cash costs but also hit the top line (not to mention the headlines) if remaining employees become disaffected.

Implementation of a redundancy exercise is well regulated by the law. Key points include:

- *Collective consultation (with unions or elected employee representatives) is required in all but small-scale exercises.*
- *Determining who is selected for redundancy needs detailed consideration to avoid employee claims.*
- *Redeployment must be considered.*
- *Individual consultation must not be overlooked.*
- *The exit package needs to be constructed in light of legal requirements and benchmarked best practice.*

Harmonisation

The information on terms and conditions emerging out of the due diligence exercise and the warranty/disclosure process in the agreement negotiation phase should allow the acquirer to do a full and detailed review of employees' terms. This can help assess the implications of harmonising terms and conditions of employment after acquisition, in terms of cost, and to find the appropriate fit for benefits going forward.

Harmonising terms and conditions of employment may be desirable. Without harmonisation, two workers doing the same job can be paid differently, which can have an adverse effect on the morale of at least one of them. Generally it is rarely desirable to operate two separate terms and conditions structures within one integrated business.

However, new terms and conditions cannot simply be imposed on staff without the risk of legal challenge, or the risk of the change being ineffective, or both. This is particularly the case when changes are linked to a TUPE transfer. Where the law currently stands, staff agreement to new terms may subsequently be able to be revoked.

It may be very costly to give both workforces the best of both sets of arrangements. Reducing benefits, on the other hand, can lead to employee resistance. A more effective solution may be the introduction of a completely new set of terms for all staff, maybe including a flexible benefits scheme. This allows the employer to demonstrate the cost of each benefit and lets the employee choose from a selection that includes their existing benefits at the existing level, as well as benefits which their opposite numbers from the 'other' business enjoyed before the deal. The benefits could include medical insurance, holidays and pension contributions.

It is more difficult and not always necessary to harmonise actual pension arrangements, particularly where there is a vendor who retains the pension scheme for other employees.

Implementation of a harmonisation of terms programme can be a complex process. There is often a trade-off between ease of process and achieving legal certainty without the risk of claims. However the task is approached, the manner of communicating the changes is vital.

Compensation strategy

Compensation strategy needs to be clearly established. This goes beyond just harmonisation of two pay and benefits systems. There is a need to agree the goals and methods of the compensation programme. For example, a statement of philosophy might be: 'Newco is committed to a compensation strategy of pay in the top 25 per cent of similar businesses in each country in which we employ staff.'

A fundamental issue will be to ensure that the overall compensation and benefits strategy reflects the market positioning within the strategy, and the overall philosophy and values of the new business, including effective rewards for the very best performers. The strategy will be ineffective if the costs are not understood and the employees are unaware of the proposals.

Normally the acquirer is allowed to participate in the vendor's pension arrangements for a period of time following the completion of the transaction (although some vendors insist on a clean break from the date of completion). Thus the purchaser may have some time after closing to establish new schemes.

However, employees can become extremely agitated about uncertainties surrounding their pension arrangements. Therefore even where a participation period in the vendor's scheme is agreed, pensions must be included in the transition planning and the development of the overall compensation strategy.

The new arrangements should then be consistent with that strategy, recognising that this can cause major concerns with employees, even if the changes represent an improvement in their arrangements. Careful communication is therefore imperative.

In putting in place any new pension arrangements, it will be necessary to communicate to employees:

- the structure of the new arrangements; and
- the options which they have in respect of their service benefits.

At a minimum, employees must be told that they will continue to participate in the existing arrangements for a period, during which time they will be provided details of the new pension arrangements.

Incentives

A company's incentive schemes, or lack of them, reveal the type of performance or behaviour that is rewarded. The scheme may speak to a small team, or the whole company or to individuals. Inherited schemes are unlikely to be exactly appropriate for the future: they must match the deal aims and the business plans.

The immediate concerns are

- whether the deal is going to trigger an early payment out of the scheme;
- whether the deal is going to make the scheme inoperable (or encourage inappropriate behaviour);
- what incentive there is for directors and employees to stay during a transition period of uncertainty;

- what incentive there is for directors and employees to support the business plan.

Share schemes are easily recognised as needing attention as the changing tax laws, the deal requirements and the company and employment law issues can raise complex puzzles to solve; and yet appropriate equity participation is one way to incentivise employees to perform in the shareholders' interests and buy them into the deal.

Bonus schemes also need attention. Performance targets may cease to be measurable, or may confer exceptional bonuses. Such schemes can often be bought out with new schemes, but some early cash will almost inevitably be necessary.

The potential for mixed messages is high particularly with retention payments. For example, if the acquisition/merger is promoted as inherently 'good for staff', then a mixed message will result if people are then apparently paid an inducement to stay. A more consistent message might focus on reward for the extra effort required to meet the challenge of bringing two businesses together whilst maintaining 'business as usual'.

In structuring new pay arrangements one must be aware that the acceptability of recognition/bonus schemes may vary between the legacy businesses, and also may vary within business units/ geographies.

Non-equity incentives need not be cash compensation based. Effective retention techniques include training and particularly pro-grammes that enhance professional development as a means of demonstrating the business' commitment to invest in the individual. Dates for such programmes could be set out ahead, providing a longer-term incentive for employees to stay.

Continued training and development

In many businesses (especially knowledge intensive businesses), development for existing and newly merged staff should remain at the core of messages going through the transition. Some 'get rights' will be:

- continued personal development/career discussions with line man-agers/directors;

- ensuring that the ability to shape work around career development objectives remains at least in line with each group's existing norms and expectations;
- ensuring that investment in training and development is not pushed aside by integration issues.

Communication and consultation

Where TUPE applies to the transaction, staff who are affected by the transfer have the right to be informed of the deal and consulted over the effects on them. This should happen at a collective level, that is, with the representatives of any trade union recognised in relation to the staff, or with representatives elected by the staff. The obligation relates to all affected employees, not necessarily just those who are the subject of the transfer (although in practice they may be the only ones affected). This exercise must occur prior to the sale, so the main obligation in relation to the transferring staff falls on the seller, as their employer. The buyer therefore needs to be aware of this obligation in its planning process.

This collective communication process needs to be considered within the overall staff communication exercise. Prior to completion of the deal, direct communication between the buyer and the target's employees is likely to be limited, firstly because of general confidentiality issues and second because the seller is unlikely to want to lose control of staff communication until the deal is set in stone.

New business leaders will need to articulate a compelling vision and quickly translate the big messages into something relevant and strong for their own areas.

In addition to leveraging 'broadcast' communications media, there is a need to plan the building of new teams as they emerge in the new organisation. This includes active attention in a number of areas, for example:

- clear messages around the strategy, direction and operation of new teams;
- director/manager time with individuals in newly forming groups;
- routine group meeting structures for planning, surfacing concerns, gaining support for changes, and taking forward ideas for change; and
- team-building events to share development of the team as an entity.

Key messages should be timed to ensure that staff, to the greatest extent possible, hear them at the same time, if not before, the public.

COMMUNICATION IS THE KEY

Written notes/memos/e-mails:
Good for more extensive or factual information (e.g. organisation issues, regulatory updates, client news). Not so good for dealing with individual concerns, or gaining support for new ideas/concepts.

Voicemessage or similar 'broadcasts':
Good for progress updates (it's very quick) and important bulletins. Not so good for long or complex messages and, at the broadcast level, not especially effective as two-way communication, nor for reaching people on a personal level.

Group meetings:
Good for local additions to business-wide messages; if run on a participative/small group basis, good for surfacing concerns, gaining support for changes, and of course taking in ideas for change. Not so good if local management is unable to add much local content, or to own local responsibility for the wider change programme.

Team building events:
Good for transforming issues into solutions, around the development of a new team; clearly less effective if there are unclear goals in terms of building the team. Likely to be essential 'technology' as a new organisation and management structure emerges.

One-to-one meetings:
Most effective in dealing with individual concerns, helping individuals to link into the transition programme, and surfacing deeper issues. Likely to be a key element of retention for individuals that are 'at risk'. Clearly not easy to use for wider messages, need to take into account consistency of messages, and require a manager/director with the skills, information and authority to deal with concerns.

The battle for 'hearts and minds' (which includes morale and retention) is won on an individual level. The more business leaders and managers can do to *listen* to their employees and address their concerns, the more likely they are to win. In this process it will be particularly important to 'capture', and then dispel, myths and misperceptions (for example 'we will all have to move to their building', 'our group will be disbanded' and 'we will all have to work in another part of the country').

One of the key issues in communication is to ensure that the correct media and vehicles are used to promote communications with the target groups concerned.

Conclusion

HR issues in acquisitions are important issue which should be dealt with by important people. It is imperative to address these from the start, to identify the risks and the costs, and to look forward to how the business will succeed from the HR perspective. Treating strategic and detailed planning, thorough due diligence and effective and timely implementation as one process is more likely to deliver business success.

Judy Brown is a principal at PricewaterhouseCoopers' Global HR Solutions.

Section Six
Turnaround

Adding strength to companies.

Arthur Andersen Corporate Finance provides
a full range of services to help companies meet the
challenges of operating in today's environment.

These include:

- Financial Restructuring
- Turnaround Management
- Post-Acquisition Integration

For further information please contact David Duggins,
David Lovett or Joanne Holland on 0171 438 3000

ARTHUR
ANDERSEN

1 Surrey Street, London WC2R 2PS

21
Turnaround

Joanne Holland
Arthur Andersen

Turnaround management

Turnaround is big business and some big businesses, as well as medium-sized and small businesses, have been in turnaround situations. Companies such as Sears and Laura Ashley are examples of companies reporting losses and requiring specialist expertise in turnaround management. Both companies appointed company doctors to implement turnaround management and financial restructuring.

There is no hard and fast definition of what constitutes a turnaround situation. It is not necessarily a cash crisis that triggers a turnaround situation. Firms or operating units whose profit performance is considerably below what one would expect for the type of business in which it is engaged have implemented turnaround plans to improve profit performance. Firms often exhibit symptoms of failure long before a crisis begins. Such firms are often stagnant businesses with under-utilised assets and ineffective management. Businesses which are in stable and mature industries with a competitive advantage that exists for largely historical reasons, and with management who do not undertake the necessary steps to adapt to the changing product market environment, could well find themselves in a turnaround situation. Alternatively a growth-oriented firm that has grown too fast may continue to be quite profitable while at the same time experiencing a severe cash flow crisis. By adopting turnaround strategies early enough, recovery can take place without the traumas usually associated with a crisis situation.

It is a commonly held but mistaken view that the primary role of a turnaround leader is short-term cost reduction. Successful turnarounds are based on addressing the strategic, operational and financial issues and involve taking control and managing the immediate crisis, rebuilding stakeholder support, fixing the business and resolving future funding.

The causes of decline

While the symptoms of decline are readily identifiable, the key issue is to identify the causes of decline. The main causes are as follows:

- poor management;
- inadequate financial control;
- relative cost disadvantages;
- operating inefficiencies;
- lack of marketing effort;
- overtrading;
- acquisitions;
- external factors.

Poor management

The personal characteristics of the Chief Executive and the key management personnel play a major role in causing decline. A dominant and autocratic Chief Executive who is unwilling to adapt to changing business conditions and who is unreceptive to new ideas from subordinates and outsiders is usually unsuccessful.

An ineffective Board of Directors can also contribute to a firm's decline, particularly where key decisions affecting the firm are poorly made or when the board fails to monitor the alignment of strategic objectives with business operations. Ineffective Boards of Directors can arise where the Chairman fails to ensure that the Board discusses key business issues or does not follow corporate governance conventions. A Board which has an unbalanced skill set or where there is lack of communication between board members will also result in an ineffective Board.

Ineffective management is one of the greatest single contributors to a firm's decline. Management that does not have the ability or the skill set to deal with change, or management that lacks the intellectual capability to deal with the problems facing them, will exacerbate decline. Other organisational problems may arise where management lacks the ability to make or implement decisions or when management neglects the core business and is distracted with issues that are not an organisational priority.

Inadequate financial control

Typically, lack of financial controls means that there is inadequate cash flow forecasting, budgetary control, costing systems and monitoring of key performance indicators. In larger firms, the problem is more typically one of inadequate systems rather than no systems at all. Often systems are complex and the information is not well understood by management. An organisation structure that hinders effective control and/or where there are poor allocations of costs, can also obstruct management from making decisions which ensure financial control.

Poor working capital management is a feature common to turnaround situations and is a consequence of poor financial control. Working capital management involves the management of debtors stocks, creditors and cash balances. Increasing stocks and debtors, and decreasing creditors, all consume cash and can lead a company into crisis.

Relative cost disadvantages

A firm that has a substantially higher cost structure than that of its major competitors is likely to be at a competitive disadvantage. With fewer funds available than competitors, they will not be able to invest so much on new product development and marketing and will therefore be less capable of building and defending their market position. However, the more common problem encountered in turnaround situations is the inability of firms to compete on price because their cost structure is too high. Cost disadvantages can also arise from the lack of ownership and control of raw material supply, lack of access to cheap labour or production know-how, or poor site location.

Operating inefficiencies

Operating inefficiencies are due largely to poor management, and affect all elements of the cost structure. Some of the areas in which inefficiencies may directly or indirectly cause higher costs are:

- low labour productivity;
- poor production planning;
- lack of adequate maintenance;
- plant layout;
- allocation of sales force time;
- allocation of advertising and promotional expenditure;
- distribution and after sales service;
- terms of trade encouraging a large volume of small orders;
- a general lack of procedures.

Lack of marketing effort

The lack of marketing effort usually emanates from a Sales and Marketing Director who is unable to provide the direction and leadership required to compete effectively in the market place. Lack of marketing effort may take many forms, but typically one finds:

- efforts not targeted at key customers and key products;
- lack of responsiveness to customers' enquiries;
- a poorly motivated sales force with a non-aggressive sales manager;
- ineffective and wasted advertising;
- poor after-sales service;
- lack of market research and knowledge of customer buying habits;
- outdated promotional material;
- weak or non-existent new product development function.

Lack of marketing effort alone may cause sales and profit to erode, but lack of marketing effort is often found in conjunction with marketing problems of a strategic nature such as severe price and product competition.

Overtrading

If a firm's sales grow at a faster rate than the firm is able to finance from internally generated cash flow and bank borrowings, this will lead to overtrading. Overtrading is a characteristic of growth firms but will arise in any firm where the focus is on sales volume rather than on maximising margins.

Acquisitions

Acquisitions are undertaken by firms to implement growth strategies in industries in which they already compete or to diversify into related and unrelated industrial sectors. There are, however, aspects of acquisitions that may cause firms to enter into a crisis situation. These situations arise where the business acquired has a weak competitive position, an unjustifiably high price is paid, or where post-acquisition implementation is weak. Poor post-acquisition management has been identified as the single most common cause of failure when making acquisitions. Acquisitions tend to be most successful when they are integrated into existing operations. Typical problems arise when the management of the new subsidiary spends time trying to resist integration and/or when duplication of resources results in high overhead costs.

External factors

External factors, which affect the firm's ability to sustain profitability fall broadly into the following categories:

- changes in market demand to which the firm does not respond (i.e. loss of one key customer);
- long-term decline in market trends which are difficult to reverse;
- cyclical market decline, especially where a number of other causal factors of decline exist.

The turnaround plan – a framework for achieving a successful turnaround

The recovery of an underperforming company depends on a robust turnaround plan. The turnaround plan identifies the fundamental problems facing the firm and provides a remedy which addresses the underlying causes. The turnaround plan must be sufficiently broad and deep to ensure that all of the critical issues are addressed. It usually involves radical rather than incremental change. A successful turnaround plan consists of the following ingredients:

- crisis stabilisation;
- strategic focus;
- organisational change and leadership;
- critical process improvements;
- financial restructuring.

The turnaround plan is usually conducted after a diagnostic review that identifies the underlying causes of the problem. From this review and analysis, a comprehensive turnaround plan is developed. The plan should clearly state the long-term goals for the business and a strategy for achieving those goals. The products and services offered by the organisation should be defined together with the target markets for those products and services. The plans should also contain a detailed programme of turnaround initiatives that should be described in terms of responsibility, proposed action, implementation timetable, resource requirement and proposed financial and operational impact. These initiatives will include cost reduction strategies together with process improvements.

The number of turnaround initiatives varies according to the size and complexity of the organisation. The recommendations may have a significant impact, such as major rationalisation of factory sites, or may be more modest, such as the hiring of key staff.

Finally, the plan should contain detailed financial projections for the first financial year of implementation and more high-level projections for subsequent years, which usually span the three to five year mark. For the plan to have the greatest chance of success, it must be adopted by the key executives who will play a part in its implementation. The turnaround plan will form the blueprint for the implementation of the turnaround over the next 18 to 24 months.

Implementation of the turnaround plan

The implementation phase concentrates on the implementation of the turnaround initiatives incorporated in the business plan. Rigorous project management is the key success factor for implementation. The plan sets out a programme of prioritised actions, allocating responsibilities and timing. The plan must be clearly understood by the key executives who will be responsible for implementing the plan in both an operational process sense and the financial impact of the turnaround plan initiatives. Progress against the plan must be monitored on a weekly basis. Weekly progress meetings supported by continuous updated implementation reports drive the management of the implementation process. Where there are insufficient resources within the organisation to implement the turnaround plan, interim management may be needed. While this may result in some initial cost, interim management may be a resource requirement solution for the short term, obviating the need to recruit long-term staff which adds to the ongoing cost structure of the firm.

Financial restructuring

The turnaround business plan is the basis of the financial restructuring plan. The financial projections accompanying the business plan will form the basis of the cash flow forecasts that are the key input into assessing the future funding requirements of the business.

The overall objective of the financial restructuring is to achieve a debt and equity structure that enables the firm to be adequately funded to implement its turnaround plans and to meet its ongoing liabilities as they fall due. The turnaround plan will need to have the support of the new or existing funding stakeholders. These stakeholders usually include debt providers and equity providers. In more recent years, Turnaround Funds have emerged as being another source of short-term and long-term funding. These Funds provide a form of mezzanine debt with some form of equity kicker.

Short-term refinancing may need to be negotiated in the very early stages and may be required during the stage of turnaround plan preparation. A crisis stabilisation plan may need to be implemented which will assess the immediate cash requirements of the business, provide plans to generate cash, establish emergency cash management controls and implement cash rationing. Preparation of detailed short-term forecasts will be required. The short-term refinancing will have provided the firm with the vital breathing space during which time the turnaround plan has been developed. The objective of the long-term financial restructuring is to provide the firm with a solvent balance sheet and an ability to implement the agreed plan whilst servicing residual or new debt. It should also restore creditor confidence, be acceptable to all stakeholders and will be key to restoring management motivation.

Equity stakeholders often take a different view to debt stakeholders in that the priority for providers of debt is to recover their loans with the appropriate risk reward profile. The equity stakeholders are usually more willing to write off unsuccessful investments but want to retain the upside on any new money going in. This leads to a tight negotiation between the stakeholders, particularly if there is to be a swap of debt for equity by the debt provider to provide balance sheet solvency. The negotiation will be driven by each of the parties' perception as to the value of their best alternative to the negotiated position. This often becomes frustrating for the company concerned. The process of financial restructuring is a lengthy and expensive process and therefore all parties should set out to achieve a final solution. Factors which influence the resulting structure, include:

- the existing capital structure;
- ongoing financial requirements of the business;
- current and potential value of the business;
- management credibility;
- the relative bargaining power of each party;
- tax considerations.

Fees and costs associated with a turnaround situation

Fees associated with a turnaround situation fall into the following categories:

- diagnostic review;
- short-term funding facilities;
- legal fees;
- preparation of the turnaround plan;
- fees associated with financial restructuring.

Legal and bank fees and charges are increasingly open to negotiation. With respect to the diagnostic review, the debt or equity provider may fund the associated fees. This is on the basis that those parties seek to determine their own financial position going forward and will wait for the diagnostic review before either taking the turnaround process further or allowing the firm to commit funds to take the turnaround process further. The company usually funds the turnaround plan.

Fees for the turnaround plan and the implementation process vary. They usually consist of a fixed fee element and a success fee element, based on successful completion of the turnaround. The success fee may be in the form of equity participation.

Section Seven

Directory of Corporate Finance Service Providers

22
Financial Advisers

3i CORPORATE FINANCE LIMITED
91 Waterloo Road
London
SE1 8XP
Tel: 0171 928 3131
Fax: 0171 975 3460

ADAM & COMPANY PLC
22 Charlotte Square
Edinburgh
EH2 4DF
Tel: 0131 225 8484
Fax: 0131 225 5136

ANDERSEN (ARTHUR)
199 St. Vincent Street
Glasgow
G2 5QD
Tel: 0141 300 6620
Fax: 0141 300 6633

BANK OF AMERICA INTERNATIONAL LIMITED
1 Alie Street
London
E1 8DE
Tel: 0171 634 4000
Fax: 0171 634 4707

BANK OF IRELAND (NIIB GROUP LIMITED)
Donegall House
9 Donegall Square North
Belfast
BT1 5LU
Tel: 01232 238111
Fax: 01232 246241

BANK OF SCOTLAND
Uberior House
61 Grassmarket
Edinburgh
EH1 2JF
Tel: 0131 243 5867
Fax: 0131 243 5948

BANK OF WALES PLC
Kingsway
Cardiff
CF1 4YB
Tel: 01222 229922
Fax: 01222 787555

BANKERS TRUST INTERNATIONAL PLC
1 Appold Street
Broadgate
London
EC2A 2HE
Tel: 0171 982 2500
Fax: 0171 283 2848

BANQUE NATIONALE DE PARIS PLC
8–13 King William Street
London
EC4P 4HS
Tel: 0171 895 7070
Fax: 0171 283 2848

BARCLAYS BANK PLC
54 Lombard Street
London
EC3P 3AH
Tel: 0171 699 5000
Fax: 0171 699 2509

BARCLAYS STOCKBROKERS LIMITED
300 Bath Street
Tay House
Glasgow
G2 4JR
Tel: 0141 352 3000
Fax: 0141 221 4951

BAUM (ROBIN F.) CONSULTANTS
53 Roupell Street
London
SE1 8TB
Tel: 0171 401 3725
Fax: 0171 401 8390

BEESON GREGORY LIMITED
The Registry
Royal Mint Court
London
EC3N 4LB
Tel: 0171 488 4040
Fax: 0171 481 3762

BERTOLI MITCHELL
Plaza 535
Kings Road
London
SW10 0SZ
Tel: 0171 349 0424
Fax: 0171 349 0338

BRITISH LINEN BANK LIMITED (THE)
4 Melville Street
Edinburgh
EH3 7NZ
Tel: 0131 243 8325
Fax: 0131 243 8324

BROWN, SHIPLEY & CO. LIMITED
Founders Court
Lothbury
London
EC2R 7HE
Tel: 0171 606 9833
Fax: 0171 796 4875

BUSINESS DYNAMICS LIMITED
The Coach House
50a Blackheath Park
London
SE3 9SJ
Tel: 0181 852 6560
Fax: 0181 852 2863

CHARTERED TRUST PLC
24–26 Newport Road
Cardiff
CF2 1SR
Tel: 01222 296000
Fax: 01222 461345

CHARTERHOUSE BANK LIMITED
1 Paternoster Row
St. Pauls
London
EC4M 7DH
Tel: 0171 248 4000
Fax: 0171 248 1998

CHASE MANHATTAN BANK LIMITED
125 London Wall
London
EC2Y 5AJ
Tel: 0171 777 2000
Fax: 0171 777 4745

CIBC WOOD GUNDY OPPENHEIMER
Cottons Centre
Cottons Lane
London
SE1 2QL
Tel: 0171 234 6000
Fax: 0171 407 4127

CITIBANK INTERNATIONAL PLC
336 Strand
London
WC2R 1HB
Tel: 0171 836 1230
Fax: 0171 500 1695

CLOSE BROTHERS LIMITED
12 Appold Street
London
EC2A 2AA
Tel: 0171 426 4000
Fax: 0171 426 4044

CLYDESDALE BANK PLC
40 St. Vincent Place
Glasgow
G1 2HL
Tel: 0141 248 7070
Fax: 0141 223 2093

CO-OPERATIVE BANK PLC (THE)
PO Box 101
1 Balloon Street
Manchester
M60 4EP
Tel: 0161 832 3456
Fax: 0161 829 5212

COUTTS & CO.
440 Strand
London
WC2R 0QS
Tel: 0171 379 6262
Fax: 0171 753 1043

DAO HONG BANK LONDON PLC
10 Angel Court
London
EC2R 7ES
Tel: 0171 606 1616
Fax: 0171 606 2900

DAVENHAM TRUST PLC
8 St. John Street
Manchester
M3 4DU
Tel: 0161 832 8484
Fax: 0161 832 9164

DELOITTE & TOUCHE
London
Stonecutter Court
1 Stonecutter Street
London
EC4A 4TR
Tel: 0171 936 3000
Fax: 0171 583 8517

Bracknell
Columbia Centre
Market Street
Bracknell
RG12 1PA
Tel: 01344 454445
Fax: 01344 422681

Cambridge
Leda House
Station Road
Cambridge
CB1 2RN
Tel: 01223 460222
Fax: 01223 350839

DEXIA MUNICIPAL BANK PLC
55 Tufton Street
Westminster
London
SW1P 3QF
Tel: 0171 799 3322
Fax: 0171 799 2117

DRESDNER KLEINWORT BENSON
20 Fenchurch Street
London
EC3P 3DB
Tel: 0171 623 8000
Fax: 0171 623 4069

DUNBAR BANK PLC
9–15 Sackville Street
Piccadilly
London
W1A 2JP
Tel: 0171 437 7844
Fax: 0171 437 3953

**EAST (JOHN) & PARTNERS
LIMITED**
Crystal Gate
28–30 Worship Street
London
EC2A 2AH
Tel: 0171 628 2200
Fax: 0171 628 4473

**FIRST TRUST BANK
(AIB GROUP NORTHERN
IRELAND)**
First Trust Centre
92 Ann Street
Belfast
BT1 3HH
Tel: 01232 325599
Fax: 01232 438338

**FLEMING (ROBERT) & CO.
LIMITED**
25 Copthall Avenue
London
EC2R 7DR
Tel: 0171 638 5858
Fax: 0171 588 7219

FORWARD TRUST LIMITED
Waterman House
101–107 Chertsey Road
Woking
GU21 5BL
Tel: 0800 328 3820
Fax: 0800 328 3823

GE CAPITAL BANK LIMITED
Trent House
Torre Road
Leeds
LS99 2BD
Tel: 0113 240 4230
Fax: 0113 240 4453

**GOLDMAN SACHS
INTERNATIONAL BANK**
Peterborough Court
133 Fleet Street
London
EC4A 2BB
Tel: 0171 774 1000
Fax: 0171 774 4510

GRANVILLE BANK LIMITED
Mint House
77 Mansell Street
London
E1 8AF
Tel: 0171 488 1212
Fax: 0171 481 3911

**GREIG MIDDLETON & CO.
LIMITED**
Glasgow
155 St. Vincent Street
Glasgow
G2 5NN
Tel: 0141 240 4000
Fax: 0141 221 6578

London
30 Lombard Street
London
EC3V 9EN
Tel: 0171 655 4000
Fax: 0171 655 4100

GRESHAM TRUST PLC
1 South Place
London
EC2M 2GT
Tel: 0171 309 5000
Fax: 0171 374 0707

**GUINNESS MAHON & CO.
LIMITED**
32 St. Mary at Hill
London
EC3P 3AJ
Tel: 0171 623 9333
Fax: 0171 283 4823

HARTON SECURITIES LIMITED
6 Lombard Street
Abingdon
Oxfordshire
OX14 5SD
Tel: 01235 535000
Fax: 01235 555796

HAWKPOINT PARTNERS
Crosby Court
4 Great St. Helens
London
EC3A 6HA
Tel: 0171 665 4500
Fax: 0171 665 4600

HODGE (JULIAN) BANK LIMITED
10 Windsor Place
Cardiff
CF1 3BX
Tel: 01222 220800
Fax: 01222 344061

HSBC INVESTMENT BANK PLC
Vintners Place
68 Upper Thames Street
London
EC4V 3BJ
Tel: 0171 336 9000
Fax: 0171 623 5768

IBI CORPORATE FINANCE
Donegall House
7 Donegall Square North
Belfast
BT1 5LU
Tel: 01232 246241
Fax: 01232 238111

IBJ INTERNATIONAL PLC
Bracken House
One Friday Street
London
EC4M 9JA
Tel: 0171 236 1090
Fax: 0171 236 0484

INVESTEC BANK (UK) LIMITED
Cannon Bridge
25 Dowgate Hill
London
EC4R 2AT
Tel: 0171 283 9111
Fax: 0171 626 1213

**INVESTEC HENDERSON
CROSTHWAITE**
Corporate Finance
2 Gresham Street
London
EC2 7PE
Tel: 0171 623 9333
Fax: 0171 283 4823

JP MORGAN & CO. INC.
60 Victoria Embankment
London
EC4Y 0JP
Tel: 0171 600 2300
Fax: 0171 325 8299

KLEINWORT BENSON LIMITED
PO Box 560
20 Fenchurch Street
London
EC3P 3DB
Tel: 0171 623 8000
Fax: 0171 475 5994

KPMG CORPORATE FINANCE
8 Salisbury Square
London
EC4Y 8BB
Tel: 0171 311 1000
Fax: 0171 311 3311

LAZARD BROTHERS & CO.
LIMITED
21 Moorfields
London
EC2P 2HT
Tel: 0171 588 2721
Fax: 0171 628 2485

LLOYDS BOWMAKER LIMITED
Finance House
51 Holdenhurst Road
Bournemouth
BH8 8EP
Tel: 01202 299777
Fax: 01202 299486

MATLOCK BANK LIMITED
1 Connaught Place
London
W2 2DY
Tel: 0171 402 5500
Fax: 0171 298 0002

MERRILL LYNCH INTERNATIONAL
BANK LIMITED
Ropemaker Place
25 Ropemaker Street
London
EC2Y 9LY
Tel: 0171 628 1000
Fax: 0171 867 2867

MIDLAND BANK PLC
Poultry
London
EC2P 2BX
Tel: 0171 260 8000
Fax: 0171 336 9500

MORGAN GRENFELL & CO.
LIMITED
6 Bishopsgate
London
EC2N 4DA
Tel: 0171 588 4545
Fax: 0171 545 7130

NABARRO WELLS & CO. LIMITED
Saddler's House
Sutter Lane
Cheapside
London
EC2V 6BR
Tel: 0171 710 7400
Fax: 0171 710 7401

NATIONSBANK EUROPE LIMITED
New Broad Street House
35 New Broad Street
London
EC2M 1NH
Tel: 0171 638 8888
Fax: 0171 282 2201

NATWEST EQUITY PARTNERS
8 Fenchurch Place
London
EC3M 4TE
Tel: 0171 374 3444
Fax: 0171 374 3580

**NCB CORPORATE FINANCE
LIMITED**
Bulloch House
2 Linenhall Street
Belfast
BT2 8BA
Tel: 01232 897777
Fax: 01232 897789

NMB-HELLER
Park House
22 Park Street
Croydon
CR9 1RD
Tel: 0181 256 1281
Fax: 0181 686 1661

NOBLE GROSSART LIMITED
48 Queen Street
Edinburgh
EH2 3NR
Tel: 0131 226 7011
Fax: 0131 226 6032

**NOMURA BANK INTERNATIONAL
PLC**
1 St. Martin's le Grand
London
EC1A 4NP
Tel: 0171 521 2000
Fax: 0171 521 3699

**NORTHERN BANK EXECUTOR
AND TRUSTEE COMPANY
LIMITED**
Causeway House
14 Howard Street
Belfast
BT2 7EB
Tel: 01232 332334
Fax: 01232 893413

PANNELL KERR FORSTER
London
New Garden House
78 Hatton Garden
London
EC1N 8JA
Tel: 0171 831 7393
Fax: 0171 405 6736

Manchester
Sovereign House
Queen Street
Manchester
M2 5HR
Tel: 0161 832 5481
Fax: 0161 832 3849

PRICEWATERHOUSECOOPERS
32 London Bridge Street
London
SE1 9SY
Tel: 0171 939 3000
Fax: 0171 378 0647

**RATHBONE BROTHERS & CO.
LIMITED**
Port of Liverpool Buildings
Pier Head
Liverpool
L3 1NW
Tel: 0151 236 8674
Fax: 0151 243 7001

REA BROTHERS LIMITED
Aldermans House
Aldermans Walk
London
EC2M 3XR
Tel: 0171 623 1155
Fax: 0171 623 2694

ROTHSCHILD (N.M.) & SONS LIMITED
New Court
St. Swithin's Lane
London
EC4P 4DU
Tel: 0171 280 5000
Fax: 0171 929 1643

ROYAL BANK OF CANADA EUROPE LIMITED
71 Queen Victoria Street
London
EC4V 4DE
Tel: 0171 489 1177
Fax: 0171 329 6144

ROYAL BANK OF SCOTLAND PLC (THE)
38 Moseley Street
Manchester
M60 2BE
Tel: 0161 236 8585
Fax: 0161 228 7625

SBC WARBURG
1–2 Finsbury Avenue
London
EC2M 2PP
Tel: 0171 606 1066
Fax: 0171 568 0901

SCHRODER (J. HENRY) & CO. LIMITED
120 Cheapside
London
EC2V 6DS
Tel: 0171 658 6000
Fax: 0171 658 6459

SCHRODER LEASING LIMITED
Townsend House
160 Northolt Road
Harrow
HA2 0PG
Tel: 0181 422 7101
Fax: 0181 422 4402

SECURE TRUST BANK PLC
Security House
23–27 Heathfield Road
Kings Heath
Birmingham
B14 7BY
Tel: 0121 693 9100
Fax: 0121 693 9101

SG HAMBROS
41 Tower Hill
London
EC3N 4SG
Tel: 0171 676 6000
Fax: 0171 702 4424

SHORE CAPITAL & CORPORATE LIMITED
1 Maddox Street
London
W1R 9WA
Tel: 0171 734 7293
Fax: 0171 734 7635

SINGER & FRIEDLANDER LIMITED
21 New Street
Bishopsgate
London
EC2M 4HR
Tel: 0171 623 3000
Fax: 0171 929 5338

SMITH & WILLIAMSON SECURITIES
1 Riding House Street
London
W1A 3AS
Tel: 0171 637 5377
Fax: 0171 631 0741

SOLOMON HARE CORPORATE FINANCE
Oakfield House
Oakfield Grove
Clifton
Bristol
BS8 2BN
Tel: 0117 933 3344
Fax: 0117 933 3345

STANDARD BANK LONDON LIMITED
5th Floor
Cannonbridge House
25 Dowgate Hill
London
EC4R 2SB
Tel: 0171 815 3000
Fax: 0171 815 3098

STANDARD CHARTERED BANK
1 Aldermanbury Square
London
EC2V 7SB
Tel: 0171280 7500
Fax: 0171 280 7636

TOKAI BANK EUROPE PLC
1 Exchange Square
London
EC2A 2JL
Tel: 0171 638 6030
Fax: 0171 457 2736

TORONTO-DOMINION BANK EUROPE LIMITED
Triton Court
14–18 Finsbury Square
London
EC2A 1DB
Tel: 0171 282 8226
Fax: 0171 638 0006

TSB BANK SCOTLAND PLC
Head Office
PO Box 177
Henry Duncan House
120 George Street
Edinburgh
EH2 4TS
Tel: 0131 225 4555
Fax: 0131 260 0127

WEST MERCHANT BANK LIMITED
33–36 Gracechurch Street
London
EC3V 0AX
Tel: 0171 623 8711
Fax: 0171 626 1610

WINTRUST SECURITIES LIMITED
21 College Hill
London
EC4R 2RP
Tel: 0171 236 2360
Fax: 0171 236 3842

YORKSHIRE BANK PLC
2 Infirmary Street
Leeds
LS1 2UL
Tel: 0113 200 1277
Fax: 0113 244 8081

23
Legal Advisers

This section contains details of legal advisers involved in merger and acquisition deals and includes an indication of the smallest and largest consideration value of these M & A deals during the last two years. For reasons of confidentiality, exact figures have not been published, but the values have been divided into the following five bands:

Band A: £0–5 million
Band B: £6–10 million
Band C: £11–20 million
Band D: £21–100 million
Band E: over £100 million

ACTONS
2 King Street
Nottingham
NG1 2AX
Tel: 0115 910 0200
Fax: 0115 910 0290
Contact: J.C. Britten
M & A range: (not supplied)

ADDLESHAW BOOTH & CO.
Leeds: Contact: Jonathan Shorrock
Sovereign House
PO Box 8
Sovereign Street
Leeds
LS1 1HQ
Tel: 0113 209 2000
Fax: 0113 209 2060
M & A range: A–E

London
60 Cannon Street
London
EC4N 6NP
Tel: 0171 982 5000
Fax: 0171 982 5060

Manchester
100 Barbirolli Square
Manchester
M2 3AB
Tel: 0161 934 6000
Fax: 0161 934 6060
M & A range: A–E

ALLEN & OVERY
One New Change
London
EC4M 9QQ
Tel: 0171 330 3000
Fax: 0171 330 9999
Contact: Guy Beringer, Alan Paul,
Richard Cranfield
M & A range: A–E

ASHURST MORRIS CRISP
Broadwalk House
5 Appold Street
London
EC2A 2HA
Tel: 0171 638 1111
Fax: 0171 972 7990
Contact: Adrian Knight
M & A range: A–E

BERWIN (S.J.) & CO.
222 Grays Inn Road
London
WC1X 8HB
Tel: 0171 533 2222
Fax: 0171 533 2000
Contact: John Daghlian
M & A range: A–E

BEVAN ASHFORD SOLICITORS
35 Colston Avenue
Bristol
BS1 4TT
Tel: 0117 923 0111
Fax: 0117 929 1865
Contact: John Townsend
M & A range: A–B

BIDDLE
1 Gresham Street
London
EC2V 7BU
Tel: 0171 606 9301
Fax: 0171 606 3305
Contact: Martin Lane
M & A range: A–D

BIRCHAM & CO.
1 Dean Farrar Street
London
SW1H 0DY
Tel: 0171 222 8044
Fax: 0171 222 3480
Contact: Paula Fagan
M & A range: A–B

BIRD & BIRD
90 Fetter Lane
London
EC4A 1JP
Tel: 0171 415 6000
Fax: 0171 415 6111
Contact: Chris Barrett, Charles
Crosthwaite
M & A range: A–E

BIRKETTS SOLICITORS
24–26 Museum Street
Ipswich
Suffolk
IP1 1HZ
Tel: 01473 232300
Fax: 01473 230524
Contact: Bob Wright
M & A range: A–C

BLAKE LAPTHORN
Harbour Court
Compass Road
North Harbour
Portsmouth
PO6 4ST
Tel: 01705 221122
Fax: 01705 221123
Contact: Kathryn Shimmin
M & A range: A–D

BLANDY & BLANDY
1 Friar Street
Reading
RG1 1DA
Tel: 0118 958 7111
Fax: 0118 956 8220
Contact: Philip Tranter
M & A range: A–D

BOODLE HATFIELD
61 Brook Street
London
W1Y 2BL
Tel: 0171 629 7411
Fax: 0171 629 2621
Contact: Chris Putt, Jonathan Brooks
M & A range: A–D

BRABNER HOLDEN BANKS WILSON
1 Dale Street
Liverpool
L2 2ET
Tel: 0151 236 5821
Fax: 0151 227 3185
Contact: Tony Harper
M & A range: A–D

Preston
7-8 Chapel Street
Preston
PR1 8AN
Tel: 01772 823921
Fax: 01772 201918

BRISTOWS
3 Lincoln's Inn Fields
London
WC2A 3AA
Tel: 0171 400 8000
Fax: 0171 400 8050
Contact: Paul Cooke, John Lace
M & A range: A–D

BRODIES
15 Atholl Crescent
Edinburgh
EH3 8HA
Tel: 0131 228 3777
Fax: 0131 228 3878
Contact: William Drummond
M & A range: A–D

BROUGH SKERRETT
99 Charterhouse Street
London
EC1M 6NQ
Tel: 0171 253 5505
Fax: 0171 253 5525
Contact: Gordon Brough
M & A range: A–D

BROWNE JACOBSON SOLICITORS
44 Castle Gate
Nottingham
NG1 7BJ
Tel: 0115 950 0055
Fax: 0115 947 5246
Contact: Rob Metcalfe, David Tilley
M & A range: A–E

BURGES SALMON
Narrow Quay House
Narrow Quay
Bristol
BS1 4AH
Tel: 0117 939 2000
Fax: 0117 902 4400
Contact: Christopher Godfrey
M & A range: A–E

CAMERON McKENNA
Mitre House
160 Aldersgate Street
London
EC1A 4DD
Tel: 0171 367 3000
Fax: 0171 362 2000
Contact: Richard Price
M & A range: A–E

CARTWRIGHTS
Marsh House
11 Marsh Street
Bristol
BS99 7BB
Tel: 0117 929 3601
Fax: 0117 926 2403
Contact: Chris Mitcher
M & A range: A–E

CHARLES RUSSELL
8–10 New Fetter Lane
London
EC4A 1RS
Tel: 0171 203 5000
Fax: 0171 203 0200
Contact: James Holder, Simon Gilbert
M & A range: A–E

CLARKE WILLMOTT & CLARKE
Bristol
The Waterfront
Welsh Back
Bristol
BS1 4SB
Tel: 0117 941 6600
Fax: 0117 941 6622
Contact: Robert Hunt
M & A range: A–C

Taunton
Blackbrook Gate
Blackbrook Park Avenue
Taunton
TA1 2PG
Tel: 01823 442266
Fax: 01823 443300
Contact: Nigel Popplewell
M & A range: A

Yeovil
Mansion House
Princes Street
Yeovil
BA20 1EP
Tel: 01935 401401
Fax: 01935 401444
Contact: Nigel Lindsay
M & A range: A–B

CLARKS SOLICITORS
Great Western House
Station Road
Reading
RG1 1SX
Tel: 0118 958 5321
Fax: 0118 960 4611
Contact: Richard Lee
M & A range: A–D

CLYDE & CO.
Beaufort House
Chertsey Street
Guildford
Surrey
GU1 4HA
Tel: 01483 555555
Fax: 01483 567330
Contact: Andrew Holderness
M & A range: A–E

COBBETTS
Ship Canal House
King Street
Manchester
M2 4WB
Tel: 0161 833 3333
Fax: 0161 833 3030
Contact: Robert Turnbull
M & A range: A–E

COLLYER-BRISTOW
4 Bedford Row
London
WC1R 4DF
Tel: 0171 242 7363
Fax: 0171 405 0555
Contact: John Bailey
M & A range: A–B

DAVENPORT LYONS
1 Old Burlington Street
London
W1X 2NL
Tel: 0171 468 2600
Fax: 0171 437 8216
Contact: Anthony Fiducia
M & A range: (not supplied)

DAVIES WALLIS FOYSTER
Liverpool
5 Castle Street
Liverpool
L2 4XE
Tel: 0151 236 6226
Fax: 0151 236 3088
Contact: Mark O'Conner
M & A range: (not supplied)

Manchester
Harvester House
37 Peter Street
Manchester
M2 5GB
Tel: 0161 228 3702
Fax: 0161 835 2407
Contact: Sue Parker
M & A range: A–E

DENTON HALL
Five Chancery Lane
Cliffords Inn
London
EC4A 1BU
Tel: 0171 242 1212
Fax: 0171 404 0087
Contact: Tony Grant
M & A range: A–E

DICKINSON DEES
St. Ann's Wharf
112 Quayside
Newcastle upon Tyne
NE99 1SB
Tel: 0191 279 9000
Fax: 0191 279 9100
Contact: John Flynn
M & A range: A–E

DICKSON MINTO W.S.
Royal London House
22–25 Finsbury Square
London
EC2A 1DS
Tel: 0171 628 4455
Fax: 0171 628 0027
Contact: Alastair Dickson
M & A range: B–E

DUNDAS & WILSON
Saltire Court
20 Castle Terrace
Edinburgh
EH1 2EN
Tel: 0131 228 8000
Fax: 0131 228 8888
Contact: David Hardie
M & A range: A–E

EDGE ELLISON
Birmingham
Rutland House
148 Edmund Street
Birmingham
B3 2JR
Tel: 0121 200 2001
Fax: 0121 200 1991
Contact: David Hull
M & A range: (not supplied)

Leicester
Regent Court
Regent Street
Leicester
LE1 7BR
Tel: 0116 247 0123
Fax: 0116 247 0030
Contact: David West
M & A range: (not suppplied)

London
18 Southampton Place
London
WC1A 2AJ
Tel: 0171 404 4701
Fax: 0171 831 9152
Contact: Simon Gordon
M & A range: (not supplied)

EDWARDS GELDARD
Dumfries House
Dumfries Place
Cardiff
CF1 4YF
Tel: 01222 238239
Fax: 01222 237268
Contact: Jeff Pearson
M & A range: A–D

EVERSHEDS
M & A range: A–E

London
Senator House
85 Queen Victoria Street
London
EC4V 4JL
Tel: 0171 919 4500
Fax: 0171 919 4919

Birmingham
10 Newhall Street
Birmingham
B3 3LX
Tel: 0121 233 2001
Fax: 0121 236 1583

Bristol
11–12 Queen Square
Bristol
BS1 4NT
Tel: 0117 929 9555
Fax: 0117 929 2766

Cambridge
Daedalus House
Station Road
Cambridge
CB1 2RE
Tel: 01223 355933
Fax: 01223 460266

Cardiff
Fitzalan House
Fitzalan Road
Cardiff
CF2 1XZ
Tel: 01222 471147
Fax: 01222 464347

Derby
11 St. James Court
Friar Gate
Derby
DE1 1BT
Tel: 01332 360992
Fax: 01332 371469

Ipswich
Franciscan House
Princes Street
Ipswich
IP1 1UR
Tel: 01473 284428
Fax: 01473 233566

Leeds
Cloth Hall Court
Infirmary Street
Leeds
LS1 2JB
Tel: 0113 243 0391
Fax: 0113 245 6188

Manchester
London Scottish House
24 Mount Street
Manchester
M2 3DB
Tel: 0161 832 6666
Fax: 0161 832 5337

Newcastle
Sun Alliance House
35 Mosley Street
Newcastle upon Tyne
NE1 1XX
Tel: 0191 261 1661
Fax: 0191 261 8270

Norwich
Holland Court
The Close
Norwich
NR1 4DX
Tel: 01603 272727
Fax: 01603 610535

Nottingham
1 Royal Standard Place
Nottingham
NG1 6FZ
Tel: 0115 960 7000
Fax: 0115 950 7111

Middlesborough
Permanent House
91 Albert Road
Middlesborough
TS1 2PA
Tel: 01642 247456
Fax: 01642 240446

FARRER & CO.
66 Lincoln's Inn Fields
London
WC2A 3LH
Tel: 0171 242 2022
Fax: 0171 831 9748
Contact: James Thorne
M & A range: A–E

FENNEMORES
200 Silbury Boulevard
Central Milton Keynes
MK9 1LL
Tel: 01908 678241
Fax: 01908 665985
Contact: Chris Robinson
M & A range: A–B

FINERS SOLICITORS
179 Great Portland Street
London
W1N 6LS
Tel: 0171 323 4000
Fax: 0171 344 5602
Contact Name: Peter Day
M & A range: A–D

FOX WILLIAMS
City Gate House
39–45 Finsbury Square
London
EC2A 1UU
Tel: 0171 628 2000
Fax: 0171 628 2100
Contact: Paul Osborne (Head of
Corporate Department)
M & A range: A–D

FRY (WILLIAM) SOLICITORS
Fitzwilliam House
Wilton Place
Dublin 2
Ireland
Tel: 00 353 1–639 5000
Fax: 00 353 1–639 5333
Contact: Paul Bale
M & A range: A–E

FURLEY PAGE FIELDING & BARTON
39 St. Margaret's Street
Canterbury
Kent
CT1 2TY
Tel: 01227 763939
Fax: 01227 762829
Contact: Christopher B. Wacher
M & A range: A–D

FYFE IRELAND W.S.
Orchard Brae House
30 Queensferry Road
Edinburgh
EH4 2HG
Tel: 0131 343 2500
Fax: 0131 343 3166
Contact: Stephen Gibb
M & A range: A–C

GOLD MANN & CO.
80 Fleet Street
London
EC4Y 1NA
Tel: 0171 822 2800
Fax: 0171 822 2822
Contact: Mark Hartley
M & A range: A–E

GORDONS WRIGHT & WRIGHT
14 Piccadilly
Bradford
West Yorkshire
BD1 3LX
Tel: 01274 202202
Fax: 01274 202100
Contact: Tim Ratcliffe (Managing
Partner)
M & A range: A–D

GOULDENS
22 Tudor Street
London
EC4Y 0JJ
Tel: 0171 583 7777
Fax: 0171 583 3051
Contact: Max Thorneycroft
M & A range: A–E

GREEN (GEORGE) & CO.
195 High Street
Cradley Heath
West Midlands
B64 5HW
Tel: 01384 410410
Fax: 01384 634237
Contact: Mr. J. O'N Robb
M & A range: A–C

GREENWOODS SOLICITORS
30 Priestgate
Peterborough
PE1 1JE
Tel: 01733 555244
Fax: 01733 347988
Contact: Sara Howard
M & A range: A–D

HALLIWELL LANDAU
St. James' Court
30 Brown Street
Manchester
M2 2JF
Tel: 0161 835 3003
Fax: 0161 835 2994
Contact: Alec Craig
M & A range: A–D

HAMMOND SUDDARDS
7 Devonshire Square
Cutler's Gardens
London
EC2M 4YH
Tel: 0171 655 1000
Fax: 0171 655 1001
Contact: Richard Burns
M & A range: A–E

HARBOTTLE & LEWIS
Hanover House
14 Hanover Square
London
W1R 0BE
Tel: 0171 667 5000
Fax: 0171 667 5100
Contact: Mark Bertram
M & A range: A–E

HARVEY INGRAM OWSTON
20 New Wall
Leicester
LE1 6TX
Tel: 0116 254 5454
Fax: 0116 255 4559
Contact: Geoff Owen
M & A range: A–B

HERBERT SMITH
Exchange House
Primrose Street
London
EC2A 2HS
Tel: 0171 374 8000
Fax: 0171 374 0888
Contact: Caroline Goodall
M & A range: B–E

**HOBSON AUDLEY HOPKINS &
WOOD**
7 Pilgrim Street
London
EC4V 6LB
Tel: 0171 450 4500
Fax: 0171 450 4545
Contact: Gerald Hobson, Max Audley
M & A range: A–E

HOWARD KENNEDY
19 Cavendish Square
London
W1A 2AW
Tel: 0171 546 8851
Fax: 0171 664 4451
Contact: Alan Banes
M & A range: A–D

HUGHES WATTON
69 Eccleston Square
London
SW1V 1PJ
Tel: 0171 416 7600
Fax: 0171 416 7601
Contact: John Watton
M & A range: A–B

JACKSON (ANDREW M.) & CO.
PO Box 47
Essex House
Manor Street
Hull
HU1 1XH
Tel: 01482 325242
Fax: 01482 212974
Contact: John F. Hammersley
M & A range: A–D

JONES DAY BEAVIS & POGUE
Bucklersbury House
3 Queen Victoria Street
London
EC4N 8NA
Tel: 0171 236 3939
Fax: 0171 236 1113
Contact: Katie Dickinson
M & A range: A–E

KENT JONES & DONE
Churchill House
Regent Road
Stoke on Trent
ST1 3RQ
Tel: 01782 202020
Fax: 01782 202040
Contact: Peter Ellis
M & A range: A–C

KIDD RAPINET
14–15 Craven Street
London
WC2N 5AD
Tel: 0171 925 0303
Fax: 0171 925 0334
Contact: Philip Wild
M & A range: A–D

KIMBELL & CO. SOLICITORS
352 Silbury Court
Silbury Boulevard
Milton Keynes
MK9 2HJ
Tel: 01908 668555
Fax: 01908 674344
Contact: Stephen Kimbell (Senior
Partner)
M & A range: A–D

KUIT STEINART LEVY
3 St. Mary's Parsonage
Manchester
M3 2RD
Tel: 0161 832 3434
Fax: 0161 832 6650
Contact: Bryan Bodek
M & A range: A–E

LEDINGHAM CHALMERS
1 Golden Square
Aberdeen
AB10 1HA
Tel: 01224 408408
Fax: 01224 408404
Contact: John Rutherford
M & A range: A–D

LEWIS SILKIN
Windsor House
50 Victoria Street
London
SW1H 0NW
Tel: 0171 227 8000
Fax: 0171 222 3486
Contact: Clare Grayston
M & A range: A–E

LINKLATERS & PAINES
One Silk Street
London
EC2Y 8HQ
Tel: 0171 456 2000
Fax: 0171 456 2222
Contact: Anthony Cann
M & A range: A–E

LINNELLS SOLICITORS
Greyfriars Court
Paradise Square
Oxford
OX1 1BB
Tel: 01865 248607
Fax: 01865 728445
Contact: Edward Lee
M & A range: A–B

LOVELL WHITE DURRANT
65 Holborn Viaduct
London
EC1A 2DY
Tel: 0171 236 0066
Fax: 0171 248 4212
Contact: Hugh Nineham
M & A range: A–E

LUPTON FAWCETT
Yorkshire House
Greek Street
Leeds
LS1 5SX
Tel: 0113 280 2000
Fax: 0113 245 6782
Contact: Bob Harrap
M & A range: A–D

MACFARLANES
10 Norwich Street
London
EC4A 1BD
Tel: 0171 831 9222
Fax: 0171 831 9607
Contact: Sarah Allington
M & A range: B–E

**MACLAY MURRAY & SPENS
SOLICITORS**
M & A range: A–E
Glasgow (Head Office)
151 St. Vincent Street
Glasgow G2 5NS
Tel: 0141 248 5011
Fax: 0141 248 5819
Contact: Magnus Swanson

Edinburgh
3 Glenfinlas Street
Edinburgh
EH3 6AQ
Tel: 0131 226 5196
Fax: 0131 226 3174
Contact: Graeme Sloan

London
10 Foster Lane
London
EC2V 6HH
Tel: 0171 606 6130
Fax: 0171 600 0992
Contact: David Cooke

MACROBERTS SOLICITORS
152 Bath Street
Glasgow
G2 4TB
Tel: 0141 332 9988
Fax: 0141 332 8886
Contact: James McGinn
M & A range: A–D

MANCHES & CO.
81 Aldwych
London
WC2B 4RP
Tel: 0171 404 4433
Fax: 0171 430 1133
Contact: Christopher Owen
M & A range: A–D

MASONS
30 Aylesbury Street
London
EC1R 0ER
Tel: 0171 490 4000
Fax: 0171 490 2545
Contact: Russell Booker
M & A range: A–E

McCANN FITZGERALD
2 Harbourmaster Place
Custom House Dock
Dublin 1
Ireland
Tel: 00 353 1–829 0000
Fax: 00 353 1–829 0010
Contact: Barry Devereux
M & A range: A–E

McGRIGOR DONALD
M & A range: A–E
Contact: Colin Gray

Edinburgh
Erskine House
68–73 Queen Street
Edinburgh
EH2 4NF
Tel: 0131 226 7777
Fax: 0131 226 7700

Glasgow
Pacific House
70 Wellington Street
Glasgow
G2 6SB
Tel: 0141 248 6677
Fax: 0141 204 1351/ 221 1390

London
63 Queen Victoria Street
London
EC4N 4ST
Tel: 0171 329 3299
Fax: 0171 329 4000

MEMERY CRYSTAL
31 Southampton Row
London
WC1B 5HT
Tel: 0171 242 5905
Fax: 0171 242 2058
Contact: Valerie Brennan
M & A range: A–E

MILLS & REEVE SOLICITORS
(NB: The offices based in Cambridge
and Norwich undertake the majority of
M & A work.)

Birmingham
Midland House
132 Hagley road
Edgbaston
Birmingham
B16 9NN
Tel: 0121 454 4000
Fax: 0121 456 3631
M & A range: (not supplied)

Cambridge
Francis House
112 Hills Road
Cambridge
CB2 1PH
Tel: 01223 364422
Fax: 01223 355848
Contact: Glynne Stanfield
M & A range: A–D

Cardiff
Temple Court
Cathedral Road
Cardiff
CF1 9HA
Tel: 01222 786440
Fax: 01222 786441
M & A range: (not supplied)

Norwich
Francis House
3–7 Redwell Street
Norwich
NR2 4TJ
Tel: 01603 660155
Fax: 01603 633027
Contact: Bryony Falkus
M & A range: A–D

MORGAN COLE
M & A range: A–E

Cardiff
Bradley Court
Park Place
Cardiff
CF1 3DP
Tel: 01222 385385
Fax: 01222 385300
Contact: Duncan Macintosh

Swansea
Princess House
Princess Way
Swansea
SA1 3LJ
Tel: 01792 634634
Fax: 01792 634500
Contact: Peter Jones

London
167 Fleet Street
London
EC4A 2JB
Tel: 0171 822 8000
Fax: 0171 822 8222
Contact: Graeme Guthrie

Newport
11 Gold Tops
Newport
Gwent
NP9 4UJ
Tel: 01633 244988
Fax: 01633 246130
Contact: Jonathan Rees

Oxford
Buxton Court
3 West Way
Oxford
OX2 0SZ
Tel: 01865 262600
Fax: 01865 721367
Contact: Joe Pillman

Reading
Apex Plaza
Forbury Road
Reading
RG1 1AX
Tel: 0118 955 3000
Fax: 0118 939 3210
Contact: Joe Pillman

MUCKLE (ROBERT) SOLICITORS

Norham House
12 New Bridge Street West
Newcastle upon Tyne
NE1 8AS
Tel: 0191 232 4402
Fax: 0191 261 6954
Contact: Ian Gilthorpe
M & A range: A–C

NABARRO NATHANSON

50 Stratton Street
London
W1X 6NX
Tel: 0171 493 9933
Fax: 0171 629 7900
Contact: Derek Reynolds
M & A range: A–E

NICHOLSON GRAHAM & JONES

110 Cannon Street
London
EC4N 6AR
Tel: 0171 648 9000
Fax: 0171 648 9001
Contact: Annmarie Pryor
M & A range: A–E

NORTON ROSE

Kempson House
35–37 Camomile Street
London
EC3A 7AN
Tel: 0171 283 6000
Fax: 0171 283 6500
Contact: Barbara Stephenson
(Corporate Finance Partner)
M & A range: A–E

OSBORNE CLARKE

Bristol
50 Queen Charlotte Street
Bristol
BS1 4HE
Tel: 0117 923 5280
Fax: 0117 927 9209
Contact: Simon Beswick
M & A range: A–E

London
Hillgate House
26 Old Bailey
London
EC4M 7HW
Tel: 0171 809 1000
Fax: 0171 809 1005
Contact: Andrew Saul
M & A range: A–E

Reading
Apex Plaza
Forbury Road
Reading
RG1 1AX
Tel: 0118 925 2000
Fax: 0118 925 0038
Contact: Richard Smerdon
M & A range: A–E

PAISNER & CO.
Bouverie House
154 Fleet Street
London
EC4A 2DQ
Tel: 0171 353 0299
Fax: 0171 583 8621
Contact: David Collins
M & A range: A–E

**PANNONE & PARTNERS
SOLICITORS**
123 Deansgate
Manchester
M3 2BU
Tel: 0161 909 3000
Fax: 0161 909 4444
Contact: Søren Tattam
M & A range: A–D

PAULL & WILLIAMSONS
Investment House
6 Union Row
Aberdeen
AB10 1DQ
Tel: 01224 621621
Fax: 01224 640446
Contact: S. Barrie
M & A range: A–E

PENNINGTONS
Godalming
Highfield
Brighton Road
Godalming
GU7 1NS
Tel: 01483 423003
Fax: 01483 424177
Contact: Robin Peile
M & A range: A–D

London
Bucklersbury House
83 Cannon Street
London
EC4N 8PE
Tel: 0171 457 3000
Fax: 0171 457 3240
Contact: Ron Allsopp
M & A range: A–E

PINSENT CURTIS
M & A range: A–E
Contact: Clare Turnbull

Birmingham
3 Colmore Circus
Birmingham
B4 6BH
Tel: 0121 200 1050
Fax: 0121 626 1040

Leeds
41 Park Square
Leeds
LS1 2NS
Tel: 0113 244 5000
Fax: 0113 244 8000

London
Dashwood House
69 Old Broad Street
London
EC2M 1NR
Tel: 0171 418 7000
Fax: 0171 418 7050

RADCLIFFES
5 Great College Street
London
SW1P 3SJ
Tel: 0171 222 7040
Fax: 0171 222 6208
Contact: Rupert Lescher
M & A range: A–D

**REYNOLDS PORTER
CHAMBERLAIN**
Chichester House
278–282 High Holborn
London
WC1V 7HA
Tel: 0171 242 2877
Fax: 0171 242 1431
Contact: Tim Anderson, Jonathan
Watmough
M & A range: A–E

RICHARDS BUTLER
Beaufort House
15 St. Botolph Street
London
EC3A 7EE
Tel: 0171 247 6555
Fax: 0171 247 5091
Contact: David Boutcher
M & A range: A–E

ROWE & MAW
20 Blackfriars Lane
London
EC4V 6ND
Tel: 0171 248 4282
Fax: 0171 248 2009
Contact: Christopher Pullen
M & A range: A–E

**SALANS HERTZFELD &
HEILBRONN HRK**
Clements House
14–18 Gresham Street
London
EC2V 7NN
Tel: 0171 509 6000
Fax: 0171 726 6191
Contact: Philip Enoch, Stephen Finch
M & A range: A–E

SHAKESPEARES
10 Bennetts Hill
Birmingham
B2 5RS
Tel: 0121 632 4199
Fax: 0121 643 2257
Contact: Charles Flint, Jill Kennedy,
Tony Jones
M & A range: A–C

SHEPHERD & WEDDERBURN W.S.
Saltire Court
20 Castle Terrace
Edinburgh
EH1 2ET
Tel: 0131 228 9900
Fax: 0131 228 1222
Contact: James Will
M & A range: A–E

SHOOSMITHS & HARRISON
Banbury
52–54 The Green
Banbury
OX16 9AB
Tel: 01295 267971
Fax: 01295 267751
Contact: John Spratt
M & A range: A

Northampton
The Lakes
Bedford Road
Northampton
NN4 7SH
Tel: 01604 543000
Fax: 01604 543543
Contact: Kit O'Grady
M & A range: A–D

Nottingham
Lock House
Castle Meadow Road
Nottingham
NG2 1AG
Tel: 0115 906 5000
Fax: 0115 906 5001
Contact: Oliver Brookshaw
M & A range: A–E

Reading
Regents Gate
Crolon Street
Reading
RG1 2PQ
Tel: 0118 965 8765
Fax: 0118 965 8700
Contact: Dean Drew
M & A range: A–D

Rugby
Bloxam Court
Corporation Street
Rugby
CV21 2DU
Tel: 01788 573111
Fax: 01788 536651
Contact: Chris Hill, David Cranfield
M & A range: A–B

SIMMONS & SIMMONS
21 Wilson Street
London
EC2M 2TX
Tel: 0171 628 2020
Fax: 0171 628 2070
M & A range: (not supplied)

SLAUGHTER & MAY
35 Basinghall Street
London
EC2V 5DB
Tel: 0171 600 1200
Fax: 0171 726 0038
Contact: Michael Pescod
M & A range: A–E

SPEECHLY BIRCHAM
Bouverie House
154 Fleet Street
London
EC4A 2HX
Tel: 0171 353 3290
Fax: 0171 353 4825
Contact: Heidie Betson
M & A range: C–D

STEPHENSON HARWOOD
One St. Paul's Churchyard
London
EC4M 8SH
Tel: 0171 329 4422
Fax: 0171 606 0822
Contact: Judith Shepherd
M & A range: A–E

TAYLOR JOYNSON GARRETT
Carmelite
50 Victoria Embankment
Blackfriars
London
EC4Y 0DX
Tel: 0171 353 1234
Fax: 0171 936 2666
Contact: Lisa Tooley
M & A range: A–E

TAYLOR VINTNERS
Merlin Place
Milton Road
Cambridge
CB4 4DP
Tel: 01223 423444
Fax: 01223 425446
Contact: (not supplied)
M & A range: A–D

TAYLOR WALTON SOLICITORS
36–44 Alma Street
Luton
LU1 2PL
Tel: 01582 731161
Fax: 01582 457900
Contact: Mr. M.G. Pettit
M & A range: A–D

THEODORE GODDARD
150 Aldersgate Street
London
EC1A 4EJ
Tel: 0171 606 8855
Fax: 0171 606 4390
Contact: Joanna Whalley
M & A range: A–E

TODS MURRAY W.S.
66 Queen Street
Edinburgh
EH2 4NE
Tel: 0131 226 4771
Fax: 0131 225 3676
Contact: David N. Dunsire
M & A range: A–D

TRAVERS SMITH BRAITHWAITE
10 Snow Hill
London
EC1A 2AL
Tel: 0171 248 9133
Fax: 0171 236 3728
Contact: Christopher Bell, Chris Hale
M & A range: A–E

TRUMPS
PO Box 8000
One Redcliffe Street
Bristol
BS99 2SD
Tel: 0117 946 8200
Fax: 0117 946 8201
Contact: Nick Moss
M & A range: A–C

VEALE WASBROUGH
Orchard Court
Orchard Lane
Bristol
BS1 5DS
Tel: 0117 925 2020
Fax: 0117 925 2025
Contact: David Worthington
M & A range: A–E

WARNER CRANSTON SOLICITORS
Pickfords Wharf
Clink Street
London
SE1 9DG
Tel: 0171 403 2900
Fax: 0171 403 4221
Contact: Ian Fagelson
M & A range: A–E

WATSON, FARLEY & WILLIAMS
15 Appold Street
London
EC2A 2HB
Tel: 0171 814 8000
Fax: 0171 814 8141/8142
Contact: Charles Walford
M & A range: A–E

WILDE SAPTE
1 Fleet Place
London
EC4M 7WS
Tel: 0171 246 7000
Fax: 0171 246 7777
Contact: Steven Blakeley (Managing
Partner)
M & A range: A–E

WITHERS
12 Gough Square
London
EC4A 3DW
Tel: 0171 936 1000
Fax: 0171 936 2589
Contact: Hugh Devlin
M & A range: A–D

WRAGGE & CO.
55 Colmore Row
Birmingham
B3 2AS
Tel: 0121 233 1000
Fax: 0121 214 1099
Contact: David Vaughan
M & A range: A–E

24
Private Equity Sources*

This section contains details of private equity sources and includes an indication of their smallest and largest investment deals of the last two years. For reasons of confidentiality, exact figures have not been published but equity values have been divided into the following five bands:

Band A: £0–5 million
Band B: £6–10 million
Band C: £11–20 million
Band D: £21–100 million
Band E: over £100 million

3i PLC
91 Waterloo Road
London
SE1 8XP
Tel: 0171 928 3131
Fax: 0171 975 3546
Contact: Patrick Dunne
Investment range: A–D

ABERDEEN ASSET MANAGERS LIMITED
10 Queens Terrace
Aberdeen
AB10 1QG
Tel: 01224 631999
Fax: 01224 647010
Contact: Hugh Little (Director)
Investment range: A

ABINGWORTH MANAGEMENT LIMITED
(Private equity provided for Biotechnological/Healthcare companies only)
38 Jermyn Street
London
SW1Y 6DN
Tel: 0171 534 1500
Fax: 0171 287 0480
Contact: J. Abell
Investment range: A

* This is not a fully comprehensive list of private equity sources; however, a full list can be obtained from the British Venture Capital Association (BVCA).

ABN AMRO DEVELOPMENT CAPITAL
7 Hanover Square
London
W1R 9HE
Tel: 0171 495 2525
Fax: 0171 491 2050
Contact: Simon Havers
Investment range: B–C

ADVENT LIMITED
25 Buckingham Gate
London
SW1E 6LD
Tel: 0171 630 9811
Fax: 0171 828 1474
Contact: Dr. Jerry Benjamin (Life Sciences), Dave Cheesman/Nick Teasdale (IT)
Investment range: A

ALBEMARLE PRIVATE EQUITY LIMITED
1 Albemarle Street
London
W1X 3HF
Tel: 0171 491 9555
Fax: 0171 491 7245
Contact: Graham Barnes, Mark Hallala, Andrew Moy, Roy Parker, David Wills
Investment range: A–B

ALTA BERKELEY ASSOCIATES
9–10 Savile Row
London
W1X 1AF
Tel: 0171 734 4884
Fax: 0171 734 6711
Investment range: A

AMADEUS CAPITAL PARTNERS LIMITED
2 Mount Pleasant
Cambridge
CB3 0RN
Tel: 01223 578365
Fax: 01223 578488
Investment range: A

APAX PARTNERS & CO. CAPITAL LIMITED
15 Portland Place
London
W1N 3AA
Tel: 0171 872 6300
Fax: 0171 636 1637
Contact: Stephen Georgiadis
Investment range: A–E

BARCLAYS VENTURES
Charles House
5–11 Regent Street
London
SW1Y 4LR
Tel: 0171 445 5900
Fax: 0171 445 5909
Contact: Jeremy Morgan, Liz Jones, Anji Gopal, Julian Viggars
Investment range: A

BARING PRIVATE EQUITY PARTNERS LIMITED
33 Cavendish Square
London
W1M 0BQ
Tel: 0171 290 5000
Fax: 0171 290 5020
Contact: Roger Gill, Mark Hawkesworth
Investment range: A–B

BC PARTNERS LIMITED
105 Piccadilly
London
W1V 9FN
Tel: 0171 408 1282
Fax: 0171 493 1368
Investment range: C–D

**BRITISH STEEL (INDUSTRY)
LIMITED**
The Innovation Centre
217 Portobello
Sheffield
S1 4DP
Tel: 0114 273 1612
Fax: 0114 270 1390
Contact: Keith Williams
Investment range: A

CANDOVER INVESTMENTS PLC
20 Old Bailey
London
EC4M 7LN
Tel: 0171 489 9848
Fax: 0171 248 5483
Contact: Stephen Curran (Chief
Executive)
Investment range: C–D

CINVEN LIMITED
Pinners Hall
105–108 Old Broad Street
London
EC2N 1EH
Tel: 0171 661 3333
Fax: 0171 256 2225
Investment range: D–E

**CLOSE INVESTMENT
MANAGEMENT LIMITED**
36 Great St. Helen's
London
EC3A 6AP
Tel: 0171 426 4000
Fax: 0171 426 4004
Contact: Simon Wilding
Investment range: A–B

**CREDIT SUISSE FIRST BOSTON
PRIVATE EQUITY**
One Cabot Square
London
E14 4QJ
Tel: 0171 888 3239
Fax: 0171 888 3477
Contact: Alec D'Janoeff
Investment range: (not supplied)

DERBYSHIRE ENTERPRISE BOARD
95 Sheffield Road
Chesterfield
Derbyshire
S41 7JH
Tel: 01246 207390
Fax: 01246 221080
Contact: Andrew Street
Investment range: A

**EGAN & TALBOT CAPITAL
LIMITED**
Investment range: A

Huntingdon
Buckden Wood
Perry Road
Buckden
Huntingdon
PE18 9XQ
Tel: 01480 812218
Fax: 01480 812981
Contact: Martin Rigby

Oxford
Oxford Centre for Innovation
Mill Street
Oxford
OX2 0JX
Tel: 01865 725244
Fax: 01865 247399
Contact: James Mallinson

ELECTRA FLEMING LIMITED
65 Kingsway
London
WC2B 6QT
Tel: 0171 831 6464
Fax: 0171 404 1533
Contact: Maria Gianoutsos
Investment range: A–D

ENTERPRISE EQUITY (NI) LIMITED
78a Dublin Road
Belfast
BT2 7HP
Tel: 01232 242500
Fax: 01232 242487
Contact: Hal Wilson
Investment range: A

EQUITY VENTURES LIMITED
Du Pont House
Bristol Business Park
Bristol
BS16 1QD
Tel: 0117 931 1318
Fax: 0117 969 5421
Contact: R. Lindemann, David Tallboys
Investment range: A

FOREIGN & COLONIAL VENTURES LIMITED
Berkeley Square House
Berkeley Square
London
W1X 5PA
Tel: 0171 825 5300
Fax: 0171 825 5399
Contact: Stephen Cavell
Investment range: A–B

GE CAPITAL, EQUITY CAPITAL GROUP EUROPE
Clarges House
6–12 Clarges Street
London
W1Y 8DH
Tel: 0171 302 6000
Fax: 0171 302 6100
Contact: Andrew Beaton (Managing Director), Henrik Olsén (Director)
Investment range: A–D

GLE DEVELOPMENT CAPITAL
28 Park Street
London
SE1 9EQ
Tel: 0171 403 0300
Fax: 0171 403 1742
Contact: Mark Wignall
Investment range: A

GRANVILLE PRIVATE EQUITY MANAGERS
Mint House
77 Mansell Street
London
E1 8AF
Tel: 0171 488 1212
Fax: 0171 481 3911
Contact: Mike Fell, Chris Harper, Mark Owen
Investment range: B–D

GRESHAM TRUST PLC
One South Place
London
EC2M 2GT
Tel: 0171 309 5000
Fax: 0171 374 0707
Contact: Trevor Jones, Paul Marson-Smith
Investment range: A–C

HODGSON MARTIN LIMITED
36 George Street
Edinburgh
EH2 2LE
Tel: 0131 226 7644
Fax: 0131 226 7647
Contact: Yvonne Savage
Investment range: A

HSBC PRIVATE EQUITY EUROPE LIMITED
Vintners Place
68 Upper Thames Street
London
EC4V 3BJ
Tel: 0171 336 9955
Fax: 0171 336 9961
Contact: Ian Forrest
Investment range: A–D

INNVOTEC LIMITED
1 Castle Lane
London
SW1E 6DN
Tel: 0171 630 6990
Fax: 0171 828 8232
Contact: Peter Dohrn
Investment range: A

LICA DEVELOPMENT CAPITAL LIMITED
102 Jermyn Street
London
SW1Y 6EE
Tel: 0171 839 7707
Fax: 0171 839 4363
Contact: Stephen Hill, Paul Sheriff
Investment range: A–B

LLOYDS DEVELOPMENT CAPITAL
50 Grosvenor Street
London
W1X 9FH
Tel: 0171 499 1500
Fax: 0171 647 2000
Contact: Julian Carr
Investment range: A–D

LTG DEVELOPMENT CAPITAL LIMITED
Chelsea House
West Gate
London
W5 1DR
Tel: 0181 991 4500
Fax: 0181 991 1678
Contact: Michael Rosehill
Investment range: A

MERCURY ASSET MANAGEMENT LIMITED
33 King William Street
London
EC4R 9AS
Tel: 0171 203 5729
Fax: 0171 203 5833
Contact: Helen Lewis
Investment range: A–D

MERLIN VENTURES LIMITED
67–68 Jermyn Street
London
SW1Y 6NY
Tel: 0171 976 1211
Fax: 0171 976 1444
Investment range: A

MIDLAND ENTERPRISE FUND FOR THE SOUTH EAST
The Cadmus Organisation Limited
King Business Centre
Reeds Lane
Sayers Common
West Sussex
BN6 9LS
Tel: 01273 835455
Fax: 01273 835466
Contact: Howard Matthews
Investment range: A

MIDLAND GROWTH CAPITAL
10 Lower Thames Street
London
EC3R 6AE
Tel: 0171 260 7935
Fax: 0171 260 6767
Investment range: A (NB: Midland
Growth Capital's maximum
investment level is £1 million)

**MIDLANDS VENTURE FUND
MANAGERS LIMITED**
The Square
Beeston
Nottingham
NG9 2JG
Tel: 0115 967 8400
Fax: 0115 967 8687
Contact: John O'Neill, Tony Stott
Investment range: A

**MORGAN GRENFELL
DEVELOPMENT CAPITAL LIMITED**
23 Great Winchester Street
London
EC2P 2AX
Tel: 0171 545 8000
Fax: 0171 545 5282
Contact: Susan Deacon
Investment range: C–E

**MURRAY JOHNSTONE PRIVATE
EQUITY LIMITED**
Investment range: A–C

Birmingham
1 Cornwall Street
Birmingham
B3 2DT
Tel: 0121 236 1222
Fax: 0121 233 4628
Contact: David Sankey

Glasgow
7 West Nile Street
Glasgow
G1 2PX
Tel: 0141 226 3131
Fax: 0141 248 5636
Contact: Neil MacFadyen

London
30 Coleman Street
London
EC2R 5AN
Tel: 0171 606 6969
Fax: 0171 606 5818
Contact: Arvinder Walia

Manchester
55 Spring Gardens
Manchester
M2 2BY
Tel: 0161 236 2288
Fax: 0161 236 5539
Contact: Gary Tipper

Sheffield
9 Meadow Court
Amos Road
Sheffield
S9 1BX
Tel: 0114 242 1200
Fax: 0114 242 6485
Contact: Sarah Pullan

**NATWEST DEVELOPMENT
CAPITAL LIMITED**
21 Castlegate
Nottingham
NG1 7AQ
Tel: 0115 959 0049
Fax: 0115 938 8400
Contact: David Lambert
Investment range: A

NATWEST EQUITY PARTNERS
8 Fenchurch Place
London
EC3M 4TE
Tel: 0171 374 3505
Fax: 0171 374 3442
Contact: David Shaw (Chief Executive)
Investment range: A–E

NATWEST IT FUND
PO Box 12264
7th Floor
1 Princes Street
London
EC2R 8PB
Tel: 0171 390 1754
Fax: 0171 390 1123
Contact: Peter Smaill
Investment range: A

NORTHERN ENTERPRISE LIMITED
6th Floor
Cale Cross House
156 Pilgrim Street
Newcastle upon Tyne
NE1 6SU
Tel: 0191 233 1892
Fax: 0191 233 1891
Contact: Mr. B.S. Hensby, Mr M.Hird
Investment range: (not supplied)

**NORTHERN VENTURE
MANAGERS LIMITED**
Northumberland House
Princess Square
Newcastle upon Tyne
NE1 8ER
Tel: 0191 232 7068
Fax: 0191 232 4070
Contact: Tim Levett
Investment range: A

PI CAPITAL
48 Hay's Mews
London
W1X 7RT
Tel: 0171 629 9949
Fax: 0171 491 1015
Contact: David Alexander
Investment range: A

PRIMARY CAPITAL LIMITED
9 King Street
London
EC2V 8EA
Tel: 0171 600 9400
Fax: 0171 600 9401
Contact: Charles Gonszor
Investment range: A

**QUESTER CAPITAL
MANAGEMENT LIMITED**
29 Queen Anne's Gate
London
SW1H 9BU
Tel: 0171 222 5472
Fax: 0171 222 5250
Contact: John Spooner
Investment range: A

**ROYAL BANK DEVELOPMENT
CAPITAL LIMITED**
26 St. Andrew Square
Edinburgh
EH2 1AF
Tel: 0131 524 8300
Fax: 0131 557 2900
Contact: Joe McGrane
Investment range: A–D

SAND AIRE PRIVATE EQUITY
101 Wigmore Street
London
W1H 9AB
Tel: 0171 290 5200
Fax: 0171 495 0240
Contact: Rupert Bell, John Hudson,
David Williams
Investment range: A

SEED CAPITAL LIMITED
Magdalen Centre
Oxford Science Park
Oxford
OX4 4GA
Tel: 01865 784466
Fax: 01865 784430
Contact: Lucius Cary
Investment range: A

THOMPSON CLIVE & PARTNERS LIMITED
24 Old Bond Street
London
W1X 4JD
Tel: 0171 491 4809
Fax: 0171 493 9172
Contact: Nathaniel Hone
Investment range: A–B

TUFTON CAPITAL LIMITED
Albemarle House
1 Albemarle Street
London
W1X 3HF
Tel: 0171 529 7800
Fax: 0171 529 7801
Investment range: A

WALES FUND MANAGERS LIMITED
50 Cathedral Road
Cardiff
CF1 9LL
Tel: 01222 230490
Fax: 01222 230491
Contact: Richard Harbottle
Investment range: A

WEST LOTHIAN VENTURE FUND
Geddes House
Kirkton North
Livingston
EH54 6GU
Tel: 01506 415144
Fax: 01506 415145
Contact: Kathy Greenwood
Investment range: A

WEST MIDLANDS ENTERPRISE LIMITED
Wellington House
31–34 Waterloo Street
Birmingham
B2 5TJ
Tel: 0121 236 8855
Fax: 0121 233 3942
Contact: Peter Collings
Investment range: A

YORKSHIRE FUND MANAGERS LIMITED
(part of the Yorkshire Enterprise Group)
Saint Martins House
210–212 Chapeltown Road
Leeds
LS7 4HZ
Tel: 0113 294 5050
Fax: 0113 294 5002
Contact: David Gee
Investment range: A

25
Stockbrokers

This section contains details of stockbrokers that deal with flotations and includes an indication of their smallest and largest flotations over the last two years. For reasons of confidentiality, exact figures have not been published but the amounts raised have been divided into the following five bands:

Band A: £0–5 million
Band B: £6–10 million
Band C: £11–20 million
Band D: £21–100 million
Band E: over £100 million

Nominated AIM advisers and brokers have been specified as such.

AUSTIN FRIARS SECURITIES LIMITED
Austin Friars House
2–6 Austin Friars
London
EC2N 2HE
Tel: 0171 256 7897
Fax: 0171 256 6346
Contact: Harmon Hardy, Peter Rickett
Flotation range: A

BEESON GREGORY LIMITED
The Registry
Royal Mint Court
London
EC3N 4LB
Tel: 0171 488 4040
Fax: 0171 481 3762
Contact: Mr. A.D. Bartlett
Flotation range: A–D
AIM adviser & broker

BLOXHAM STOCKBROKERS
IFSC
2–3 Exchange Place
Dublin 1
Ireland
Tel: 00 353 1–829 1888
Fax: 00 353 1–829 1877
Contact: Peter O'Carroll, Angus
McDonnell
Flotation range: A–B

BURROUGH JOHNSTONE LIMITED
24–25 Cliffe High Street
Lewes
BN7 2AH
Tel: 01273 486244
Fax: 01273 486225
Contact: Charles Dampney
Flotation range: B–D
AIM broker

BUTTERFIELD SECURITIES
29–30 Cornhill
London
EC3V 3NF
Tel: 0171 648 8700
Fax: 0171 648 8724
Contact: Clive Carver
Flotation range: A–B
AIM adviser & broker

**CHARTERHOUSE TILNEY
SECURITIES LIMITED**
1 Paternoster Row
St. Paul's
London
EC4M 7DH
Tel: 0171 248 4000
Fax: 0171 334 3601
Contact: Peter May
Flotation range: C–D

COLLINS STEWART (CI) LIMITED
PO Box 8
TSB House
Le Truchot
St. Peter Port
Guernsey (C.I.)
GY1 4AE
Tel: 01481 726511
Fax: 01481 700476
Contact: Andrew Duquemin
Flotation range: A–B
AIM broker
(also specialists on Channel Islands
Stock Exchange listing work.)

**COOKE (HENRY) CORPORATE
FINANCE LIMITED**
Flotation range: A–D
Contact: Philip Johnson

Manchester
One King Street
Manchester
M2 6AW
Tel: 0161 832 2288
Fax: 0161 832 6024

Leeds
West Riding House
67 Albion Street
Leeds
LS1 5AA
Tel: 0113 243 9011
Fax: 0113 242 5731

CREDIT LYONNAISE SECURITIES
Broadwalk House
5 Appold Street
London
EC2A 2DA
Tel: 0171 588 4000
Fax: 0171 588 0278
Contact: Nicholas Donaldson
Flotation range: C–E
AIM adviser & broker

CREDIT SUISSE FIRST BOSTON DE ZOETE & BEVAN LIMITED
One Cabot Square
London
E14 4QJ
Tel: 0171 888 6010
Fax: 0171 888 6017
Contact: Nicholas Brigstocke
Flotation range: B–E

DAVY CORPORATE FINANCE LIMITED
Davy House
49 Dawson Street
Dublin 2
Ireland
Tel: 00 353 1–679 7788
Fax: 00 353 1–679 1423
Contact: Tom Byrne
Flotation range: D–E

DRESDNER KLEINWORT BENSON
20 Fenchurch Street
London
EC3P 3DB
Tel: 0171 623 8000
Fax: 0171 623 4069
Flotation range: D–E
AIM adviser & broker

DURLACHER LIMITED
4 Chiswell Street
London
EC1Y 4UP
Tel: 0171 459 3601
Fax: 0171 628 2749
Contact: Mr. G.H. Chamberlain
Flotation range: A–B
AIM broker

ELLIS & PARTNERS LIMITED
Talisman House
16 The Courtyard
East Park
Crawley
RH10 6AS
Tel: 01293 517744
Fax: 01293 521093
Contact: Richard Feigen
Flotation range: A
AIM broker

FISKE & CO. LIMITED
Salisbury House
London Wall
London
EC2M 5QS
Tel: 0171 638 4681
Fax: 0171 256 5365
Contact: C. F. Harrison
Flotation range: A–C
AIM broker

GOLDMAN SACHS INTERNATIONAL
Peterborough Court
133 Fleet Street
London
EC4A 2BB
Tel: 0171 774 1000
Fax: 0171 774 1550
Contact: Andrew Learoyd
Flotation range: D–E

GOODBODY CORPORATE FINANCE
122 Pembroke Road
Ballsbridge
Dublin 4
Ireland
Tel: 00 353 1–667 0420
Fax: 00 353 1–667 0410
Contact: Kevin Keating, Brian O'Kelly, Liam Booth
Flotation range: A–B
AIM broker

GREIG MIDDLETON & CO. LIMITED
Flotation range: B–D
AIM adviser & broker

Glasgow
155 St. Vincent Street
Glasgow
G2 5NN
Tel: 0141 240 4000
Fax: 0141 221 6578
Contact: Ralph Catto, Hugh Nash

London
30 Lombard Street
London
EC3V 9EN
Tel: 0171 655 4000
Fax: 0171 655 4100
Contact: Robert Clinton

HAWKPOINT PARTNERS LIMITED
4 Great St. Helens
London
EC3A 6HA
Tel: 0171 665 4500
Fax: 0171 665 4600
Contact: Annette Nason-Waters
Flotation range: (not supplied)

HENDERSON CROSTHWAITE INSTITUTIONAL BROKERS LIMITED
2 Gresham Street
London
EC2 7PE
Tel: 0171 623 9333
Fax: 0171 283 4823
Contact: Clive Richardson
Flotation range: A–E
AIM adviser & broker

HOARE GOVETT LIMITED
4 Broadgate
London
EC2M 7LE
Tel: 0171 601 0101
Fax: 0171 374 7064
Contact: Nigel Mills
Flotation range: (not supplied)

HOARE (T.) & CO.
4th Floor
Cannon Bridge
25 Dowgate Hill
London
EC4R 2YA
Tel: 0171 220 7001
Fax: 0171 929 1836
Contact: T. Hoare
Flotation range: A–D
AIM adviser & broker

HSBC SECURITIES
Thames Exchange
10 Queen Street Place
London
EC4R 1BL
Tel: 0171 621 0011
Fax: 0171 621 0496
Contact: Krishna Patel
Flotation range: (not supplied)

INVESTEC HENDERSON CROSTHWAITE
32 St. Mary at Hill
London
EC3P 3AJ
Tel: 0171 772 7084
Fax: 0171 772 7112
Contact: J. Greenall, Mr. M. Stranks
Flotation range: B–D
AIM adviser & broker

KEITH, BAYLEY, ROGERS & CO.
Ebbark House
93–95 Borough High Street
London
SE1 1NL
Tel: 0171 827 9988
Fax: 0171 403 3536
Contact: Mr. A.H. Drummon, Mr. D.
Crowhurst
Flotation range: A–C

MARSHALL SECURITIES LIMITED
Crusader House
145–157 St. John Street
London
EC1V 4RE
Tel: 0171 490 3788
Fax: 0171 490 3787
Contact: John Webb
Flotation range: D
AIM adviser & broker

NCB STOCKBROKERS LIMITED
IFSC
3 George's Dock
Dublin 1
Ireland
Tel: 00 353 1–611 5611
Fax: 00 353 1–611 5766
Contact: John Conroy
Flotation range: A–D
AIM broker

PEEL, HUNT & COMPANY LIMITED
62 Threadneedle Street
London
EC2R 8HP
Tel: 0171 418 8900
Fax: 0171 972 0112
Contact: C. Holdsworth Hunt
Flotation range: A–D
AIM adviser & broker

RAPHAEL ZORN HEMSLEY LIMITED
Cheapside House
138 Cheapside
London EC2V 6LH
Tel: 0171 776 1500
Fax: 0171 776 1555
Contact: Charles Crick
Flotation range: C–D
AIM adviser & broker

ROWAN DARTINGTON & CO. LIMITED
Colston Tower
Colston Street
Bristol
BS1 4RD
Tel: 0117 925 3377
Fax: 0117 927 2067
Contact: Barrie Newton
Flotation range: A
AIM adviser & broker

SG SECURITIES (LONDON) LIMITED
Exchange House
Primrose Street
London
EC2A 2DD
Tel: 0171 522 1075
Fax: 0171 588 6144
Contact: Andrew Dawber
Flotation range: B–E
AIM adviser & broker

SHARP (ALBERT E.) SECURITIES
Flotation range: A–C
AIM adviser & broker
Birmingham
Temple Court
35 Bull Street
Birmingham
B4 6ES
Tel: 0121 200 2200
Fax: 0121 683 7305
Contact: John Folliott Vaughan

London
Pinners Hall
105–108 Old Broad Street
London
EC2N 1ET
Tel: 0171 638 7275
Fax: 0171 614 8889
Contact: Eddie McCutcheon

Manchester
1 St. James' Square
Manchester
M2 6DN
Tel: 0161 827 7000
Fax: 0161 834 1474
Contact: Dr. Kevin Wilson

SHORE CAPITAL STOCKBROKERS LIMITED
1 Maddox Street
London
W1R 9WA
Tel: 0171 734 7292
Fax: 0171 734 7635
Contact: Graham Shore, Jonathan Elstein
Flotation range: A–C
AIM adviser & broker

STANLEY (CHARLES) & CO. LIMITED
25 Luke Street
London
EC2A 4AR
Tel: 0171 739 8200
Fax: 0171 739 4307
Contact: Philip Davies, Robert Howard
Flotation range: A–C
AIM adviser & broker

SUTHERLANDS LIMITED
Dashwood House
69 Old Broad Street
London
EC2M 1NX
Tel: 0171 628 2030
Fax: 0171 628 2090
Contact: Trevor Inglis
Flotation range: B–D
AIM broker

TEATHER & GREENWOOD LIMITED
12–20 Camomile Street
London
EC3A 7NN
Tel: 0171 426 9000
Fax: 0171 621 1504
Contact: Ken Ford
Flotation range: A–E
AIM adviser & broker

TOWNSLEY & CO.
44 Worship Street
London
EC2A 2JT
Tel: 0171 377 6161
Fax: 0171 895 8128
Contact: Barry Townsley, Simon Fox
Flotation range: A–C
AIM broker

WARBURG DILLON READ (Investment Banking Division of UBS AG)
1 Finsbury Avenue
London
EC2M 2PP
Tel: 0171 567 8000
Fax: 0171 247 4984
Contact: Michael Lacey-Solymar
Flotation range: C–E

WESTLB PANMURE LIMITED
New Broad Street House
35 New Broad Street
London
EC2M 1SQ
Tel: 0171 638 4010
Fax: 0171 588 5297
Contact: Tim Linacre
Flotation range: C–D

W.H. IRELAND LIMITED
11 St. James's Square
Manchester
M2 6WH
Tel: 0161 832 6644
Fax: 0161 661 9098
Contact: David W. Youngman
Flotation range: A–B
AIM broker

WILLIAMS DE BROE PLC
6 Broadgate
London
EC2M 2RP
Tel: 0171 588 7511
Fax: 0171 588 8860
Contact: Tim Worlledge
Flotation range: A–B
AIM adviser & broker

WISE SPEKE
PO Box 512
National House
36 St. Ann Street
Manchester
M60 2EP
Tel: 0161 839 4222
Fax: 0161 832 1672
Contact: Robert Race
Flotation range: A–C
AIM adviser & broker

Index

Index of Advertisers